CHARACTERS AND THEIR LANDSCAPES

By the same author

A Treasonable Growth
Immediate Possession
The Age of Illusion
Akenfield
The View in Winter
Divine Landscapes

Anthologies

Writing in a War: Poems, Stories and
Essays, 1939–1945
Aldeburgh Anthology
Places

CHARACTERS
AND THEIR
LANDSCAPES

RONALD BLYTHE

A Helen and Kurt Wolff Book
Harcourt Brace Jovanovich, Publishers
San Diego   New York   London

Originally published in Great Britain as *From the Headlands*

Library of Congress Cataloging in Publication Data
Blythe, Ronald, 1922–
Characters and their landscapes.
Original title: From the headlands.
"A Helen and Kurt Wolff book."
1. Literature, Modern—History and criticism—
Addresses, essays, lectures. I. Title.
PN710.B576   1983   820′.9   83-7890
ISBN 0-15-116792-3

Printed in the United States of America
First American edition 1983

A B C D E

BT 14.95 / 8 96 . 5/84

820.9
BlyThe

for JAMES HAMILTON-PATERSON

Acknowledgements

I am most grateful to the following for their kind permission to include *An Inherited Perspective* (Nobel Symposium, Royal Society of Arts, Gothenburg), *My First Acquaintance with William Hazlitt* and *Thomas Hardy's Marriage Novel* (Penguin Books Ltd), *The Writer as Listener* and *The Dangerous Idyll* (Royal Society of Literature), *Death and Leo Tolstoy* (from Tolstoy's *The Death of Ivan Ilyich*, translated by Lynn Solotaroff, published by Bantam Books, Inc.; translation copyright © 1981 by Bantam Books, Inc.; all rights reserved), *Dinner with Dr Stopes* (New Statesman), *Thomas Hardy's Courtship Novel* (Macmillan Ltd), *Country Christmas* and *Interpreting the Shades* (The Listener), and *Roads to Debach* (The Observer).

Acknowledgement is also made to the following for permission to reprint copyright material: Jonathan Cape Ltd and Mrs Sheila Hooper for excerpts from *Kilvert's Diary* edited by William Plomer (published 1938–40); Allen & Unwin Ltd for an excerpt from 'Dawn on the East Coast' in *Ha! Ha! Among the Trumpets* (1946) by Alun Lewis; David Higham Associates and Faber & Faber Ltd for an excerpt from *Wednesday Early Closing* by Norman Nicholson (1975); New Directions Publishing Corporation for an excerpt from 'Canto XIII' from *The Cantos of Ezra Pound*, copyright © 1934 by Ezra Pound; Bantam Books, Inc., New York, for an excerpt from Tolstoy's *The Death of Ivan Ilyich*, translated by Lynn Solotaroff, translation copyright © 1981 by Bantam Books, Inc., all rights reserved; Oxford University Press and the Estate of the late W. J. Turner for an excerpt from 'Words and Ideas' in *Fossils of a Future Time* (1946) by W. J. Turner; David Higham Associates and Hamish Hamilton Ltd for excerpts from *Journals* (1952) by Denton Welch edited by Jocelyn Brooke.

Contents

Introduction

After living as a writer for many years, I have noticed that a pattern made up of the supporting writing, as it were, begins to show itself. Criticism, plus all the comment on friends, places and experiences which has run parallel to the writing of the books, takes on a completeness of its own. This book reflects some of the ideas and happenings that were affecting me while the main work was being done. In order to give such a selection a pivot, I have confined it to writing which 'doubles' certain literary and personal reactions to readings and events. Thus, for example, the chapter on Thomas Hardy's courtship novel, *A Pair of Blue Eyes*, is here because it contains a great deal of inner knowledge of its landscape due to the many visits I made to my old friend the poet James Turner in North Cornwall during the nineteen-sixties, when he – and occasionally Charles Causley – introduced me to 'Off Wessex'. Similarly, the chapter on Tolstoy's attitude to death, although quite incidentally, happened to be the one I had begun work on when my life-long friend John Nash himself lay dying and I was nursing him.

The native element, naturally, is omnipresent. I still occasionally speculate what it can be like to live somewhere where the signposts are not all pointing to the towns and villages of childhood. It is not as if, as some writers have, I made a vow to stick to the home ground, for I never did, and have often thought that there could be benefits from giving it the slip for a decade or two. I could say that it had had some kind of pull, etc., but inertia comes into it. On the other hand (I justify myself) if a writer has stayed at home, there is no doubt that he suffers certain home pressures, and his way of coping with such stresses and strains can be the strength of his work. And so I have included various explanations of the so-called 'local' writer's position, with all its rooted advantages and complexities, stability and unease, imagination and inescapable painful realities.

Solitude, although it is a state which I rarely think about, has always been a very real part of it too, and so there are chapters which derive from solitary habits, such as chronic reading and those uncontrollable thought-runs which have a way of taking one over when slaving away in the huge gardens of little farmhouses, and the like. Also from such favourite activities as a kind of haphazard wandering-walking off across the county. No plan, no sensible route, no time to the day. Because two of my books have been about what other people have said of things which I have seen or felt, or have to some extent been myself involved in, I have included my own interpretation of how a writer listens.

A few of these essays have been previously published in the scattered way of such things, and quite a few of them have not. Being given this opportunity to bring them together does allow them to show a linkage of mood, thought and autobiographical facts.

R.B.

An Inherited Perspective

'Any landscape is a condition of the spirit,' wrote Henri-Frédéric Amiel in his *Journal Intime*. As a Swiss he could have been reproaching all those British intellectuals and divines who abandoned what their own country had to offer by way of transcendental scenery, the Lake District beginning to lose its efficacy as a spiritual restorative by the mid-nineteenth century, for the Jungfrau and the Matterhorn. *Any* landscape is a condition of the spirit. A few months ago I happened to glance up from my book as the train was rushing towards Lincoln to see, momentarily yet with a sharp definition, first the platform name and then the niggard features of one of the most essential native landscapes in English literature, John Clare's Helpston. I had not realised that the train would pass through it, or that one could. It was all over in seconds, that glimpse of the confined prospect of a great poet, but not before I had been reminded that he had thrived for only as long as he had been contained within those flat village boundaries. When they shifted him out of his parish, although only three miles distant – and for his own good, as they said – he began to disintegrate, his intelligence fading like the scenes which had nourished it. Of all our poets, none had more need to be exactly *placed* than John Clare. His essential requirements in landscape were minimal and frugal, like those of certain plants which do best in a narrow pot of unchanged soil.

I observed this tiny, yet hugely sufficient, world of his dip by under scudding clouds. A church smudge – and his grave an indefinable fraction of it – some darkening hedges, probably those planted after the Enclosure Act had stopped the clock of the old cyclic revolutions of Helpston's agriculture, thus initiating Clare's disorientation, a few low-pitched modern dwellings, and that was all. It was scarcely more impressive in Clare's lifetime. A contemporary clergyman, gazing at it, said that 'its unbroken tracts strained and tortured the sight'. But not the poet's sight, of course. This it nourished and extended with its modest images. He liked to follow the view past the 'lands', which he disliked because of the way they overtaxed the strength of his slight body when he laboured on them, to where the cultivation dropped away into a meeting with heath and fen. From here onwards the alluvial soil swept unbroken to the sea. It was this landscape of the limestone heath, he said, which 'made my being'. And thus it was in this practically feature-less country that genius discovered all that it required for its total expression. From it Clare was to suffer a triple expulsion. The first entailed that fracture from his childhood vision of his home scene – something which we all have to endure. The second was when the fields and roads of Helpston were radically redesigned in 1816, evicting him from all its ancient certainties. The third, and quite the most terrible, was when it was arranged for him to live in the *next* village, a well-meaning interference with an inherited perspective which, in his special case, guaranteed the further journey to Northampton lunatic asylum.

To be a native once meant to be a born thrall. Clare's enthralment by Helpston presents the indigenous eye at its purest and most naturally disciplined. By his extraordinary ability to see furthest when the view was strictly limited, he was able to develop a range of perception which outstripped the most accomplished and travelled commentary on land-scape and nature, of which in the early nineteenth century there was a great deal. He had no choice. He did not pick on Helpston as a subject. There was no other place. As a boy, like most children, he had once set out from his village to find 'the world's end', and got lost.

So I eagerly wanderd on & rambled along the furze the whole day till I got out of my knowledge when the very wild flowers seemd to forget me & I imagind they were the inhabitants of new countrys the very sun seemd to be a new one & shining on a different quarter of the sky

is how he described this adventure in his *Autobiography*. And twice more in this book, when he was aged fifteen and when he was aged twenty, he tells of a kind of geographical giddiness, such as that which one has when being spun round blindfold in some game, when he had to leave the balanced centre of his native village to look for work in nearby market towns, and his sense of psychic displacement went far beyond that which could have been brought on by the strain of interviews and so forth. Here is Clare again, as the universe itself careens out of control because he is unable to use his village reference points.

I started for Wisbeach with a timid sort of pleasure & when I got to Glinton turnpike I turned back to look on the old church as if I was going into another country Wisbeach was a foreign land to me for I had never been above eight miles from home in my life I coud not fancy England much larger than the part I knew . . .

I became so ignorant in this far land that I coud not tell which quarter the wind blew from & I even was foolish enough to think the sun's course was alterd & that it rose in the west & set in the east I often puzzled at it to set myself right . . .

'I became so ignorant in this far land . . .', 'to set myself right' – these are the telling words. Beyond his own parish boundary Clare felt that he was ignorant. He felt his intelligence desert him and that another man's scene – even another man's sun – could not be understood. When the success of his two collections of published poems brought him into contact with literary London, an event for which many a provincial writer prayed in the hope that their work would provide the exit visa from the limitations which had inspired it, Clare reacted very wisely indeed. 'It seems', says John Barrell in his excellent study, *The Idea of Landscape and the Sense of Place: An Approach to the Poetry of John Clare*, 'that the more the poet began to understand about literary London, the more tenacious became his desire to write exclusively about Helpston.' London's literary landscapes knew no bounds at all. They swept back in immense, formal vistas carrying the educated eye to valleys in Thessaly and to Roman farms. Knowing that he could never be entirely free at home and accepting an element of imprisonment as the major condition for his being a poet, Clare chose the local view.

I believe that, whether with a feeling of relief or despair – or both – the majority of what are called regional poets and novelists come to a similar decision. Their feeling for nature and the landscape of man deepens when it remains hedged about by familiar considerations. Paradoxically, they discover that it is *not* by straying far from the headlands that they are able to transport their readers into the farthest realms of the imagination and its truths, but by staying put.

I find that I have two states of local landscape consciousness. The first I would call instinctive and unlettered, a mindfulness of my own territory which has been artlessly and sensuously imbibed. On top of this I have a country which I have deduced or discovered from scientific, sociological, aesthetic and religious forays into its depths. Of course, like the rest of us, I want to have my cake and eat it too. I do not want the first knowledge, wherein lies all the heart and magic, to give way entirely to the second knowledge, wherein lie all the facts. It is the usual dilemma of intuition versus tuition and how to reconcile the one with the other without patronising either. Because my boyhood East Anglia was by far the major source of all the references which have directed me as a writer, I find myself constantly hankering after primordial statements which still float around in my memory, and which seem to say something more relevant about my own geography than anything my trained intelligence can tell me, yet which tantalisingly avoids definition. All the same, I must say something about the fields and streams and skies, the cottages, gothic churches, lanes and woods of Suffolk as I first recognised them. This could have been the time when I knew the river but did not know its name. Certainly it is a verifiable fact that much which can be seen now could be seen then – when I was ten or twelve. Or two or three. When does one begin to look? Or does landscape enter the bloodstream with the milk?

'Local' – a limited region, says the dictionary. And 'location', the marking out or surveying of a tract of land. Also a position in space. So, early on, we begin to take stock of our limited regions, marking them out, and with never a suspicion that they at this period could be marking *us* out. I took stock of flowers first, then paths and then architecture. I do not know that I ever at this time took stock of weather or of inhabitants. The latter were thin then, pared down to the high cheek-bone by the long agricultural depression and with skins polished by the winds. But however great the omissions, I saw enough to lay in a lasting stock of feeling and emotion, for as Lord Holland said, 'There is not a living creature . . . but hath the sense of feeling, although it hath none else.' We, of course, are taking feeling beyond such an elementary sensation and into human sensibility. It is this proto-sensibility created by the impact of nature on our earliest awareness that intrigues us later on. We know that climates create cultures and cultures create types, but an individual voice within us says that there is more to it than this, conceit notwithstanding.

'Those scenes made me a painter', wrote John Constable, acknowledging the river valley in which I now live and just above which I was born. It has been said that from these scenes he fashioned the best-loved landscapes of every English mind. Thomas Gainsborough too, another local boy pushed into art by scenery, was born in this valley and was sketching along the same footpaths in the eighteenth century as I, when a child, was wandering in the twentieth. Indeed, my old farmhouse is roughly perched at the frontier of these two artists' territorial river inspirations. Gainsborough's landscape was upstream and flowing back in golden-brown vistas to the Dutch masters; Constable's was downstream and flowing forward to the French Impressionists. When I was an adolescent, these two local painters dominated my equally native landscape to an alarming extent, often making it impossible to see a field for myself. And I was further alarmed when I heard that Sickert had called the entire district a sucked orange. Would there be anything left for a writer to feed on, or would I be like someone attempting to take an original view of Haworth or Egdon Heath? Ancestry decided it. Not that I knew much about the centuries of farming fathers stretching away from me, perhaps into Saxon days, but the realisation that our eyes had repeatedly seen the same sights began to promote a way of looking at life which was vigorous and questioning, and which did not depend on past conclusions.

And so what was my inherited perspective? What, particularly, was I recognising before I was educated in history and ecology and, most potently, in literature? Or even in local loyalty, for in all the provinces, in every hamlet, one might say, there is this beaming self-congratulation of those who have been born there and who indicate that it would be superfluous to ask more of life. Although not quite as restricted as Clare in mileage terms, as a boy in those immediate pre-World War Two days from a rural family apparently existing on air, I saw a very little world indeed. Until I was twelve or so, East Anglia was for me no more than a small circle of villages round a small town, plus an annually visited beach, or rather a slipping, clinking wall of cold shingle, monotonously piled up and pulled down by the North Sea. The landscape of Crabbe, in fact, who had made the definitive statement about it. Benjamin Britten was able to say something else about it in another medium. I saw this beach as the edge to my interior landscape, disregarding the distance in between. From the beginning I was laying claim to a broader scenic inheritance than some writers.

The Cumbrian poet Norman Nicholson has not only restricted himself to Millom, his home town, but finds himself far from cramped, creatively speaking, in the modest house where he was born and where his grandparents' wallpapers lie beneath his own interior decoration like a palimpsest of their domesticity. Nicholson warns us, particularly writers, of how we tend to overload infant experience with intelligence of a later date. At the beginning of his autobiography he gives a remarkably convincing apology for the merest squint of landscape being adequate for a child's imaginative growth. In comparison with his first contemplation of nature, mine was on the scale of the Grand Canyon. His confession is all the more interesting because just a mile or two away from where he was making do with a creeper on a brick wall rolled landscape with a capital L, Wordsworth's landscape of the Lakes! During his early years this great scene had been bricked out without cost. It was the bricked-in prospect which became so perversely satisfying and which made his blood thunderous with imagination. Nicholson wrote of this backyard behind his father's tailor's shop as

a little Eden, a Garden Enclosed. Even today I survey it with a complacency equal to that of any Duke of Devonshire looking out from Chatsworth . . . seen from the yard, there was only the sky, broken by two telephone poles and a pulley for a washing-line. And when you looked out of the window of the little back bedroom, you could see the explanation of this emptiness, for the whole length of the other side of the street was taken up by the wall of the old Millom Secondary School, almost every corner of which could be kept under watch from our house . . . But if I climb up to our second storey and push my head out of the fanlight in the back attic, I can look . . . and see what I used to see, the St George's Hall, the scraggy, slag-clogged fields, the old mines at Hodbarrow, the hills of Low Furness across the estuary [though] the view and even the school playground were all too far away to mean much to me at that age. I rarely ventured out into the street . . . I stayed behind the back door, teasing the dog, trotting up and down the slate slabs that paved the yard or dibbling a fork into the few clods of soil we called our garden. For when my father first came to The Terrace, he had up-ended a row of black tiles, cemented them to the slate paving about a foot away from the wall, and filled in the space between tiles and wall with soil dug up with a pen-knife on his walk round the fields and carried home carefully in brown paper bags. In this he had planted a few cuttings of Virginia

Creeper [which] has routed its black arteries all over the walls, giving them the withered, sinewy look of an old coal miner's arms . . .

Lying unclaimed and ignored, and within walking distance of this artfully skimped outlook, was the view proper, the massive outcrops of the Lake District rock and the broad Irish Sea. Nicholson waited until he was grown-up before entering into this inheritance, and later he has half-mockingly rejoiced in being fashioned by a minimal view in one of the world's maximum areas of the literary imagination, and to have succeeded in getting himself awakened by it without having any idea that Wordsworth and Coleridge were crying 'Awake!' so profoundly a mile or two away.

My own powerful landscape inheritance was not walled off from me until I grew up. There was no pittance to start with in the shape of an elementary soil brought home in paper-bags, no rationing of the sky, no ignoring of the native scene's prophets, one of whom was no less than the foremost artist of the English romantic movement, John Constable. And yet, like all children, how little of it I comprehended as a boy! Looking back, I am as much intrigued by my blindness to the obvious, as by the way I sometimes instantly grasped some central truth. There seems to be a considerable osmotic action in landscape, particularly one's native landscape, which causes it to be breathed in as it thrusts against our earliest senses. Being there, right under our noses, we inhale it as well as comprehending it with our intellects. For some it is a fatal air, for others a kind of inescapable nourishment which expands the soul. Quite where the emotional – I will not say mindless – absorption and the instructed viewpoint began to fuse in myself, I find it impossible to say. Nor can I tell if I have continued all these years, living as I have among the first earthly patterns and colours I ever saw, to absorb them instinctively as well as intellectually. But I do recall some of those instances in which the obvious says nothing to the child. For example, I climbed a road called Gallows Hill every day and never once did it say something agonising, macabre and morbid to me. What it said was freedom, running loose. Gallows Hill was the path to the white violet and cowslip sites – for plants remained undisturbed in their locations for generations then, and village people of all ages saw them as a form of permanent geography by which the distance of Sunday walks could be measured, or where tea or love could be made, or, in my case, where books could be read. These special flowers in their hereditary places were solidly picked, I might add, but there were always just as many next year. Had the victims of Gallows Hill picked them in the years before they picked pockets? I expect so.

Gallows Hill also led to Froissart and Malory for me, for just above stood a little moated manor with a castellated tower and swans on the dark water, and even now I see this as an annexed scene, as a house which does not belong to its residents, but to my most personal country-side. So do the aged village relations who sat four-square in their lush gardens like monuments, as if growing out of the Suffolk clay itself, their bodies wooden and still, their eyes glittering and endlessly scanning leaves and birds and crops, their work done and their end near. I remember very distinctly how these old country people were not so much figures in a landscape, as local men and women who, in their senescence, were browning and hardening back into its simple basic elements.

As a rule, children draw back from the illimitable, except when they catch such suggestions of it in the experience of running down grassy slopes with open arms on a windy day, and prefer the secret, the clandestine and the enclosed. I had to grow up to see that East Anglia was not a snug den but a candid plain, an exposed and exposing place. Once it was all manageable privacies and concealments, each memor-ably furnished with its particular stones, flora, water and smells. In this secret range I included the North Sea, for although it was all of thirty miles off and seen so rarely, perhaps only once a year, I felt the same parochial tenderness about it as I did about the meadows – fields, really, gone to weed due to the agricultural depression – which led to my grandmother's house. As I sighted this quite unimaginably immense liquid wall at the end of the coast road, with the Rotterdam shipping riding its horizon, I can remember how it revoked all the feelings I had for the interior. The sea makes us treacherous; it captures our senses and makes us faithless to the land. I found myself in a different state by the sea; not freed, but in another kind of captivity. I lived by it briefly when I first became a writer and felt myself both in my own deeply-rooted country and on the edge of things. The entire ecology changes long before one even suspects the presence of the Suffolk sea. A twelve-mile belt of light soil, which we call the sandlings, produces heath and coniferous forests, and pale airy villages, dyked meadows and vast stretching skies, and by the time one has reached the rattling beach, still guarded by forts built to repel Bonaparte and Hitler, the interior seems remote. This is the land of our seventh-century Swedish kings who lie buried in their great ships at Sutton Hoo and whose palace is under a Nato bomber base. Screaming sea-birds and screaming planes on practice runs, and often profound silences, this is the indigenous periphery. Also a cutting wind and an intriguing marine flora which between them force the gaze to the ground. This is Benjamin Britten's rim of country. When, at the end of his life, he worked for a brief spell in a cottage sunk in the cornlands of Suffolk, he told me how utterly different the imaginative stimulus was, and I realised that we had shared similar experiences of territorial disorientation within the home area, but from opposite directions.

What half-entranced, half-shocked me about the coast was its prodigious wastefulness. Here nature was humanly unmanageable, and I was not deceived by breakwater and drain or the sly peace of the marshes. There was another kind of wastefulness in the central clay country which, to my child's eye, was transmuted into a private harvest of benefits. Every hollow held water, and in the ancient horse-ponds and moats, under coverlets of viridescent slime starred with water ranunculus, lay the wicked pike, fish of legendary size, cunning and appetite which we believed were a century old, and which grew fat on suicides. The small heavy land fields had not then been opened up to suit modern machinery, and most of them possessed what the farmers called 'muddles', or uncultivated scraps which were crammed with birds, insects, flowers, shrubs, grasses and animals. Towering quickset hedges from enclosure days survived as well as mixed shrub hedges from Saxon, Norman and Tudor times, all still containing the oak trees which Shakespearean ploughmen must have used to set their first furrow. The surface of the land was littered with flint, and no matter however much was picked up for making churches and roads, no field was ever cleared, even when it had been hand-quarried for a millennium. It was a kind of catch-crop which worked itself up to the surface from its silican depths to provide assured hard labour for each succeeding generation of country people. Its permanency was like that of the mountains to field-workers in the north. 'So light a foot will ne'er wear out the everlasting flint,' says the

priest as Juliet approaches to marry Romeo. We expended a massive
amount of energy splitting these weighty stones to find the toad which
was said to live inside them. We also spent hours in vast old gravel-pits
searching for 'dawn stones' (eoliths, as I was to learn in my gradual
enlightenment), but which then I was convinced meant the first stones
warmed by the sun in the first chapter of Genesis. We would spend
whole days in these workings, many feet below the peripheral corn,
scraping away at the partly-known and the unrealised, but really at our
ultimate ancestry, the Scandinavian Maglemose forest folk who, ten
thousand years ago, before the sea washed us away from the continental
mainland to which we were tenuously attached by salty lagoons, walked
to Suffolk and began agricultural pattern-making on its fertile clays. We
learned that they were followed by the Windmill Hill folk and the
Beaker people, and these homely appellations would cut through time as
the blade cut through June grass, making hay of its density. Distant past
has moments of tangibility to a native, particularly to one who has not yet
encountered the written history of his area. I can remember the need or
compulsion I had to touch stones. I suppose I felt them for their
eloquence and because an adjacent artifact told me that a Windmill boy
might have done the same. Later, I came to love the stoniness of the
symbolism in the poetry of Sidney Keyes, one of the best poets of the last
war, who died in African sand, aged twenty-one.

It must be added that, seascape or richly dilapidated clayscape, the
natural history of my childhood was marvellously impacted with mystery. There were swaying rookeries and barns like dust-choked temples
almost within the precincts of our market town, behind the main streets
of which ran a maze of courts and yards fidgety with sullen life.
Naphtha flares blazed over the banana stalls and cheapjacks in the
square, whilst mediaeval bells burled their sound for miles along the
river valley when the wind was right. Having the wind right for this or
that was something one heard a lot about. It was the bitter wind of a dry
country and you had to stand up to it, they said. Vagrants and itinerants
brewing up in the shelter of marl-pits fought a losing battle against it,
and the silk factory operatives, sweeping in and out of their villages on
bicycles, were swept along by it like pedalling birds. The scene was one
of stagnant animation. One would catch the eye of a solitary worker
among the sugar-beet, and it would be strangely hard and transparent,

like glass. Extremes were normal. I once saw twenty men joyfully and silently clubbing scores of rats to death in a stackyard. No words, only rat-screams. Only a few yards from this spot Gainsborough had posed Mr and Mrs Robert Andrews against a spectacle made up of trees and towers and bending stream, and painted what Sir Sacheverell Sitwell has called the finest English domestic portrait. The young husband is seated between his gun and his wife. And once on this hill I heard the rarest, most exquisite aeolian music when the wind was right. It was a sound that made one weightless and emancipated, and I had that momentary sensation of *being* nature – nothing less or else.

Richard Jefferies used a nineteenth-century language to describe this transition of man into landscape and landscape into man in *The Story of My Heart*. We may have a later language or no language at all to put this feeling into words, but we have shared the experience. This is his way of putting it:

Moving up the sweet short turf, at every step my heart seemed to obtain a wider horizon of feeling; with every inhalation of rich pure air, a deeper desire. The very light of the sun was whiter and more brilliant here. By the time I had reached the summit I had entirely forgotten the petty circumstances and the annoyances of existence. I felt myself, myself. There was an intrenchment on the summit, and going down into the fosse I walked round it slowly to recover breath . . . There the view was over a broad plain, beautiful with wheat, and inclosed by a perfect amphitheatre of green hills. Through these hills there was one narrow groove, or pass, southwards, where the white clouds seemed to close in the horizon. Woods hid the scattered hamlets and farmhouses, so that I was quite alone. I was utterly alone with the sun and the earth. Lying down on the grass, I spoke in my soul to the earth, the sun, the air, and the distant sea far beyond sight. I thought of the earth's firmness – I felt it bear me up . . .

Recognisable in this post-Darwinian, pre-Freudian landscape con- fession is that confusion of the newly articulate response and incom- municable sensation which all of us have known. Jefferies was often exasperated by not being able to find a natural way to talk about nature. He saw that men operated on the assumption that nature was something which surrounded them but which did not enter them. That, glorious though it was, and inspiring, they were outside its jurisdiction. When they spoke of the influence of environment on a person, they meant some aspect of men's social environment, not climate and scenery. The man who, for some reason or other, remains on his home ground, becomes more controlled by the controlling forces of all that he sees around him than he could wish or realise. Jefferies sought such a control in a quasi-religious and poetic pilgrimage to the grassy heights above his Wiltshire farm, and Thomas Hardy and Emily Brontë created immense dramas by allowing their characters to be activated as much by weather and place as by society. These, and many other writers and artists, shock us by showing us the malignancy of the native scene, how it imprisons us as well as releases us. Jefferies and Hardy, of course, were cynically amused that we should imagine it would be interested in doing either.

However, because we have had such a considerable hand in the actual arrangement of the local view, we must be allowed some subjectivity. Over the centuries we introduced the non-indigenous trees and flowers and crops, we made the roads, fields and buildings, and we filled in the heath with forests and levelled the woods for corn. What we see is not what nature, left to its own devices, would let us see. To be born and to die in an untouchable scene, in the wild mountains, for example, is quite a different matter. Comparatively few people do this. And so what the majority of us celebrate as natives is native improvements. The shapes, colours and scents have an ancestral significance, and what moves us is that the vista does not radiate from some proto-creation like a dawn-stone but that it is a series of constructions made by our labouring fathers. Within these, the normal partisan provincial will insist, must lie all that the inner and outward life requires.

Landscape and human sensibility can come to shallow terms in villages, which are notorious for the resentment they display when some indigenous guide, poet or painter, presents them with the wider view. The field workers who saw Cézanne and Van Gogh painting, and John Clare writing, believed that they were in the company of blasphemers. In a letter to his publishers Clare complains how isolating it is to be in possession of a literate landscape.

I wish I livd nearer you at least I wish London woud creep within 20 miles of Helpstone I don't wish Helpstone to shift its station I live here among the ignorant like a lost man in fact like a man whom the rest seem careless of having anything to do with – they hardly dare talk in my company for fear I should mention them in my writings & I find more pleasure in wandering the fields than mixing among my silent neighbours who are insensible of everything but toiling and talking of it & that to no purpose.

And yet, ironically, it was only by keeping their faces to the earth could these neighbours and their forebears carve out the sites where the poet's intelligence could dwell. The average home landscape entailed more looking down than looking around. As for the agreeability of a used countryside, as the poet and critic Geoffrey Grigson said, 'When I see men, and women, bent over the crops, I realise it isn't so agreeable for them. '*C'est dur l'agriculture*' (read Zola in *La Terre*). I like seeing machines which keep the human back from bending, as in the last five thousand years.'

When I was writing *Akenfield*, and thinking of the old and new farming generations, it struck me that I was seeing the last of those who made landscapes with their faces hanging down, like those of beasts, over the soil. Grigson also notes how artists and poets push landscape forward, thrust it into view and make contact with it unavoidable. In the past the figures which inhabited it were both gods and mortals, Venus and the village girl, Apollo and the shepherd. The scene was both natural and supernatural. And the indigenous man will occasionally look up from his disturbance of the surface of his territory as he earns his living, to draw into himself all that lies around him in a subconscious search for transcendence. From childhood on, what he sees, he is. Flesh becomes place. Although it was said of my East Anglian countryman, George Borrow, that he could look at nature without looking at himself. What an achievement!

My First Acquaintance
with William Hazlitt

A conspiracy of caution has grown up around William Hazlitt. Unquestionably a 'great author' in the system which measures writers for posterity, he has to be admitted, yet grudgingly, warningly. An impression persists of a man at odds with all and everything, someone to whom his friends had to offer an almost saintly response if they were not to get their heads bitten off. He was a bitter creature, a malcontent. Equally persistent is the hint of scandal: a rumour about making a fool of himself over young girls which, in the case of Herrick, say, carries with it amusement and forgiveness, but which in connection with Hazlitt is loaded with Sunday newspaper innuendo. He was an irritant and a grit in the eye of his contemporaries. But he wrote as marvellously as an essayist who was not Montaigne could, so his work has always received high praise. Yet, in spite of this, most of the assessments of Hazlitt have a certain maggoty quality and are eaten through with reservation.

In the many editions of his work there are numerous attempts to present him in the best light. Because there was in his fretful nature a sublime streak of joy and serenity which allowed him to write perfectly about human happiness, the essays in which he does so have been singled out for constant reprinting, with the result that the average Hazlitt-taster has not met the real flavour of this extraordinary man. His great hedge of thorny comment, which runs parallel with the retreat-from-revolution politics of the early nineteenth century, has too often been chopped away in order to show a calm view of a journalist-philosopher hanging 'Great Thoughts' on the typeline and meditating on such absolutes as fame, time, death and nature. Yet the very essence of Hazlitt is his dangerousness, and not only with respect to the reactionary climate of his own day, but when and wherever freedom and truth are compromised by those actions which are summed up as the 'art of the possible'. These were what he called 'the lie', and it was his refusal to either take or give 'the lie' which turned him into the uncomfortable creature he was. This, the very kernel of his character, has been seen as a kind of aberrant grumpiness, a tiresome failing in an otherwise excellent prose stylist. So his work has been tilted until it squares up to what is expected of an inexhaustible aphorist, and again it is wholesome Hazlitt, rather than the whole Hazlitt, which is presented.

What was it, both in his own day and after, which makes him one of literature's separated brethren, which sees to it that he is critically acclaimed but which leaves him outside the full warm fellowship of what were once called trusted writers? 'I want to know why everyone has such a dislike of me?' he asked Leigh Hunt. Edmund Gosse, giving the general nineteenth-century answer, put it all down to cussedness: 'Eccentricity, violence and a disregard of the conventions were at no time unsympathetic to Hazlitt.' Except for his telling inclusion of that key-word 'violence', the rest of Gosse's statement takes up the central position and is a nervous cheer for a writer who made the Olympian winning post, though handicapped. 'In his own time and way he was a transmitter of the sacred fire.' Like so many critics before and since, Gosse tries to stay neutral. But Hazlitt leaves no one neutral. Disturbed himself by every ecstatic, political and tragic aspect of the human condition, he could never believe that there were those who managed to get through life without feeling and knowing these things in all their intensity. He could not understand the rules of selection which made some of the subjects on which he wrote praiseworthy and socially acceptable – art, Shakespeare (although once his analysis of Desdemona brought shouts of 'obscenity!'), the countryside – and others – class, war, money, slavery, sex – taboo. His England had been at war with France for twenty years and had, like the rest of Europe, been fed on cruelties. His London was famous for its prostitutes. The great mass of his fellow men were near starvation. Yet he was to be polite in print and draw the line. It was impossible.

'Hazlitt was not one of those non-committal writers who shuffle off in a mist and die of their own insignificance,' wrote Virginia Woolf.

His essays are emphatically himself. He has no reticence and he has no shame. He tells us exactly what he thinks, and tells us – the confidence is less seductive – what he feels. As of all men he had the most intense consciousness of his own existence, since never a day passed without inflicting on him a pang of hate or of jealousy, some thrill of anger or pleasure, we cannot read him for long without coming in contact with a very singular character – ill-conditioned yet high-minded; mean yet noble; intensely egotistical yet inspired by the most genuine passion for the rights and liberties of mankind. So thin is the veil of the essay as Hazlitt wore it, his very look comes before us. No man could read him and maintain a simple and ur.compounded idea of him.

There is a noticeable broadening of judgement here but it is still 'less seductive' to know what Hazlitt feels than what he thinks. He is all right until he allows his private life to run so unchecked onto the page. But of course it is when Hazlitt is most privately concerned that he touches on those public affairs which involve political, sensual, happiness-seeking, disappointment-finding mankind. The reader, encountering this form of literary nakedness, must either acknowledge its reality or join the prissy mob which defines what is permissible. But whatever his reaction to that 'brow-hanging, shoe-contemplative, *strange*' creature of Coleridge's jittery description, ordinary, conforming, tax-paying, shibboleth-swallowing man must inevitably encounter guilt, cowardice and regret when he encounters William Hazlitt. The oil which runs the smooth society was not for him. Nor did he ever pretend otherwise:

> I am not in the ordinary acceptance of the term, *a good-natured man*, that is, many things annoy me besides what interferes with my own ease and interest. I hate a lie; a piece of injustice wounds me to the quick, though nothing but the report of it reaches me. Therefore I have made many enemies and few friends; for the public know nothing of well-wishers and keep a wary eye on those that would reform them.

William Hazlitt was born in Maidstone on 10 April 1778, the fourth child of an Irish Unitarian minister. The Reverend William Hazlitt and Grace his wife were revolutionaries and intellectual deists, thoroughly familiar with the teachings of Franklin, Priestley, Price and Godwin. Having such direct access to this radical spring was to create in their son what he described as 'that unfortunate attachment to a set of abstract phrases, such as liberty, truth, justice, humanity, honour . . .' Weaned on absolutes, quite unable to judge anything without the use of both head and heart, Hazlitt inherited a code which lacked all social flexibility. What was not truth was a lie. And what made the world swing, far more terribly than merrily when the movement was honestly examined, was, for him, chiefly a set of myths. What was not liberty was slavery. Where and what was compromise? It was a word on which he stumbled, never seeing it, never able to convince himself of its uses. 'If we only think justly,' the good father told the son, 'we shall easily foil all the advocates of tyranny.' Hazlitt believed this and continued to believe it to the end of his life; and long after the great dream of replacing kingdoms (government by superstition) with republics (government by reason) was being repudiated as a kind of youthful excess by his friends. For them it was just a phase, and to remind them of it became a breach of good manners. Students and young writers said wild things. The sign for them to accept the world as it was came when Napoleon crowned himself in Notre Dame. Their loyalties, they then knew, were elsewhere.

Hazlitt, dedicated to the revolution, became a lone voice speaking against the full blast of windy rhetoric needed to prosecute a national war. Allied to his revolutionary politics there were notions of personal freedom which not only disturbed and shocked, but which could endanger the kind of blanket patriotism required during a national emergency. He insisted that to deny discussion of any aspect of the human condition was cant. His contemporaries disagreed. What they could not bear in the public sense they called 'sedition' and what they shrank from in the personal sense they termed 'filth'. Hazlitt met invective with invective. His abuse was an art in itself. It coruscated with brilliant side issues. This was the Hazlitt who believed 'in the theoretical benevolence, and practical malignity of man', and who was able to turn every dirty thrust with such skill and panache that reading his rage and abuse at this length of time is still as exhilarating and disturbing as watching an immense gale. Both enemy and friend hoped that these periodic great uproars, with their close engagement with life as it was, would somehow loosen Hazlitt from his untenable ideals and bring him into the ordinary arena of debate. Somewhere where his white face and black looks did not spoil the comfort of the day. But he could not be drawn into any cosy circle. He remained on the edge to remind friends who had done a deal with the establishment of the time when they would have refused to settle for little improvements on earth and pious hopes of heaven. Humanity might have had its heart's desire, as the young Wordsworth had plainly stated,

Not in Utopia . . .
But in the very world, which is the world
Of all of us – the place where in the end
We find our happiness, or not at all!

The chance to 'find happiness in the world of all of us' had occurred in a rare and wonderful way during Hazlitt's lifetime. Then had come this blank refusal on the part of the very heralds of change. How could they have gone back on all the bright promises? He was unable either to understand or forgive:

I have never given the lie to my own soul. If I have felt any impression once, I feel it more strongly a second time; and I have no wish to revile or discard my best thoughts. There is at least a thorough *keeping* in what I write – not a line that betrays a principle or disguises a feeling.

Hazlitt's youth had spanned an incredibly ecstatic moment in human history. Shackling traditions were being overhauled; the *status quo* questioned. The American colonies had freed themselves with surprising ease from Britain and the French people had rejected the hereditary principle in government. He was still a boy when Captain Tournay had ridden against the very symbol of the old power, the Bastille, and it had fallen. Hope reached out far beyond Paris at this event and involved radicals everywhere in the actual possibility of creating a society which up until this moment had seemed to belong to the geography of romance, or the hereafter. It was the first of Hazlitt's personality-shaking, soul-forming experiences. Others were to come and each would exalt and afflict him for the rest of his days. His anger was only equalled by his astonishment when, later on, others were to describe similar experiences and the commonsense way they had grown out of them. Enthusiasm – a word then used to sum up a well-meaning but weak-headed eagerness – should not be applied to the new and the untraditional. Yet some had never presented enthusiasm more magnificently:

For mighty were the auxiliars which then stood
Upon our side, we who were strong in love!
Bliss was it in that dawn to be alive
But to be young was very heaven!

This was the clear trumpet-note which Hazlitt heard in his head and felt in his heart until he died. He had stayed, the rest had retreated. (He had actually advanced, that was his trouble. Although so exactly late-Georgian man, there was that in his nature which anticipated radical concepts and behaviour which are only now being accepted as possible alternatives to the existing structure.) He was often so far ahead politically that he was fighting evils which his contemporaries simply could not see. He called their conduct cant – a favourite epithet – but it was true that they often did not know what he was so angry about. When his strictures became too much, too outside anything they could comprehend, it became charitable to call him mad.

But for him there were worse things than being called mad. Nicknames. 'A nickname is the hardest stone that the devil can throw at a man. It will knock down any man's resolution. It will stagger his reason. It will tame his pride. . . . The unfavourable opinion of others gives you a bad opinion of yourself.' As so often happens, the least apt, the most moronically inspired nickname cut deepest. In March 1818 he was described as 'Pimpled Hazlitt' in *Blackwood's Magazine*. The fact of his notoriously sharp, set face with its pale clear skin became irrelevant. He believed that his entire image in the eyes of the world had become pustulate and obscene because of this false description. It heralded the grand attack on him and he met it with the most dazzling set pieces of invective which, with the exception of Swift's, can be found in the language. But the damage was done all the same and, as he confessed to Bryan Procter ('Barry Cornwall'), 'it nearly put me underground.' Procter tragically summed it up when he said that Hazlitt 'was crowned by defamation'. There was another young friend who had reason to take sides with the figure in the pillory. Why should not Hazlitt speak out on anything and everything? What was the fear – it could be nothing less – which made the *Quarterly*, for instance, attempt to reduce his influence by declaring that his essays were dished up in 'broken English' and left behind them a trail of 'slime and filth'? Since when was the world unable to endure the truth? 'Hazlitt,' cried John Keats '. . . is your only good damner, and if ever I am damn'd – damn me if I shouldn't like him to damn me.'

But however deep the wounding, Hazlitt was never changed by it. Society was never to teach him a lesson. Sweet reason and threats alike could not sway his commitment, whether to an individual or a cause.

'These bargains are for life,' he said of his decisions, once made. Had not his father been equally uncompromising? Old Mr Hazlitt's outspokenness had forced him out of his comfortable living at Maidstone, and his protests about the barbarous treatment given by the English garrison to American prisoners of war in Ireland had made it necessary for him to leave that country. Greatly daring, he had in 1783 emigrated to the new and hopeful republic of the United States of America, only to find as much bigotry in Boston as in Kent or County Cork. William, aged eight, thought so little of his new land that, writing to his father, he said, 'that it would have been a great deal better if the white people had not found it out'. His only memory of America, from which he returned a year later, was the taste of barberries. In 1788 the family settled in Wem, Shropshire, Mr Hazlitt's gradual withdrawal from 'the world of all of us' to a dreamier habitation is described by William with absolute tenderness, and without accusation. A note of wistfulness, too, intrudes. Hazlitt, though never an agnostic, has parted from the comfort of his father's God. There will be no such retreat for him when the world becomes unendurable:

After being tossed about from congregation to congregation . . . he had been relegated to an obscure village, where he was to spend the last thirty years of his life, far from the only converse that he loved, the talk about disputed texts of Scripture, and the cause of civil and religious liberty. Here he passed his days, repining but resigned, in the study of the Bible, and the perusal of the Commentators – huge folios, not easily got through, one of which would outlast a winter! . . . Here were 'no figures nor no fantasies' – neither poetry nor philosophy – nothing to dazzle, nothing to excite modern curiosity; but to his lack-lustre eyes there appeared . . . the sacred name JEHOVAH in capitals: pressed down by the weight of style, worn to the last fading thinness of the understanding, there were glimpses, glimmering notions of the patriarchal wanderings, with palm-trees hovering in the horizon, and processions of camels at the distance of three thousand years . . . questions as to the date of the creation, predictions of the end of all things; the great lapses of time, the strange mutations of the globe were unfolded with the voluminous leaf, as it turned over; and though the soul might slumber with an hieroglyphic veil of inscrutable mysteries drawn over it, yet it was in a slumber ill-exchanged for all the sharpened realities of sense, wit, fancy or reason. My father's life was comparatively a dream; but it was a dream of infinity and eternity, of death, the resurrection, and a judgment to come!

Although Hazlitt had, at fifteen, rejected his father's wish that he should become a Unitarian minister, his awakening to faith had about it much of the detail of the classic Christian conversion, word, angel and all. The latter had luminous eyes, a mighty brow and large, soft childish lips only partly concealing bad teeth. At twenty-six, Samuel Taylor Coleridge had not had the same difficulties as Hazlitt in combining religion with intellectual freedom, and in 1797 was considering the offer of a Unitarian living in Shrewsbury. In January 1798 Hazlitt was now nineteen and had done little since leaving college four years before except to hide away in his room or in a field and read *Tom Jones* (another bargain for life), Rousseau and Burke; having read Coleridge's 'Ode on the Departing Year', and having heard that he was a revolutionary, he walked the ten miles from Wem to Shrewsbury to hear him preach. Neither he nor the world as yet knew that this magical young man had completed *The Ancient Mariner* or that he had begun the regular use of drugs. The sermon was spectacular. Coleridge's text was 'And he went up into the mountain to pray, HIMSELF, ALONE.' It was about the real Christ-path, about pacifism (Britain was expecting to be invaded by Napoleon), poetry and isolation. Hazlitt listened and was both crushed and elated by the personal implications the sermon had for him. The following Tuesday Coleridge came to Wem for a dinner of Welsh mutton and boiled turnips, and stayed the night. Hazlitt walked with the poet as far as the sixth milestone when he returned to Shrewsbury in the morning. Hazlitt's walk was straight and Coleridge's meandering and constantly crossing the younger man's path. Hazlitt saw that they did not collide and listened to the quite unimaginable flood of talk. All was changed, all was new. His confusion and dullness had gone. His joy in Coleridge was almost like that of a lover at times, making him sick and exhilarated by turn. When, on parting, the poet invited him to visit him in Somerset, where he and Wordsworth were collaborating on a book of poems – the *Lyrical Ballads* – Hazlitt's happiness was overwhelming.

Years later, in one of the most wonderful descriptions of a turning-point in life – 'My First Acquaintance With Poets' – Hazlitt recalled the moment exactly.

On my way back, I had a sound in my ears, it was the voice of Fancy: I had a light before me, it was the face of Poetry . . . I had an uneasy, pleasurable sensation all the time, till I was to visit him. During these months the chill breath of winter gave me a welcoming; the vernal air was balm and inspiration to me. The golden sunsets, the silver star of evening, lighten me on my way to new hopes and prospects. *I was to visit Coleridge in the spring.* The circumstance was never absent from my thoughts, and mingled with all my feelings. I wrote to him at the time proposed, and received an answer postponing my intended visit for a week or two, but very cordially urging me to complete my promise then. This delay did not damp, but rather increased my ardour. In the meantime I went to Llangollen Vale, by way of initiating myself in the mysteries of natural scenery; and I must say I was enchanted with it . . . That valley was to me (in a manner) the cradle of a new existence . . . !

Thus the first meeting with Coleridge and Wordsworth possessed all the dramatic power of a curtain rising on a tragedy whose first scene is a deceptive and lulling idyll. Yet, in spite of what was to follow, when Wordsworth, sunk deep in reaction and apprehensive of what the world would think of his youthful friendship with a man who was now a notorious radical, was not above spreading gossip about Hazlitt's sex life in an effort to discredit him, and Coleridge, as marvellous during this period as his own drinker of the milk of Paradise, had sunk into a comfort-seeking hulk, the essayist allowed nothing to dim or qualify the glory of his twentieth year. 'What I have once set my hand to, I take the consequences of . . .' We see Coleridge at this moment as one who commits others to great doctrines which he is unable to follow himself, and we see Hazlitt's frightening vulnerability for the first time. 'My First Acquaintance With Poets' reveals, as well as happiness, that ultimate defencelessness which marks all his writing.

It was art, however, and not literature which received its fillip from this meeting, although in Hazlitt's mind at this time the two activities had begun their inseparable fascination for him – 'Till I began to paint, or till I became acquainted with the author of *The Ancient Mariner*, I could neither write nor speak.' But painting for Hazlitt was to be neither a career nor a mere interest. Mania might best describe it. It is doubtful if any words – his beloved Shakespeare's excepted – were ever to involve him heart and soul as did Rembrandt, Titian and Raphael. Throughout his life he thrust these masters forward like a salvation-bringing icon, insisting 'Believe! believe!' It was not enough that he should become rapturous in picture galleries: he had to bring others to this state, for he knew nothing to equal it. A few weeks after meeting the poets he left home to become an art student in London. His hero now – for Hazlitt was a man who insisted on heroes – was James Northcote.

Hazlitt's conception of painting was strictly retrospective. The nearer it turned back to its sublime source – Titian, Rembrandt, Raphael – the greater it became. Northcote's special attraction was that he had known Sir Joshua Reynolds and his circle, and, as one who had had direct contact with an artist who had reaffirmed the inviolable laws of art, he possessed a special mystique for Hazlitt. Eventually he Boswellised the gossipy old man in *Conversations of James Northcote*, a book which contains many amusing anecdotes, including one about Romney and a painter friend first seeing the Sistine Chapel, and the friend gasping, 'Egad, George, we're bit!' Hazlitt, the entirely open and inquiring, the radical and the sceptic in most matters connected with human activity, became fiercely orthodox and academic the moment he entered a gallery. Nor could he ever see a picture without needing to place a written description beside it. He quite baffled old Northcote – 'Very odd – very odd! I can make nothing of him. He is the strangest being I ever met with.' But when, in 1821, he published his essay 'On the Pleasure of Painting', the need for such an enthusiasm is explained. Reading it in the light of his multiple tragedy, his inability to relate to everything, from the accepted pattern of politics to the average notions of love, we see his faith in painting as a great stabilising factor in his sad, triumphant life. Old Mr Hazlitt, after half a lifetime's engagement with callousness, had sought Jehovah's arm. His son, fighting the same evils but never to know a moment's rest, found in landscapes the portraits harmonious statements from which he could draw strength. Art was for Hazlitt a mixture of religion and medicine, and he envied those engaged in it.

No one thinks of disturbing a landscape painter at his task: he seems a kind of magician, the privileged genius of the place. Whenever a Claude, a Wilson, has introduced his own portrait in the foreground of a picture, we look at it with interest (however ill it may be done) feeling that it is the portrait of one who was quite happy at the time, and how glad we should be to change places with him.

Where his own painting was concerned, Hazlitt was a fundamentalist, restating the dictums of the old masters as faithfully as he could. He painted his father in the manner of Rembrandt, and Charles Lamb in the style of Titian. On two occasions, in 1802 and 1824, he visited the Louvre. No one in search of Europe's great pictures need have gone further, for Napoleon had looted the Continental galleries and palaces of their treasures and had heaped them up in Paris. There had never been so great a concentration of the major European schools, and certainly not one so easily available to the ordinary people. Hazlitt, a shabby student of twenty-four when he first sat copying one of his beloved Titians in rooms so recently closed to all but the privileged few, felt that he was present at some kind of response in the frustrating rules governing humanity. 'You have enriched the museum of Paris with 300 masterpieces . . . which it required thirty centuries to produce,' Napoleon had told his troops. For Hazlitt, this was not the customary spoils of war but a taking of art out of the exclusive hereditary sector and making it available to all. In France, he heard tales of the Emperor's taste, charm, courage and general superiority at every hand, and there began that process – and one involving the hero of all heroes – by which he could accept Napoleon as the enemy of absolutism and all the stale systems developing from it.

Wordsworth, who was also in France in 1802 – the Peace of Amiens had brought the British across the Channel in their thousands, all eager to see this sensationally transformed nation – watched Napoleon's imperialism and lost all belief in revolution. He wrote sneeringly of the eagerness of the recent destroyers of the Bourbons to

> bend the knee
> In France, before the new-born Majesty!

For Hazlitt, Napoleon remained the hope of the world and when, at Waterloo, the final crushing came, his despair was terrifying. 'It is not to be believed how the destruction of Napoleon affected him,' wrote Benjamin Robert Haydon:

He seemed prostrated in mind and body, he walked about unwashed, unshaved, hardly sober by day and always intoxicated by night, literally, without exaggeration, for weeks; until at length, wakening as it were from a stupor, he at once left off all stimulating liquors, and never touched them after.

(This latter teetotalism was not the good thing it might appear, for Hazlitt took to drinking green tea of such strength and in such quantities that it probably contributed to the stomach cancer which was to kill him.) Another witness of Hazlitt at this time was Thomas Talfourd, the first biographer of Lamb. 'When I first met Hazlitt in the year 1815,' he wrote, he was staggering under the blow of Waterloo. The reappearance of his imperial idol on the coast of France, and his triumphant march to Paris, like a fairy vision, had excited his admiration and sympathy to the utmost pitch; and though in many respects sturdily English in feeling, he could scarcely forgive the valour of the conquerors . . .

He added, 'On this subject only was he "eaten up with passion", on all others, he was the fairest, the most candid of reasoners.'

Hazlitt's last great task was a monumental *Life of Napoleon Buonaparte*. It was mostly written in Paris and he intended it as both a vindication of Bonaparte and the pinnacle of his own career. He also relied on it to bring him some real money and to put a stop, at least for some time, to the hand-to-mouth existence of essay writing. But whereas these had seemed to simply fly into print with no difficulty beyond that created by Rightist cliques, the great *Life of Napoleon* seemed hardly able to totter from the press. Nor was this all. Like some hideously uncalled-for blow from a person for whose sake one has endured much, the publishers went bankrupt, involving Hazlitt in a loss of £200 when, with his last illness approaching, he was in desperate need of money. The Emperor who had alighted like the bird of promise had turned into a albatross. Hazlitt could have found reasons for getting Napoleon off his neck. It would have made life easier. It would certainly have widened his influence as a radical journalist, for there were those who saw his defence of Napoleon as something which at the best was irrational and at the worst, mad. But, as he wrote to William Gifford.

The reason why I have not changed my principle with some of the persons alluded to Wordsworth, Coleridge and Southey is, that I had a natural inveteracy of understanding which did not bend to fortune or circumstances. I was not a poet, but a metaphysician; and I suppose that the conviction of an abstract principle is alone a match for the prejudices of absolute power. The love of truth is the best foundation for the love of liberty. In this sense, I might have repeated –

> 'Love is not love that alteration finds:
> O, no! it is an ever-fixed mark
> That looks on tempests and is never shaken.'

Besides, I had another reason. I owed something to truth, for she had done something for me. Early in life I had made (what I thought) a metaphysical discovery; and after that it was too late to think of retracting. My pride forbad it:

my understanding revolted at it. I could not do better than go on as I had begun. I too, worshipped at no unhallowed shrine, and served in no mean presence. I had laid my hand on the ark, and could not turn back!

To trace the second disastrous strand in Hazlitt's life, we have to return to his second meeting with the poets. This occurred in the summer of 1803. They were kind and welcoming, but they were *different*. They sat to the almost penniless artist for their portraits, but when they introduced him to their benefactor, the High Tory Sir George Beaumont, a famous patron, he disgraced them by airing his radical views and contradicting Coleridge, Sir George's latest protégé, in his – Sir George's – actual presence. Other complications followed. Hazlitt drifted along with the poets, now including Southey, all that autumn, becoming more and more bewildered by the great change which had come over his friends, and feeling upset. On 14 December 1803 he left. Southey, writing at the time, makes it sound a perfectly ordinary departure, and even goes so far as to describe Hazlitt as a painter 'of real genius'. Wordsworth, writing twelve years later, had a very different tale to tell. Hazlitt, the moralist on all things, had when staying with the poets in the Lake District attempted to violate a village girl against her will and it was only through the generosity of his friends that he had escaped from the indignant country youths, and possibly from transportation. Charles Lamb, who received this news from Wordsworth in December 1814, laughingly reduced it to a pastoral frolic, but Henry Crabb Robinson, who actually heard the details from Wordsworth's own lips, was so fascinated by them that, in the selfish manner of educated prudes, he resorted to Latin when setting them down in his diary. An obscene gossip proliferated at once from this story and from now until the close of his life Hazlitt's name carried with it the overtones of depravity.

Wordsworth's motive for making the serious charge stemmed from his political *volte-face* of 1802–3. Both he and Coleridge had sided with France during the first half of the Napoleonic war because they regarded their own country's action as a war against the birth of democracy. But they changed sides when the second war was decided upon because they saw that Napoleon was no more democratic than the Bourbons and was in fact planning a great imperial military adventure. Eagerness to begin this second war, which had actually been declared by the time Hazlitt reached Keswick, was rowdily apparent and he saw, to his disgust, that Coleridge of all people was in the van of 'the war-whoop', as he called it. Coleridge had, in fact, invented Napoleon's most damaging nickname – 'the Corsican'. Such fervent patriotism was reassuring to Sir George Beaumont, and came as a natural relief to Wordsworth in his new mood of Olympian withdrawal to the Cumberland mountains. Hazlitt's disgust at their revised positions when he arrived in 1803 was one thing, but his morbid pursuit of them in print as turncoats – something they could not have imagined the confused young artist would ever be able to do – was another. Hazlitt, fighting his own private war for liberty, was a menace. The note of accusation never ceased. The accuser needed to be accused – but of what?

Because his enemies so often reached through his private life in order to discredit his politics and, in Wordsworth's case, even his literary opinions – for one reason why the Lakes escapade was made public in 1814 was fear of what Hazlitt might write about *The Excursion*, which was published that year – it is necessary to take a brief look at Hazlitt and women. They were very important to him, but his neglect of 'manner' in his approach to them and what seemed like a tacit assumption on his part that they would reciprocate his feelings without going through the usual charade of high-flown talk and artificial gestures got him no-where. His lack of success, and subsequent fear and hostility towards 'young ladies', was well known among his friends, who found it very amusing. Crabb Robinson had seen his nervous confusion and shock when, still a boy, some well-bred girls had teased him during a holiday at Bury St Edmunds. It enabled the diarist to state, when the outcry against him as an immoralist was at its height, that 'Like other gross sensualists, he had a horror of the society of ladies, especially of smart and handsome and modest young women.'

Hazlitt was married twice, each time to a 'lady'. But an early Rousseau-like idealisation of simple, unsophisticated girls, a conception of companionship which at first had for him a dreamy innocence, grew naturally into a sexual desire for such women. Although they let him down every bit as much as the ladies, his forgiveness of their inability to accept him as a lover showed that in these encounters he was not self-blind. P. P. Howe, his best biographer, sees the Keswick incident as the sketch, as it were, of the marvellous and remorselessly worked-out *Liber Amoris* story in which both the bathos and the splendour of obsessional sexual love have been set down on the page in their entirety. It is the type of love which those who have not experienced it call infatuation because to them it is undignified and pathetic. Hazlitt in love was, to his friends, a comic sight; to his enemies, a disgusting one. Hazlitt did not pretend to find love, as he recognised it, in either of his wives. The first union, to Sarah Stoddart, was almost as much an arranged marriage (by Charles and Mary Lamb) as if the bride and groom had been Chinese. Lamb, for whom Hazlitt's sex life was the only thing about his friend he could never take seriously, laughed so much during the wedding that he was nearly turned out of church. Sarah was to bring Hazlitt little happiness in herself but she gave him a son, whom he both mothered and fathered, his wife being cold in such matters and, anyway, frequently away from home on great walking tours. Neither lover nor homemaker, she was yet what he vaguely wanted a woman to be – a free agent, an untrammelled soul. Sarah Hazlitt was, in fact, a New Woman born a century before her time. How she would have enjoyed 'rational' clothes for all that hiking! By the time of their – inevitable – divorce, in Edinburgh, her craving for the open road forced her to walk nearly 150 miles through the Scottish countryside during the proceedings. As well as his adored son, she gave her husband one other thing that pleased him, a small cottage in Winterslow, Wiltshire.

It was from this address, immediately after his marriage in 1808, that he began to bombard the London editors with outlines for literary projects, and that he wrote his *Memoirs of the late Thomas Holcroft*. The choice of subject was interesting. Thomas Holcroft, who had died the year before, had been a friend of Tom Paine and a believer in Godwin's revolutionary ideas. He had also been a stable-boy who had become a successful novelist and playwright.

But neither painting, his wife's fortune of £80 a year, nor the solid books he was managing to turn out, met the expenses of married life, and in the autumn of 1812 Hazlitt, with Lamb's help, became parliamentary reporter for the *Morning Chronicle*, a Whig newspaper edited by James Perry, whose snobbery and scant scholarship did not prevent him from becoming one of the most progressive figures in nineteenth-century journalism. Within a year of accepting this job, Hazlitt was filling the columns of the *Morning Chronicle* with far more exciting things than could be heard in the House of Commons, essays such as 'On the

Love of Life' and brilliant accounts of what was taking place on the London stage. Both these discursive essays, in which profound and extraordinary matters were dealt with wittily and with a personal conviction which made an immediate contact with the reader, and the dramatic criticism, were of a kind previously unknown to journalism. The excellence and unusualness of his work provided Hazlitt, now in his early thirties, with the influence which he could never have hoped to have derived from any other literary activity. Whatever the world thought of his politics, both his style and the strangely intimate tone of his arguments were things which no one cared to miss. 'Once he had started,' says P. P. Howe, 'we find his dramatic criticisms, art criticisms, political letters and leading articles, "Common-places", and contributions from "An English Metaphysician", all going up together in Mr Perry's columns.'

As this hardly-to-be-expected burst of literary power and excellence coincided with such national self-examinings as the meaning of patriotism, inquests on the value of the French Revolution and what to do with Napoleon, a reactionary Britain – including the Lake District – saw with horror that a Daniel had come to judgement. Worse, Hazlitt's very catholicity, his perverse refusal – or inability – to specialise in a subject, as other men did, made him hard to handle. A piece that, when produced by the eighteenth-century essayists and their followers, would have contained a few ounces of elegantly wrapped morality, often contained an ethical explosion when it left Hazlitt's hand. He lacked all restraint. Anything which threatened the total liberty of the individual, the little deceits by which society managed to get by, the areas of human behaviour which it was 'civilized' to ignore, speciousness of all kinds and *cant* – his four-letter word for describing the talk which covered the naked truth – these were his natural targets. He attacked them with a mixture of gaiety and rage. Those who had reason to fear waited nervously for his blow. His concept of truth as a once-revealed thing to which a man remained loyal no matter what happened later on placed everybody in the somewhat religious position of either the 'faithful' or the 'apostates'. Southey, who at nineteen had written a revolutionary play called *Wat Tyler*, was aghast to find something he hoped the world had forgotten being reissued by a pirate-publisher at the very moment he had accepted the Laureateship. Hazlitt gave no quarter in this affair, and others with radical pasts which, up to now, they thought well-buried, shivered. He was no believer in the woolliness which society permitted to shelter public and private lives, but however much people might deplore his stark honesty, they could not forbear to look.

Yet he was never simply out for a scoop, and journalism in the ordinary sense of news plus comment meant little to him. A magnificent writer who would have preferred to work quietly on philosophical treatises in the tradition of Locke and Hobbes, he was driven to the newspapers and the magazines by the need to make money. He wrote spasmodically and with a certain resentment. He was daydreaming and indolent. His real pleasure never stemmed from work but from drifting, idling, unplanned days made up of lying on the chalky turf of the Wiltshire downs, playing racquets on the St Martin's Street court, and chatting to strangers or chance acquaintances. Like so many artists, he was never reconciled to one or another in the choice between the country and the town. His compassion for the village people of England during their extreme misery of the 1820s also indicated his personal fear of them. As a village intellectual on and off for the best part of his life, he could not forget the countryman's narrowness and meanness of spirit, and as a townsman he could never be sufficiently man of the world to exist without shock amidst scenes of accepted greed, indifference and hypocrisy. In both village and town he recovered his shaken belief in life by reading the poets and by looking at pictures.

Yet, although shy of contact with the masses and often scathing about them, he saw them as few people did at the time – as the real England, crushed by the land evictions, reduced and starved by the famine caused by the war, and tragically inarticulate. His emergence in 1807 as a trenchant and controversial writer came with his attack on Malthus in *A Reply to the Essay on Population*. The Reverend T. R. Malthus was exactly what the establishment needed after the drums of revolution had petered out, a clergyman-prophet able to supply fact and figure for the inevitability of inequality in human society. For the ruling class Malthus had provided a mandate for going on as before. To back his theory he had put forward a plan for dealing with 'the poor', that inconvenient nine-tenths of the nation. This included, among many other things, notions for restraining fatherhood among rural males and the blue-print for extensions of the Poor Law which was to harass countless simple families right up to the First World War. Hazlitt's attack on Malthus was violent and emotional but it displayed his freedom, and less apprehensive friends than Wordsworth and Coleridge came forward to acknowledge him. Among these was Charles Lamb, Hazlitt's senior by only three and a half years, but in whose (much tried) relationship there was a stable, protective element suggesting a much older man. The great difference, in fact, between Lamb and Hazlitt was that the former seemed to have received the gift of perpetual early middle-age and the latter, with his moodiness, his iconoclasm, his physical energy, his hero-worship, his passionate love and his general recklessness, appeared to have been cursed with everlasting youth. To outgrow innocence – one's initial reflexes to important matters – was for Hazlitt a sin. James Knowles, one of his disciple-like young friends, said, 'There was ore in him, and rich, but his maturer friends were blind to it. I saw it. He was a man to whom I would have submitted my life.'

From 1816 onwards Hazlitt's work has to be seen against the churning unrest which provoked the government to suspend Habeas Corpus in 1817 and which was violently epitomised in the massacre at Peterloo on 16 August 1819. His collected essays from the *Examiner* were published under the title of *The Round Table*, and dedicated to Lamb. The essays so excelled the usual literature of radical protest that one critic described the collection as being 'like a whale's back in a sea of prose'. We have a number of glimpses of him at this period, including the one Haydon painted in his enormous *Entry into Jerusalem*, where Hazlitt is shown 'looking at Christ as an investigator'. The same year as this portrait appeared, Wordsworth was writing to the artist, 'The miscreant Hazlitt continues, I have heard, to abuse Southey, Coleridge and myself in the *Examiner*. I hope you do not associate with the Fellow, he is not a proper person to be admitted into respectable society . . .' A less hostile witness gives this vivid description.

His face was indeed indifferent, and his movements shy and awkward; but there was something in his earnest, irritable face, his restless eyes, his black hair, combed backwards and curling (not too resolutely) about a well-shaped head, that was very striking . . . At home, his style of dress (or undress) was perhaps slovenly, because there was no one to please; but he always presented a very clean and neat appearance when he went abroad. His mode of walking was loose, weak and unsteady; although his arms displayed strength, which he used to put forth when he played at racquets with Martin Burney and others . . . His violence (if violence he had), was of very rare occurrence. He was extremely patient . . . Had he been as temperate in his political views as in his cups, he would have escaped the slander that pursued him through life.

Temperance, however, was not something which Hazlitt understood. 'When I see a spirit of intolerance I see a great Devil,' he said.

This, then, was how he looked at the moment when he was at the height of his power as a writer. The man who in life so disliked being touched and human contact generally, and accepted friendship on chilling terms – and then complained of lack of warmth: 'I want to know why everybody has such a dislike of me' – was, on the page, to generate a glow which admitted the reader at once to his intimate presence.

In 1820 Hazlitt and Lamb were contributing to the *London Magazine* the wonderful essays which were to become, respectively, the first volume of *Table Talk* and *The Essay of Elia*. It was also the year of disaster. Hazlitt lost all hope – 'I believe in the theoretical benevolence and practical malignity of man' – and eventually almost lost his reason. Why? Because at forty-three he had fallen in love at first sight with the nineteen-year-old girl who waited on him in the two back rooms of a lodging-house in Southampton Buildings. 'Love at first sight is only realising imagination that has always haunted us . . . our dream is out at last . . .' At twenty-six, the Lakes girl had led him on, laughing, and (according to Wordsworth) he had struck her. Now he was middle-aged, Sarah Walker was to do the same, with 'mock embraces' and lips 'as common as the stairs'. Yet sometimes she smiled, and in analysing the effect this had on him, he had immortalised her. His refusal not to treat the situation rationally – with a straightforward sexuality – bewildered Sarah and puzzled his friends, to whom he was compelled to pour out his troubles. Strangers, too, had to listen to every humiliating detail of the affair, for he was an obsessed creature, 'the fool of love'. It was the kind of behaviour which appeared to justify De Quincey's later verdict that Hazlitt 'wilfully placed himself in collision with all the interests that were in the sunshine of this world . . .' The love affair, grotesquely compounded with divorce proceedings concerning the other Sarah, and followed by a nervous breakdown during which he considered suicide, produced the extraordinary *Liber Amoris*. Once he had been merely bitter when a simple girl let him down – 'Choose a mistress from among your equals . . . Those in an inferior station to yourself will doubt your good intentions . . . They will be ignorant of the meaning of half you say, and laugh at the rest' – now he gave himself up to a total declaration of the nature of the only sexual love he understood. The *Liber Amoris* endorsed posterity's claim to distrust him long after his politics had ceased to offend. Robert Louis Stevenson thought of writing Hazlitt's biography, then discovered this book and withdrew in horror. Augustus Birrell was simply astonished that a grown man could let himself in for anything so idiotic – 'The loves of the middle-aged are never agreeable subject matter . . . a fool at forty is a fool indeed . . .' He added, '*Liber amoris* now sinks below the stage, and joins the realm of things unspeakable . . .' Charles Morgan, in an excellent introduction to the book (1948), reminds us that Hazlitt's unguarded account of love and sexual madness was published at the same time as Stendhal's *De l'amour*, and he says that 'the whole story of the *Liber amoris* is a flawless example of Stendhal's theory of crystallization'. To write it, Hazlitt had to abandon the only thing which could have made it even remotely socially acceptable – dignity. It was not 'manly', declared *Blackwood's*. This it all too shatteringly was. Love is frequently a pitiable state.

Recovered from the débâcle, he settled down to his familiar unsettled life, working when he must but now with a greater sense of his own coherence. In 1825 came *The Spirit of the Age* and a year abroad with his second wife, the all but unknown Isabella Bridgwater. Also a meeting with Stendhal – 'my friend Mr Beyle'. He returned looking ill. His writing grew in its intensity, breaking in on the privacy of those who read it with irresistible and sometimes unbearable news. There was no escape from his meaning; the language which conveyed it shone with precision – 'I hate to see a load of bandboxes go along the street, and I hate to see a parcel of big words without anything in them.' The exposition of an idea would start out on the page in light, happy phrases which threatened no man's complacency, and then the skilful strengthening would begin, and intellectual involvement would bind the reader. Each essay shows the build-up of numerous small climaxes, such as are sometimes employed in the novel. Excitement and expectation mount. Hazlitt is the word-juggler who never misses; his almost casual use of ornament, epigram and fancy is hypnotic. Some, like De Quincey, resented that they should be morally got at by this 'abrupt, insulated, capricious . . . and non-sequacious style'. Hazlitt's method of writing essays had something in common with his action on the St Martin's Street fives court. He would begin by pleasantly spinning his subject around, work along various entertaining possibilities until he found a possible break-through, then score for all he was worth. He never regarded journalism as an inferior literary activity. His only regret was the voracious way it had of swallowing up work, and thus the time he would have preferred to spend in a kind of unambitious reverie. 'All that is worth remembering of life is the poetry of it.' Yet it was, as Virginia Woolf saw, the chafing and goading of many of life's unpoetic asides which kept Hazlitt on the stretch. Although he is primarily the spokesman for the inarticulate, the exploited, the self-deceived and the less brave inhabitants of George IV's England and the conscience of an era, he has also an uncanny ability to involve us across the generations in his hopes, hates, enthusiasms, fury and sensuality. It is also possible to see in him the warring extremes of the Puritan nature. He is a writer who must always remain more than 'works', and it is both thrilling and sobering when one investigates the latter to find so much flesh and blood, so much anger and so very much love. His was a uniquely rounded life. For him, writing never took the place of living.

He died of cancer on 18 September 1830 in a poor little room at 6 Frith Street, Soho. Bryan Proctor heard him speaking his last words in a voice 'resembling the faint scream I have heard from birds'. He was fifty-two.

The Writer as Listener

It was William Sansom who used to give 'Watching' as his hobby in *Who's Who* and it is true that writers are as watchful as cats. But what of listening? Or is listening an integral part of watching? I would like to isolate listening from the writer's general function of incessant observation and ask, do we, as poets, novelists and historians, ever attempt to examine or assess our own individual ear? Have we any idea of the range of our listening or of its selectivity? We know that we have long since become quite unashamed about our eavesdropping and we know that there is a subtle difference between what we set out to hear for the purposes of literature, and what we hear involuntarily. We even accept that, like Milton's Comus, there are times when we are all ears in order to take in strains that might create a soul, and when we are especially alert to any passing voice which might suggest a new character. But what we do not know is the extent and pattern of our listening generally. It seems easier to describe what we normally *see* than what we normally hear. Even in the physical sense we allow the eye ranges and limitations which, unless we suffer from very considerable loss of hearing, we deny to the ear. Yet it is likely that the solitary nature of the act of writing, and the accumulative quiet in which most of us spend our working lives, affect our listening capacity, intensifying it in some, distorting it in others. In the long run, of course, the only people who can tell us what we hear are our readers. Our veracity is proved this way for, as Thoreau said, 'It takes two to speak the truth, one to speak, and another to hear.'

Listening in the strict sense of the word means to hear attentively. Yet literature abounds with remarkable things which the writer heard because he was not paying this kind of classroom attention, and by this I do not mean inner voices and the like, but actual sounds, usually sentences, floatingly acquired. Those speaking these sentences, did they but know that they were being so effortlessly intercepted, could say, 'I am not talking to *you*'. But as every writer knows at such a moment, they are – and in riveting tones. His thoughts build up around these syllables which he could have missed had he been listening 'attentively' and his creativity comes into play. Or he might tell himself, 'That's it! I have heard the voice of this decade, or of my time; I have caught its cadence and I can hear how we speak *now*.'

Havelock Ellis in his beautiful essays, *From Rousseau To Proust*, a book which led me to French novels and poetry when I was a boy but which, I fancy, is pretty unknown now, wrote, 'When we are young we do not immediately know where we shall hear those voices of our own time to which our virginal hearts will deeply and instinctively respond. They must come from figures of our own time, older than we are or they would not have found expression, but not old enough to have "arrived".' Thus, even if we write into old age, which we should (for there is a rich language which can only be heard then and which needs to be put down) it is important to read young writers of promise. For it is usually only they who can authenticate the present, who can convey its tone.

Attentive, as opposed to unconscious, listening by a writer demands the close hearing of someone else's story for the sake of the story which he has to tell. Although for various reasons he may wish to, he will not be able to hear such a story with detachment. Everything from his critical fascination with the narrative itself to the emotion of hearing from another's lips some confession or incident either long withheld or, until now, thought too uninteresting to describe, connects him to the speaker. Such emotion is equal in the force of its impact, even if varied in its origins, should the story come from a father, a friend or a stranger. Each individual speaker in the telling of it will unmask a little, and will add something to the writer's file on human variety and mystery. A man telling one how he makes a wheel – or a fortune – will inadvertently tell one much more. The main thing here is whether the writer possesses a context for what he is being told or whether it is completely out of his academic or social range. The listening writer is frequently drawn back to the voices of his childhood because he knows that they are saying things about his maturity which he will never hear elsewhere. Unlike many a professional interviewer, he finds the guardedness of those he listens to as rewarding as their frankness for, as was said of Proust, 'the power of observation only develops highly in the individual who has a personality to defend'. People can be as reticent about their aspirations as about their crimes, yet one is often struck by the precision and liveliness which accompanies some confessed longing. 'To tell one's dreams one must be infinitely awake,' wrote Paul Valéry, and fantasy is apt to make its owner exceedingly alert. The writer as listener rarely needs the whole tale, and the story-teller often sees little or nothing in what he has to offer, but, as Racine remarked when he had to reply to critical complaint about the emptiness of his *Bérénice*, 'All creation is out of nothing and what God on the seventh day saw as very good, for an unseeing eye (or unhearing ear) it would have still been nothing.' We can repeat Christ's pun after he had told his simple harvest tale about the ears of corn. 'Ye that have ears to hear, let him hear.'

Listening was until very recently a somewhat fugitive occupation for the writer. Whether he held what he had heard in his head until diary-time, as Boswell and others did, or whether he took it all down in immediate shorthand, there could be no actual repetition of a story which contained those rests and rushes which created its first impact. But now the writer as listener can hear the original talk on tape – hear it over and over again, pick over its contents and its semantics at his leisure, and could, not only reduce what he once heard with his creative ear to an automatic strip of information, but be in danger of losing the ear itself. Would Boswell have used tape? – had it been invented, that is. No, because the Doctor would not have let him. Who should use it? Chiefly those imaginative and creative writers who regard it as an advance on shorthand notes for the collecting of basic information, and oral historians with their philological skills. However, words are words, and the disembodied voice in the writer's study can resurrect a face, a gesture, an attitude, and before he knows where he is his special intelligence is at work, and he is telling us what he specifically heard.

I suppose that this process could come under the general title – 'Innovation in Literature'. When I wrote *Akenfield* I attempted to over-hear what had been said in and around my family for close on a rural century, using neighbourly surrogates for those whom death had silenced. It did not strike me as being innovatory at the time – just a method allowing both them and myself to speak. I remember when I began, and in great trepidation, never having done anything remotely like it before, trying it out on the dog, so to speak, or old Len, whom I had seen since a child. And then, after he had said his piece, as he called it, the shock and humiliation at discovering that I had never 'seen' him and never 'heard' him – not once in all my life. What I had heard and seen was a stocky little outline in the local fields, not this lucid rural intelligence with one foot caught in Cobbett's world and the other capable of finding a purchase in that of the E.E.C., had he lived long enough. From that day on I have regarded even the most open, colourful or predictable people as merely displaying the tip of the iceberg where their full reality is concerned. Not that most writers can hope to discover much more than a fraction of such a reality, yet, by listening to a particularly individual pattern of words, catching a tell-tale emphasis, or recognising that something is being said which the speaker may not ever have been able to say before, there is a recognition of the infinite possibilities and experiences lying just under the surface of things.

A striking description of what could happen to a writer who is completely cut off from human voices occurs in Michel Tournier's *Friday, Or the Other Island*. This vivid novel, like Jean Rhys's *Wide Sargasso Sea*, offers an audacious sequel to a previous work of genius, in this case *Robinson Crusoe*. Robinson, as Michel Tournier calls him, does not think of himself as writer but the brilliant extracts from the Journal he is allowed to keep convinces the reader that he is one. But, until Friday appears, Robinson's ears ache for spoken words; without them he realises that he is being diminished, gradually squeezed of response and literary interpretation.

'I know now,' writes Robinson on his silent island,

that every man carries within himself – and as it were above himself – a fragile and complex framework of habits, reflexes, preoccupations, dreams and associations, formed and constantly transformed by perpetual contact with his fellows ... My fellow men were the mainstay of my world ... Each day I measure my debt to them by observing the fresh cracks in my personal structure. I know what I would suffer should I lose the use of words ... [Here] there is only one viewpoint, my own, deprived of all context ... Language in a fundamental manner evoked the *peopled* world, where other men are like so many lamps casting a glow of light around them within which everything is, if not known, at least knowable. Those lights have vanished from my consciousness ... Since I have been here I have become something of a specialist in silence, or in silences, as I should say. With my whole being intent like a single ear I note the particular quality of the silence at a given moment.

Ironically, when Friday appears he fills Robinson's silences, not with language but with laughter, and directs his listening to what a 'civilized' ear no longer hears, the sensuous clamour of the natural universe. Mystic writers, of course, have their listening habits redirected in a similar fashion. A further irony which Michel Tournier employs when he forces the reader to contemplate what the wordless effect of a desert island must have on a writer whose ear is instinctively greedy for speech is to remind us that Robinson Crusoe was brought up in the Quaker religion, a faith which prohibits too much talk. Is it a divine rebuke for his conversation-craving, therefore, that when Robinson does find someone to listen to, he should be a 'savage' and thus in eighteenth-century terms not much advance on a talking dog? How Friday's human voice gradually penetrates an ear which has so long been stuffed-up with written ethics that it has forgotten the spoken give and take of our common humanity has its lessons for all of us.

Great novelists in particular have always revealed historic movement and social change and transition in a kind of build-up of seemingly casual talk. Immersed in their own artistically contained world, the characters of Sterne, Jane Austen, Flaubert and Thackeray also tell us about their world at large, though not in so many words. Yet their times are there. In order to convey the ceaseless shifts of society – and thus the ceaseless changes in the texture of its talk – Dickens created a marvel-lous series of party scenes ranging from the benign (Dingly Dell) to the grotesque (the evening entertainments laid on by Mr and Mrs Veneer-ing and Mr and Mrs Podsnap in *Our Mutual Friend*, masterly cross-currents of solecism as the newly enriched victors of the industrial revolution heave their way into the ranks of the upper bourgeoisie).

Some years ago I was shown the minute-books of the Great Yarmouth Literary Club and was enthralled to discover that now and then both Lord Nelson and Charles Dickens signed in as honorary guests. But even more enthralling was the familiar note of jollity and affability sounded by the secretary in his copper-plate hand. It was like voices-off saluting 'Pickwick' or the cosy mumbling from coffee-rooms with closed baize doors. Dickens had not begun to write his comic master-piece then, but no doubt he was all ears at Great Yarmouth. The affability which resounded among the 'bran-new' possessions of Pod-snap and Veneering required a very different interpretation – and got it. We laugh now at the dazzling invention and brio of it all, but how it must have lacerated hosts of Dickens's contemporaries as it caught the very accent of their pretensions and their materialism! Much has been said of his night walks in search of copy through London's rookeries but, in another sense, the language he listened to among the rising middle-class of the mid-nineteenth century offered an equal challenge to his genius. Have you noticed how the children of what one might call the talkers-in-transition in *Our Mutual Friend* reveal a different attitude, and often accent, to that of their parents? Although finer, it is less confident. Or, as in Miss Podsnap's reply to Mrs Lammle, it is a decision to shut-up, once and for all. But, if Mrs Lammle or anyone else persisted, Miss Podsnap would give her something to talk *about*, though not with her. (It is one way of crippling a conversation.)

Mrs Lammle was overjoyed to escape into a corner for a little quiet talk.

It promised to be a very quiet talk, for Miss Podsnap replied in a flutter, 'Oh! Indeed, it's very kind of you, but I am afraid I *don't* talk.'

'Let us make a beginning,' said the insinuating Mrs Lammle, with her best smile.

'Oh! I am afraid you'll find me very dull. But Ma talks!'

. . . 'Fond of reading perhaps?'

'Yes. At least I – don't mind that so much . . .'

'M-m-m-m-music.' So insinuating was Mrs Lammle that she got half a dozen m's into the word before she got it out . . . 'Of course you like dancing? . . .'

'Oh no, I don't . . .'

'No? With your youth and attractions? Truly, my dear, you surprise me!'

'I can't say,' observed Miss Podsnap, after hesitating considerably, and stealing several timid looks at Mrs Lammle's carefully arranged face, 'How I might have liked it if I had been a – you won't mention it, *will* you?'

'My dear! Never!'

'No I am sure you won't. I can't say then how I would have liked it, if I had been *a chimney-sweep on May-day.*'

Then we come to Thomas Creevey, listener extraordinary to the Regency, and insatiable recorder. It is now well-nigh impossible for us to understand how it came about that this plump little lawyer from nowhere, socially speaking, was such a hit with his contemporaries, from the Royal family down. Yet it is to him that we are indebted for every cough and rustle of those years. Of course, there are the Greville Memoirs, but Greville's ear had an official tilt to it and was more analogous to that of a Dick Crossman than to the artist in gossip. Mr

Creevey had the entrée because he had no fish to fry and because there was virtually nothing too small or insignificant in what another person had to say for it not to engage his undivided attention. He was thus uniquely qualified for being invited everywhere, which he was. Those who will listen with undisguised sympathy and an unprofessional keenness to trifles will be told, on occasion, History with a capital H.

Among Mr Creevey's recordings of the latter, none is more astonishing or impressive than what emerged from his casual encounter with the Duke of Wellington immediately after Waterloo. The Duke, you will remember, had left the battlefield and returned to Brussels after writing half of his dispatch. ('I came back' – that is from another room in the inn at Waterloo where he had visited a wounded friend – 'had a cup of tea and some toast, wrote my dispatch, and then rode into Brussels [where] I met Creevey . . . and he called out to me, "*What news?*"'

And that, I think, was the secret of Creevey's success, the triumph of his nature – to possess not only a tongue but a presence which made everyone he met feel that they had news to give. He was all ears to all men, which is why he became a perpetual guest and welcome everywhere until the day of his death. 'He possesses nothing but his clothes,' wrote Greville. 'He has no home, no servant, no creditors and no ties . . . I think he is the only man I know in society who possesses nothing.' Except the confidences of his age, one should add, a vast ocean of talk channelled into his *Journal* in handwriting so dreadful that it might almost have acted like a code.

But back to one of Mr Creevey's major scoops. The Duke, having won the battle which settled the fate of Europe for the next hundred years, and having had his tea and toast, was standing pensively in his hotel window when who should be staring up at him but Mr Creevey, the very man everyone had to tell everything to, and thus the Duke beckoned, and poured it all out in his 'short, natural, blunt way . . . and without the least approach to anything like triumph or joy'.

"It has been a damned serious business, Blücher and I have lost 30,000 men. It has been a damned nice thing – the nearest run thing you ever saw in your life . . ." He repeated so often its being *so nice a thing – so nearly run a thing*, that I asked him if the French had fought better than he had ever seen them do before? – "No," he said, "they have always fought the same . . ." Then he said, "By God! I don't think it would have done if I had not been there."

When Creevey sent the letter containing this talk home (in the same bag as that carrying Wellington's dispatches on his victory), he omitted the last sentence as 'It did not seem fair to the Duke to state it without full explanation, as there was nothing like vanity in the observation in the way he made it.' But when seven years later the Duke became 'very foolishly, in my opinion, a politician', Creevey replaced the sentence. The writer as listener had discovered an area in which talk is rigged, and the talker premeditated and cautious. Creevey's collection of Waterloo talk instances his brilliant selectivity of material for in the midst of this vast drama and its comment – its screams, too, for immediately after the battle he wandered across the field – he heard a military doctor say that the thousands of wounded left there two whole nights stood a better chance of recovery than those unfortunate enough to have been taken to hospital.

Nor can we leave this splendid listener without a word about his wife. Did he recognise in her a similar craving, or did she catch it from him? Or was she his pupil? She was a widow and the mother of six when she married him, and they seemed to have divided their engagement book, with Mrs Creevey covering those dinners and routs which coincided with his, and sending him by way of letters everything she saw and heard. But the listening was different. What is said is a kind of telling fragmentation set in a sparkling narrative, like curls in a locket.

Oh, this wicked Pavilion! we were there till $\frac{1}{2}$ past one this morng., and it has kept me in bed with the headache till 12 today . . . When the Prince appeared, I instantly saw that he had got more wine than usual, and it was still more evident that the German Baron was extremely drunk. The Prince came up and sat by me . . . and talked a great deal about Mrs Fitzherbert . . . Afterwards the Prince led all the party to the table where the maps lie, to see him shoot with an air-gun at a target placed at the end of the room. He did it very skilfully, and wanted all the ladies to attempt it. The girls and I excused ourselves on account of our short sight; but Lady Downshire hit a fiddler in the dining-room, Miss Johnstone a door and Bloomfield the ceiling . . . I soon had enough of this, and retired to the fire with Mac . . . At last a waltz was played by the band, and the Prince offered to waltz with Miss Johnstone, but very quietly, and once round the table made him giddy, so of course it was proper for his partner to be giddy too; but he cruelly thought of supporting himself, so *she* reclined on the Baron.

There is a familiar note in what Mrs Creevey hears and we recognise it –

in Thackeray. Mr Creevey cannot achieve this insouciance, this dashing-off of the deplorable. Just a week after this romp she is with the Prince at Brighton Pavilion when: 'Harry Grey has just come in with news of a great victory at sea and poor Nelson being kill'd . . . What will this do? not, I hope, save Pitt . . .' She picks up a conventional sentence or two to illustrate Prinny's grief, which was very real, but she lacks the right antennae for such profound tidings and cannot convey their effect. Her ear is actually corrupted, though economically so, by the chatter into which her marriage to Mr Creevey has hurled her. Moreover, what her husband can accept as the necessary rituals of the great world she, with her womanly commonsense, sees as a charade. Each listens intently but what Mrs Creevey hears is so absurd that only a dashing, throwaway style can fix what she hears on to the page. Together, they form a balanced witness of their age.

Among modern novelists who knew how to hear beneath the conversational surface of life the announcements of inescapable change was the late Paul Scott, a writer whose importance is only now being recognised. What he heard as a young soldier during the last war in India began a process of major penetration into the rich mysteries of the Anglo-Indian dialogue which has succeeded as few other works of fiction have in showing our imperialism in crisis. As with the nineteenth-century novelists he resembles in scope and mounting detail, Scott's Raj Quartet is one of those mines of social and political information which have been made accessible by brilliant story-telling and illumined by authentic conversations between representatives of the two countries about to cut adrift. The books move along with a solid narrational power which is chiefly generated by observation and an interior monologue, but their power seems to derive from scatterings or little bursts of very ordinary speech. Too ordinary, maybe, like that heard by Pinter and Beckett, for any but the extraordinary ear. Like these writers Paul Scott understands that we proceed colloquially by untidy repetitions. Particularly when we have got something important to say. We learn all we need to know about Miss Crane the spinster missionary and her colleague Mr Chaudhuri in one of these little tumbles of talk. The latter has urged her to step hard on the accelerator as their car approaches the rioters, but she cannot. To injure someone, to kill him . . . she cannot.

'They weren't going to move, they'd have died. I'm sorry.'

'Don't speak,' Mr Chaudhuri said. 'Now leave it to me. Don't speak.' He put a hand on her wrist. 'Trust me,' he said. 'I know you never have, but trust me now. Do whatever I say. *Whatever* I say.'

She nodded. 'I trust you. I'll do what you say . . . But don't run risks. I'm not worth risks. I'm old and it's all gone and I've failed . . . If this is where it ends for me, let it end.'

'Please, Miss Crane,' he said, 'don't be ridiculous.'

In this flutter of words the novelist makes us hear Miss Crane personifying the Raj at the moment when it hands over its authority. Although he is dealing with vast events, he is anti-epic in his account of them. There is a constant element of surprise in all this. His innovation is to move us profoundly by quietly excellent though orthodox prose and a dispassionate vision. Had he been a great journalist I suppose he would have been described as having his ear to the ground. But his listening was never confined to this or to any other basic level. He spoke of the 'mood of childish irritation brought on by yet another critical comparison of the novels I write about India and the novel which E. M. Forster wrote' and of how in the end every word which Forster heard there became for him the utterly dull 'bou-oum' or 'Ou-boum' of the Marabar cave. The essential difference between himself and Forster, he said, was that 'my India made me talkative, and his stunned him into silence'.

It is a broad description of how current events affect our current literary responses. Except that in the case of our hearing only bou-oum or ou-boum, our silence must be short-lived, for the poet, the novelist and the historian never needs to listen more creatively than when he suspects that there is a hollow at the heart of things. What made the void? What drained from it? What has to flood back into it? To ask such questions isn't to take the now unfashionable optimistic view but to state the obvious – that you can't make brick without straw. A few have attempted it in their experimental way and have intrigued us, or out-raged us, or taught us a thing or two en route, but the majority of us desire and demand to hear talk that makes us talkative. There never was an age without a voice – however lacking in eloquence the previous age accuses it of being. And it is only by a true – and dispassionate, if you like – hearing of this voice that we can artistically create both the individual speaker and the relentlessly shifting social atmosphere from which he can never escape. There could be desperate results, as with a Mandelstam, a Sylvia Plath or a Solzhenitsyn.

> Oh dreadful is the check, intense the agony
> When the ear begins to hear, and the eye begins to see.

wrote Emily Brontë in her poem 'The Prisoner', and we with our daily helping of media-conveyed sounds and sights of a mostly suffering world could find it all too much. But when we remember that what we write is a form of self-extension, we know that we cannot reach everywhere and everyone, and that to have defined our personal territory is common sense.

No great writer in Britain defined his personal territory more absolutely than Thomas Hardy, and none was more personally generous (self-indulgent, some have said) as to what it had to contain. Briefly, it consisted of the social realities of Dorset and the West Country during the first half of the nineteenth century, for his vision was retrospective and, like that of most villagers, ever harking back, plus the reality of his immense literary imagination. Hardy thus heard his own people speaking through his own intricate culture and wrote down what it sounded like. His first reviewers had never heard anything like it in their lives, and said so. R. H. Hutton, reviewing *Far From the Madding Crowd* in the *Spectator* in 1874 said, more in sorrow than in anger, for he admitted that Mr Hardy had a turn for an 'amusing and original story', how much he deplored the author's habit of making an intellectual graft on coarse and vulgar thoughts. 'The reader who has any general acquaintance with the civilisation of the Dorsetshire labourer, with his average wages and his average intelligence, will be disposed to say that a more incredible description of them than that which Mr Hardy has given us can hardly be conceived,' and the reviewer particularly distrusts 'the curious flavour of mystical and Biblical transcendentalism' in the rustic talk. How can a servant say to Bathsheba as the field men arrive for their wages, 'The Philistines are upon us!' and what business have labourers to converse in a peculiar style which is deeply infiltrated with this kind of moral irony? Why isn't Mr Hardy like George Eliot, who never confused her own ideas with those of her dramatic figures? Well, to answer all this would involve a long and familiar explanation. I only mention Hardy now because I have been long involved with him during the recent editing of his matchless novels. And also because these old criticisms reminded me of certain criticisms of *Akenfield*. An American reviewer proved my literary infiltration of what had been said by my Suffolk villagers by quoting the last sentence of Len Thompson's talk as an impossible thing for a farmworker to say, that I was a poet and that I had involved Len in my poetry. But Len did in fact say, 'I have these deep lines on my face because I have worked under fierce suns.' It certainly was an odd and untypical remark but it came out of an emotion which our meeting had unwittingly released.

What I am saying, and probably rather obviously, is that the writer's ear, like Prospero's island, is full of noises. The spoken words of his day drift ceaselessly across the words spoken in the myriad, and often haphazardly encountered, books which have brought him his culture. Stories which have *given* him an ear for more stories. We listen to them within the containing bounds of a time and a circumstance but the sentences in them, even when they are blunted clichés, act as litmus as they flare through our imagination, touching off brighter connections, for we are incorrigibly allusive. Yet, for all this, there *is* a language of the hour and whether we are twenty or eighty years old, and whether we like it or despise it, it is always curiously exciting to recognise it. To do so is essential to an understanding of fiction and history particularly, and no one has paid the latter's debt to the language of the hour better than the present Professor of Modern History at Oxford, Richard Cobb, who connects his readers with that of eighteenth-century France as though the simple people speaking it were at the end of the telephone. Cobb says that the historian has much the same assignment as Proust, but as he does not have the advantage of Proust's own memory, he has to construct, then pillage, other people's.

The contemporary novelist and poet, listening to the language of the hour, do not need to construct before they pillage. The words which they are hearing, and which are coming to them with a certain inimitable emphasis simply because it is *now*, are the expression of a social structure which is all around them. Often while standing at bus-stops or in bars, or even in the gallery of the House of Commons, or the home of an old friend, the writer is amazed to hear vivid forms of common speech which are clearly widely used, though not by him. He asks himself, where was he when everybody else was picking it up? Puzzled by the emergence of some new manner of saying things, some not quite definable note in the talk generally which seems to suggest that society has begun to enter one of its soul-searching phases, the writer will return to read books by the reputed spokesmen of his generation, only to discover that, besides being ever so slightly out of date, these spokesmen all arrange current speech in stylish literary patterns which are only joined by the vaguest contemporaneity with the speech he just heard. Or overheard usually, for we are less analytical when we are not eavesdropping. If the altered way of talking persists, as in the clearly different way educated young people talk compared with the educated over forty-fives, a novelist will feel that he must learn the cadence of this speech in order to understand his own times. And so he will make his own patterns of dialogue and monologue, strictly as he hears them, although ignoring the fact that by fixing spoken words to the page we can uplift them or degrade them – or even make them sound as if they had never been in common circulation. Each of us, too, remains faithful to certain 'spokesmen of our time' in the highest literary sense. Whether they warned us or dazzled us, or whether the people in their stories talk in the only way we find acceptable – even now, decades on, they stay part of ourselves.

And so do, though more mysteriously, those audacious masters who seized the strands and inner meanings, the surface glitter and sad heart of communication, into their own hands and made what they would of it. Writers like Carroll, Firbank and Ivy Compton-Burnett, and those belonging to the experimental school of novelists who developed in the 'sixties, who declared – and often proved – that naturalism is not enough. Some of these have pressed and lobbied for innovation, others have been innovators unawares, and a few have done what they had to do, as they say in a Western film, and have ignored the world's amusement or fury at their mannerisms.

This brings me to the literary respectability of innovation. It has a slightly dubious ring about it which suggests the stretching of a point here or there, or adding gewgaws that catch the eye, or that the writer lacks integrity in dismissing the standard practice and introducing his own. And yet I believe that most of those great innovators (and these include what we call minor writers) who have listened to the talk of their day and then subjected it to their artistry, were never experimentalists.

They did not try out some method of literary renewal; they were simply the victims – or victors – of a unique ear which was in perfect collaboration with a unique pen. The novel in particular advances because the new pressures of his day sometimes force the novelist to express them in a new way. *It is nearly always via dialogue.* If an analysis was made of kaleidoscopic change and development in English writing over the past century – and we must exclude poetry – it would show that nearly all of it related to the treatment of dialogue. Do we hear differently because of all these fluctuating patterns made by spoken words on the page? I think we do. In its best sense, to innovate means to make new, but I think that it is its botanical meaning which is best applied to the writer – the formation of a new shoot at the apex of a stem or branch, especially that which takes place at the apex of the thallus of mosses.

Death and Leo Tolstoy

In *The Death of Ivan Ilyich* Tolstoy takes what was for him the tremendous imaginary leap of analysing the reactions of a man who, until the surprising pain of his terminal illness began, had never given the inevitability of his own dying so much as a passing thought. A man who thus was as unlike Tolstoy as it was possible to be. For Tolstoy himself was a lifelong death-watcher. He had, in fact, a vast experience of death and had compulsively observed it from a thousand angles both physically and metaphysically. He could not resist looking at it even when the sight of it terrified him. Ivan Ilyich on the other hand had taken no look and had made no search. Death had announced itself to him in a trivial fashion which, as a worldly careerist, he found idiotic and at first quite unbelievable. He had bumped himself slightly whilst hanging up curtains; how could such a thing spell annihilation? Was an early-middle-aged high court judge to be swept away by such a trifle? To the judge the notion is as unjust as it is absurd. However, dissolution starts, casually and even delicately at first, then ravenously. One critic of this little novel, whose vast theme makes it into a masterpiece of literary compression, said that instead of descending into the dark places of the soul in this story, Tolstoy 'descends with agonising leisure and precision into the dark places of the body. It is a poem – one of the most harrowing ever conceived – of the insurgent flesh, of the manner in which carnality, with its pains and corruptions, penetrates and dissolves the tenuous discipline of reason.'

In a chilling, plain language which has been shorn of most of the descriptive richness of his customary prose style, Tolstoy tells with bleak honesty what it is like to die when the mind is body-bound. He knew what being body-bound meant from his own strenuously earthy instincts, but at least he had developed a spirituality to put these instincts into some kind of focus. But what of a man whose existence had no focus? What happened to *him* when the little pain which wouldn't go away arrived? And so Tolstoy stares remorselessly through the orifices of the death-mask of a man whose social and moral features have nothing whatever in common with his own, a conventional jack-in-office with blunted feelings and a sharp eye for the main chance. That such a person should preside over such a mighty thing as justice only adds to the irony. But we know his type; we see him everywhere still, on the board as well as on the bench, in politics and in advertising, always in the swim, so far as he can manage, a tenth-rate exerciser of power over others. Yet Tolstoy raises this dull and rather despicable man up until something about him shines sufficiently for the reader to catch a glimpse of both himself and of the immortality reflected in him. He proves how, when the body is almost eaten up by disease and frightful to contemplate, and when pain is searching out the breaking-point of the intellect, another factor, call it soul or spirit or the true self, emerges.

The German physician and literary critic A. L. Vischer has investigated the parallel relationship which exists between a man's total personality and his relationship to death. 'Simple, uncomplicated souls,' he wrote,

who do not attach such great importance to their own life, are able to accept their illness, because they accept their fate: life and heart have done their work, time for them to go. By contrast, successful and self-assured people are usually at a complete loss when faced with the reality of physical collapse.

And he goes on to describe that popular and macabre theme of the Middle Ages when death suddenly partners the living in a dance. The beautiful, the young, the important, the rich, the saintly are each approached 'spitefully, brutally, without warning' and are stopped in their tracks:

Today the concept of a blind fate is probably the concept of the first half of life. A man who is in its grip will react by falling back on certain set formulae. He will speak of 'inscrutable ways', of the 'cruel whims of fate', i.e. of the all-powerful Moira (the idea of a pre-ordained fate against which it was useless to struggle, and which dominated the death-thinking of the ancient Greeks). Such people exist in a perpetual present, their unreflecting lives given over to one long round of activity . . . their unmistakeable progress lacks a sense of time.

Nearly all this applies to Ivan Ilyich, although Tolstoy's own particular difficulty was caused by his long being unable to accept that death must partner him as it partnered all men. Just how would *he* behave when death tapped him on the shoulder on some ordinary day when he was decorating a room, or doing a deal, or blotting a page? He cannot imagine how – it is too altogether impossible and horrible, and this in spite of his Christianity. And so he imagines it happening to a man he could never be, Ivan Ilyich, an opportunist lawyer on the make, with his starved emotions and crude vision. Gradually, as disease consumes him, the victim becomes Tolstoy's – and the reader's – spiritual brother and the equal of all humanity, the worst and the best.

The Death of Ivan Ilyich marked the close of Tolstoy's great crisis of faith which preoccupied him for nearly the whole of the 1870s and during which the thought that he must die harassed him almost to the point of insanity. The very rationality of death became for him the most irrational thing of all. He could not say, like Michelangelo, 'If we have been pleased with life then we should not be displeased with death, since it comes from the hand of the same master,' because his entire nature cried out against death as a *fact*. He felt he could not live if there was death. Men have frequently complained over the way in which death interrupts their work or play. Casanova on his deathbed resented being thrust out of life before the end of the show, and Simone de Beauvoir states that the reason why death fills us with anxiety is that it is the inescapable reverse of our projects. But Tolstoy's anti-death mania went far beyond such thinking and led him into a labyrinth where, just when by means of some religious or philosophical trick he thought he had shaken his pursuer off, he would turn a corner and meet death face to face. Not Moira, the fate a man had to accept, but the fiend which had to be fought every inch of the way until breath stopped, or the heart burst. Ivan Ilyich's terrible screaming resistance to death would have met the approval of Dylan Thomas who urged his father to 'rage, rage against the dying of the light', and it forms an unforgettable description of how Tolstoy thought he himself could behave in such a plight. Such resistance is rare. Although the dying are sad about losing out they are also usually passive. The acceptance of death transforms death, wrote Paul-Louis Landsberg in his *Essai sur l'Expérience de la Mort*, which is something neither Tolstoy nor Ivan Ilyich could accept. Both the novelist during the 1870s and his pathetic hero were like naked victims, impotent at the mercy of a fate which their entire instincts fought and denied. Tolstoy, for whom everything that ever happened to him was grist to the literary mill, had to examine this denial of death.

He found a way of doing so after hearing about the death of a provincial judge named Ivan Ilyich Mechnikov. The death had been described to him in some detail by the judge's brother. Mechnikov had presided at the court at Tula, a town near the Tolstoy estate and from whose railway station the writer often watched the victims of Tula justice set out in chains, and with shaved heads, for Siberia. Count Tolstoy, burning with Christ-like identification with these poor outcasts, many of them young boys and aged men, had imagined the kind of professional detachment which made it possible for officials like Mechnikov to treat their fellow creatures so inhumanly, and then return to dinner with their families and friends. Comforting the prisoners on Tula station, Tolstoy had been amazed by the triviality of their offences: 'One hundred and fourteen persons sent away for failure to possess a passport . . . Two accused of nothing; they're just being deported . . . Two convicts sentenced to hard labour for life, for brawling and manslaughter . . . they were crying. A pleasing face. Appalling stench . . .' he noted.

Then suddenly, perhaps one ordinary morning when he was running through the list for the day, Mechnikov himself had been sentenced to the dark and to the cold, he who had so unfeelingly and for so long doled out death or a half-life to others. What happened inside Mechnikov from then on? At first Tolstoy thought he would set out the effects of this terminal illness in the shape of a diary entitled 'The Death of a Judge', then he changed his mind. His own death fears must be incorporated in this book because the chief reason why we can tolerate death in others, even in those near to us, is that it pushed it away from ourselves. In this story he would join a man in his death to the limits of his literary power. 'Take the saving lie from the average man and you take his happiness away,' said Ibsen. The biggest saving lie is to accept a friend's death and not one's own.

From childhood onwards Tolstoy's diaries, letters and books reveal how it intrigued him. His death 'notes' range from the detailed studies he made of slaughter on the battlefield to an execution in Paris, from the animal-like acceptance of death by the muzhiks on his estates, to the greatly varying reactions he had to the many deaths of his own family.

These, as was customary at all times until our own, included the frequent deaths of children. Sometimes he showed uncontrollable grief over the death of one of his little boys, sometimes almost a callousness, as though he was keeping death in its place. He was fascinated to discover that death annoyed him as much as it saddened him, and in *The Death of Ivan Ilyich* there is a lot of plain ordinary irritation to be found. Neither the dying man nor those attending him have any time for death, and they are vexed when they are forced to give it their full attention.

Tolstoy was remembering how put out he had been when his brother Dmitry died and how, in his youthful defiance of the etiquette of bereavement, he had behaved very badly. Yet he had not been able to stop himself. When he had come to his brother's sickroom and seen this terrible object with 'his enormous wrist as though soldered to the bones of his fore-arm', he felt that what he was seeing was no more than a miserable, useless part of himself, and so he freed himself from it with what he considered then was a natural revulsion. This brother's life, brief though it was, had been Tolstoy's spiritual journey in reverse. First of all Dmitry had been extravagantly chaste and pure, and then, at twenty-six, extravagantly sexual and debauched. So total had been his sensuality that, rather like Genet, he had transformed it into a sacrament. Tolstoy, staring down at him before he hurried away, saw that 'his face had been devoured by his eyes.' Later, picking away at his motives for deserting his brother at such a moment, he wrote, 'I felt sorry for Mitya [Dmitry] but not very . . . I honestly believe that what bothered me most about his death was that it prevented me from attending a performance at Court to which I had been invited.' In Jane Austen's *Mansfield Park* a young man is furious when a play he is about to take part in is cancelled because of the death of a grandmother, and in Proust's *The Captive* someone pretends that news of a death hasn't reached him so that he need not cancel a party. Mourning customs in the West have been reduced to the minimum in order that 'life may go on'. Religious people will talk glibly of their belief in resurrection to excuse this disregard, but as Paul Tournier, a real Christian, observes, 'Resurrection does not do away with death. It follows it. I cannot minimise death because I believe in resurrection.'

With all but two exceptions those surrounding Ivan Ilyich at his end feel sorry for him, 'but not very'. Sorrow is a formality, and he himself knows it. Nearly everything in his life has been a formality – his outlook, his marriage, his work and his hopes – and he is hurt but not surprised by the conventional reaction to his tragedy. When his colleagues first heard the news 'the death of a close acquaintance evoked in them all the usual feeling of relief that it was someone else, not they who had died. "Well isn't that something – he's dead, but I'm not." ' And then the tedious demands of propriety, as Tolstoy calls them, have to be obeyed, and all the familiar protective rituals set in motion, not so much for the dear departed as for the safety of his friends. Have they not been grimly dragged away from food and money, sex and conversation, power and ambition to a muddy hole in the ground? No small part of Ivan Ilyich's suffering is caused by his understanding of all this. He knows, for instance, that he is no longer the head of the house but an obstacle to his family 'and that his wife has adopted a certain attitude towards his illness and clings to it regardless of what he said or did.' In one of the novel's poignant moments, the sheer desolating aloneness of dying is evoked when 'after supper his friends went home, leaving Ivan Ilyich alone with the knowledge that his life had been poisoned and was poisoning the life of others. He had to go on living like this, on the brink of disaster, without a single person to understand or pity him.'

It is death *as it is watched by the dying* that Tolstoy probes here. Death as it is glimpsed by the healthy or imaginatively understood by the artistic is not his theme. Neither is it death as seen by doctors, for these he despises. What he concentrates on is the plight of a man who has a coldly adequate language for dealing with another's death but remains incoherent when it comes to his own. When death actually begins to happen, when one has to say, like Ivan Ilyich, that it's not a question 'of a kidney, but of life . . . death. Yes, life was there and now it is going, going . . .', what then? What words? What useful clichés even? What soothing talk about us all having to go sometime? That remarkable though neglected novelist John Cowper Powys once gave the bitter answer in these words.

He it is who – and make no mistake, my friend, the poor devil is yourself – who now, very now, visualises the inflamed condition of his prostate gland and the curves of the pattern on his lavatory floor. There is the appalling possibility that the 'I' upon whom this whole world of intimate impressions depends will soon have to face its absolute *annihilation*. The sun will rise as before, and the winds will blow as before. People will talk of the weather in the same tone. The postman will knock as he did just now and the letters will fall on the mat. But *he* won't be there. He, our pivot and the centre of everything, will be nowhere at all.

In *The Death of Ivan Ilyich* Tolstoy puts the same realisation thus:

'Yes, life was there and now it's going, going, and I can't hold on to it. Yes. Why deceive myself? Isn't it clear to everyone but me that I'm dying, that it's only a question of weeks, days – perhaps minutes? Before there was light, now there is darkness. Before I was here, now I am going there. Where?' He broke out in a cold sweat, his breathing died down. All he could hear was the beating of his heart. 'I'll be gone. What will there be then? Nothing. So where will I be when I'm gone?'

Maurice Maeterlinck, the Belgian poet who was born a generation later than Tolstoy, and who lived long enough to see the holocaust of both world wars, often attacked the convention by which we allow a whole range of expressions for dealing with the deaths of strangers, neighbours, friends, parents – even our children and lovers – but almost none at all for the death which must come to ourselves. When Ivan Ilyich realised that he was lost, that there was no return, 'that the end had come, the very end', he didn't use words at all but began three days of incessant screaming. He screamed with an O sound, wrote Tolstoy. It reminds us of Edward Munch's famous work 'The Scream', painted in 1893, and which has been described as a John the Baptist-like cry to an unprepared world, to unmindful minds. The totally alone figures in the paintings of Francis Bacon also echo this solitary noise which is both protest and prophecy.

Earlier in his mortal illness Ivan Ilyich had 'cried about his helpless-ness, about his terrible loneliness, about the cruelty of people, about the absence of God,' etc. About articulate concepts and ideas which were now letting him down. Although bitter and indignant, like a little boy in his tears and rage, he yet retained a belief that one or all of these temporarily unkind forces would stop hounding him, that they would even show him their benign side and comfort him and kiss him better. The nightmare would pass because, up until now, nightmares had always passed. Then there returns the plain black fact – he is dying. Ironically, he can only attract the attention of his friends and of his God by acknowledging this. But acknowledgement is horrifying, and thus the adult screaming, the most dreadful of all sounds.

Maeterlinck was amazed by the crudeness of Western man's thought when it came to the subject of his own death. The fatuity and shallowness of his philosophy then appalled him. 'We deliver death into the dim hands of instinct,' he wrote in *La Mort*,

and we grant it not one hour of our intelligence. Is it surprising that the idea of death, which should be the most perfect and the most luminous, remains the flimsiest of our ideas and the only that is backward? How should we know the one power we never look in the face? To fathom its abysses we wait until the most enfeebled, the most disordered moments of our life arrive.

Ivan Ilyich certainly does this, and Tolstoy even goes so far as to create in the dying judge a hint of actual frustration when, his screaming done and his hour come, it occurs to him that now he won't have time to explore the fascinating, and no longer hideous, territory of his own death. Yet only an hour before this intellectual peace descends, Ivan Ilyich is experiencing the peak of terror as he finds himself in the strange conflict of appearing to be thrust into a black hole and yet, at the same time, not being able to be engulfed in it.

What prevented him from getting into it was the belief that his life had been a good one. This justification of his life held him fast, kept him moving forward, and caused him more agony than anything else. Suddenly some force struck him in the chest and the side and made his breathing even more constricted: he plunged into the hole and there, at the bottom, something was shining. What had happened to him was what one frequently experiences in a railway car when one thinks that one is going forwards, but is actually moving backwards, and suddenly becomes aware of the right direction. 'Yes, all of it was simply not the real thing. But no matter. I can still make it *the real thing* – I can. But what *is* the real thing?' Ivan Ilyich asks himself.

The real thing involves a recognition of death as a natural corollary of life. It is no good being platitudinous about it, or brave and witty like Epicurus – 'How should I fear death? When I am, death is not; and when death is, I am not.' Neither will the steadily increasing application of modern hygienics make it disappear, like a stubborn stain under a detergent. Present trends are to make us conscious of death as a social tragedy which could be conquered by means of compassion, economics, and improved medicine. Multiple death in wars, famines, epidemics, accidents – even as a statistic issued by the anti-smoke and drink lobbies – is shown as not incurable, and talk of this death sends no shiver down the individual spine. But private death, individual death, one's own death – that is quite another matter! The language for this has become repressive and full of clinical taboos. There were some who preferred this slurring and dimming of the eloquence of death even during the century when Tolstoy was writing. Napoleon complained that 'the doctors and the priests have long been making death grievous.' For this professional slayer it was clearly nothing much to grieve about. We too are anxious to play the whole subject down and discourage morbidity. It's all best left unsaid, unfelt now for as long as possible, and, with the help of last-minute drugs, forever, if we are lucky. Don't look, it is death, is what we are told now. Call in the people who deal with that kind of thing, there will be terminal and disposal problems. Best leave it to the experts.

Yet nature, art, religion, literature – all the great progenitors of our living awareness – tell us that death is a positive and quite individual occurrence, and to refuse to look at it is the most certain way of shrinking our responses to everything else. 'Be absolute for death,' insisted Shakespeare, adding that by doing so we will make life as well as death the sweeter. And George Herbert, writing during the seventeenth century when our own scientific society was emerging, could say without any of the revulsion which overtook Ivan Ilyich when he discovered 'that horrid, appalling unheard-of something that had been set in motion within him,' that he felt death was at work within him 'like a mole'. Maeterlinck endorses this acceptance. It is not the arrival of death but life that we must act upon, he says.

Evils rise up from every side at the approach of death, but not at its call; and though they gather round it, they did not come with it . . . We impute to it the tortures of the last illness . . . but illnesses have nothing in common with that which ends them. They form part of life, and not of death. We easily forget the most cruel sufferings . . . and the first sign of convalescence destroys the most unbearable memories of the room of pain. But let death come, and at once we overwhelm it with all the evil done before it. Not a tear but is remembered as a reproach, not a cry of pain but it becomes a cry of accusation.

Death for Ivan Ilyich is his cancer right up until the penultimate moment of his life, when, briefly and tantalisingly, he perceives something altogether different and entirely acceptable. The Christian-scientific philosopher Teilhard de Chardin prayed that he might have an understanding of the terminal process when God was painfully parting the fibres of his being in order to penetrate to the marrow of his substance and bear him away within Himself. Tolstoy's own egotism made it impossible for him to accept death in these passive mystical terms, and Ivan Ilyich's dreadful struggles are an honest description of how he thought he himself might have behaved in similar circumstances.

Acceptance of death when it arrives is one thing, but to allow it to upstage the joys of living is ingratitude. Ivan Ilyich's grey tragedy is that of a man who debased life and who tried to fight off death. Tolstoy presents the judge's life in coldly accurate terms which might almost be a summary heard in his own court. It is shot through with accusation. What did you do with this divine asset, life? demands Tolstoy. You made no attempt to live it outside the meanest terms. You played safe according to the most selfish rules. You took care to see that everything you did was done with 'clean hands, in clean shirts, and with French phrases'. You never put a foot wrong and so you never stepped out of your rut. Your life has been 'most simple and commonplace – and most appalling'. The bleak indictment continues with Ivan Ilyich's opportunism, marriage of convenience, vanity and limitation – and then, with astonishment, the reader finds himself beginning to quite like this conventional man and to be sorry when he starts to lose out to death. Heroes can be certain of admiration and anti-heroes of love. In sympathising with the judge, cut off in his prime, as he thought, although the average expectation of life for a man in the 1880s was only forty-one years, we are sympathising with ourselves and all the little hopes and aspirations we have, which are so despicable or laughable when put into our dossier or official record, but which are so precious to us. Ivan Ilyich's death remains one of the most self-identifying deaths in all literature, his death in life, his death as transient flesh, they are still visibly exact reflections of our own deathliness. It is not a period piece except in such things as comparative terminal nursing. That screaming might be tranquillised now but not the ignorance of death which caused it. Ivan Ilyich sees that

the awesome, terrifying act of his dying has been degraded by those about him to the level of a chance unpleasantness, a bit of unseemly behaviour (they reacted to him as they would to a man who emitted a foul odour on entering a drawing-room): that it had been degraded by that very 'propriety' to which he had devoted his entire life.

We too play death down when it is happening and, later, simply clean it up, pushing its profundity out of sight.

Tolstoy was fifty-seven when he published *The Death of Ivan Ilyich*. Since the wild success of *Anna Karenina* – which had come out in instalments between 1875–7 and in book form in 1878 – he had been caught up in what his wife called 'a disease', or an experiment in living according to the actual rules laid down by Christ and his followers, a faith which he believed had quite disappeared under centuries of myth, politics, the orthodoxy of religious institutions and mere social convenience. It was an experiment which was to eventually lead him to excommunication, as well as to the meaning of death, pain and the conflict between loving life and having to accept that it was temporal. 'Leo is still working,' wrote his wife to her sister,

but, alas, all he is producing are philosophical disquisitions! He reads and writes until it gives him a headache. And all in order to prove that the Church does not accord with the Gospels. There are not ten people in Russia who can be interested in such a subject. But there's nothing to be done. My only hope is that he will soon get over it.

She was only part relieved when she heard that he had begun a story called 'Death of a Judge', because during the years which had elapsed since he worked regularly as a novelist attempts at fiction had come to nothing. However, when the long short story now entitled *The Death of Ivan Ilyich* appeared, all Countess Tolstoy's faith in her husband as a writer of genius returned.

Although from now on he would let his imagination, and not religious and political theories alone, dictate his work, like the great artist he was, these years marked a gradual parting of the ways between Tolstoy and his Countess. They would end in his flight from her and his quite impossible to imagine death in the station master's cottage at Astapovo surrounded by some of the first mass-media publicity of the twentieth century. News of his dying had spread across the world and immense crowds controlled by police and the militia attended his end. Barred from his bedside, his wife's flattened face stared through the window until someone hung a blanket up to prevent their eyes meeting. Here the similarity to the stress between Ivan Ilyich and his wife is prophetic. The Countess's adoration of the genius who had abandoned her was neurotic but total; but Ivan Ilyich knows that his wife doesn't love him and so can't go very far with him along the black road which stretches ahead. Only near the end, as the acceptance of death creates understanding and forgiveness, does he come close to her, but until then 'he hated her with every inch of his being'. Tolstoy too died with difficulty. His disciples, the 'Tolstoyans', heard his last words – 'The truth . . . I care a great deal . . . How they . . .' But in spite of a solemn promise to ask him about death as it occurred, they said nothing themselves. Tolstoy said that when he was dying they were to ask him if he saw life as he usually saw it, or whether he saw it as a progression towards love and God. 'If I should not have the strength to speak, and the answer is yes, I shall close my eyes, if it is no, I shall look up.' But none of them troubled him. The dying are in the hands of the living, who generally remain more loyal to deathbed conveniences than to deathbed revelations. It comforts them to know that the dead person knew and felt nothing. 'He felt nothing,' they will later tell each other, forgetting that there are more things to feel than pain and fear. Yet men have always thought of a conscious death as their mortal birthright and have prayed that they 'would not die as the unconscious things, the frozen sparrow under the hedge, the dead leaf whirled away before the night wind . . .' But we, confronted by a glimpse of infinity and threatened by last words, cling fast to clichés and hygiene. Feel nothing, say nothing, we advise the dying, smoothing the rubber sheet, adjusting the drip.

In the West twentieth-century habits surrounding our entering and leaving the world are determined by these exits and entrances no longer taking place in the home, but in the hospital. When children were born and parents died in the actual marriage-bed, where first and last cries were heard in the very same room, where the first things looked at were often the last things seen, where the corpse lies where the lover's body moved, when the entire intimacy of life from start to finish was confined to the family house, and not to maternity wings, ending-up wards and funeral parlours, death itself possessed dimensions and connotations which are now either forgotten or lost. Everyone until recently knew the actual smell of death. In a big family during the nineteenth century it was not unusual for it to be an annual smell and to take its position in the odorous year along with springtime beeswaxing, summer jams and winter fires. When death came, it was the family who dealt with it, not the specialists. Death's mysteries and its chores became inseparable.

Tolstoy wrote through, as it were, numerous family deaths, and he lost one small son while actually at work on *Ivan Ilyich*. His reactions to these periodic losses fluctuated wildly from desolation and horror to a coldly grandiloquent form of acceptance. He either went to pieces over a bereavement or became unfeelingly stoical. There was one occasion in 1873 when his little son Petya died when he actually panicked and fled from his house to Moscow because he thought he might catch death as one caught an infection. Yet, some time later, when the four-year-old Alexis followed his brothers to the grave in one of those repetitive little processions which regulated the old parenthood, Tolstoy found a quite different way of stepping out of death's path, this time by applying hard logic.

All I can say is that the death of a child, which I once thought incomprehensible and unjust, now seems reasonable and good ... My wife has been much afflicted by this death and I, too, am sorry that the little boy I loved is no longer here, but despair is only for those who shut their eyes to the commandment by which we are ruled.

Quite the worst period for dealing with death for him were the years 1873–5, when he lost three children and two adored aunts.

'It is time to die,' he wrote sombrely. 'That is not true. What *is* true is there is nothing else to do in life but die. I feel it every instant. I am writing, I'm working hard ... but there is no happiness for me in any of it,' he told his brother. 'Every minor illness, every death among his acquaintances, brought him back to the thought of his own end,' wrote his biographer Henri Troyat, describing the time when Tolstoy's fame as a novelist and his powers as an artist soared in reverse ratio to his confidence in staying alive:

Why was fate dogging his heels like this? He felt as though he were skirmishing with some animal – intelligent, powerful and vindictive – that had been trained to snap at him. In a moment of abject anxiety he wrote to a friend, 'Fear, horror, death, the children laughing and gay. Special food, agitation, doctors, lies, death, horror – it was torture!' *Death was* and yet he had to stay sane and work and earn money and look forward to Easter and cut the hay ...

'One strange thing in both *Anna Karenina* and *War and Peace*,' says

Troyat, '. . . it is the exceptional, glittering beings, those marked by some metaphysical sign, who disappear, and the average, even insignificant ones who survive and trudge along their little paths, halfway between good and evil.' Ivan Ilyich is the exception. Here it is meanness of spirit which is made to produce its own pathos. In spite of what we first felt about him, we find ourselves sorrowing for a man for whom we have no natural sympathy. The traditions governing death in nineteenth-century fiction are broken page by page. This is how it really happens, Tolstoy is saying, this is what the outrage of the ego is like.

The novel is masterly in its brevity and in the use made of dramatic foreshortening. The reader rapidly finds out that he lacks all the usual perspectives for looking at the familiar nineteenth-century deathbed scene and that he is at once plunged into realities concerning himself. He is forced to look down to a ledge where a man clings without dignity and out of reach of help. Above the man, only just beyond his grasp, stands everything which once held him safe and sound, home, job and society. Below him lies a spinning darkness. Agony is created by those above accepting the situation, by even being rational about it. Something which obscured his identity has moved across their usual view of him like a filter and already, with the breath still in him, he is outside their comprehension. Tolstoy's theme is about the inability of the dying to communicate and of the sick to remain inside the old circle of relationships. The very first hint that Ivan Ilyich is poorly begins the process of expulsion, as wife, children and colleagues prepare to live in a world which will no longer contain him. Self-interest reigns. Gain runs parallel with loss. It is a busy period for everyone and there really isn't much time for being sad. Afterwards, when he has slipped from the ledge out of sight, empty words are politely muttered in the empty space he has left. There is coarse honesty when the dead man's friend takes the opportunity to fix up a game of whist while viewing the corpse. The widow acts out the grief she is supposed to feel and receives the condolences of those who are not sorry. It is finished – a life that proved to have no meaning for anyone except him who possessed it, and who parted with it with fear and incredulity.

Ivan Ilyich is the climax of Tolstoy's death-writing. It also acted as the great purgative to his own extreme fears of death which reached their crescendo during a visit he made to the town of Arzamas. The incident is crucial to Tolstoy's obsessional fascination by death in all its variety. Shortly after the publication of *War and Peace*, when his body had never felt more vigorous or his mind more active, with praise and success ringing in his ears, and when his life should have been bursting with a sense of wellbeing, he fell into a deep despair which took the form of being irreconcilably opposed to the inevitability of his own death. Henri Troyat has described Tolstoy's fear as animal, visceral, chilling. 'It came on him all of a sudden – he began to tremble, sweat broke out on his forehead, he felt a presence behind his back. Then the jaws of the vise loosened, the shadow passed on, life tumbled in upon him, the tiniest vein in his body rejoiced at the surge of new blood,' and he felt safe. But only temporarily. So he plunged into activities which he hoped would be a hedge against death. Ordinary, practical, earthy matters, such as extending his estate with the royalties from *War and Peace.* There was land for sale hundreds of miles away from Yasnaya Polyana, the ancestral home, and so he travelled there with a servant of whom he was particularly fond, a laughing, attractive high-spirited boy named Sergey. It was not Count Tolstoy the saint but Count Tolstoy the capitalist on this opportunist jaunt – 'I was looking for a seller who was an imbecile with no business sense and it seemed to me that I had found one.'

The trip began happily enough; then the frightfulness started to return, dogging his footsteps, catching up with him just when Sergey's cheerfulness and goodness promised protection. Saying nothing to the boy, Tolstoy took a room at the inn at Arzamas, and there the classic existentialist nightmare overwhelmed him. The room itself was death and he was in it. 'I was particularly disturbed by the fact that it was square,' he wrote. It was full of torment and the torment was irrevocable. What was in the room with him *had to be* – this was the delirium of it. There *was* no escape, no way out – or in, if it came to that. He was. Death was. 'Where am I? Where am I going? What am I running away from?' he thought – a thought which he never allowed Ivan Ilyich. Later, in a short story called *Notes of a Madman*, Tolstoy set out the whole terrible experience.

'This is ridiculous,' I told myself. 'Why am I so depressed? What am I afraid of?'

'Of me,' answered Death. 'I am here.'

A cold shudder ran over my skin. Yes, Death. It will come, it is already here, even though it has nothing to do with me now . . . My whole being ached with the need to live, the right to live, and, at the same moment, I felt death at work. And it was awful being torn apart inside. I tried to shake off my terror. I found the stump of a candle in a brass candlestick and lighted it. The reddish flame, the candle, the candlestick, all told me the same story: there is nothing in life, nothing exists but death, and death should not be!

The 'square white and red horror' Tolstoy found himself in was his tomb. All rooms were tombs. All talk was part of the everlasting silence, all movement no more than a slight twitching of the thick stillness, all horizons but walls. This was the shattering message of Arzamas. Soon after turning it into *Notes of a Madman*, Tolstoy began to apply his death-findings to his neighbour, Judge Mechnikov, the kind of man he could never be, turning into someone who knew nothing about rooms being tombs – until a window-knob prodded him to draw his attention to the fact.

The two major existentialists, Jean-Paul Sartre and Martin Heidegger are in conflict about Tolstoy's room. For Heidegger it is an anteroom, stark and dreadful certainly, but leading on to what we are too mortal to imagine, though not black and destructive. For Sartre (who confessed that the idea of death haunted him during his childhood because he did not love life) death is simply a hard fact like birth. 'It is absurd that we should be born, it is absurd that we shall die . . . Life, so long as it lasts, is pure and free of any death. For I can conceive of myself only as alive. Man is a being for life, not for death.' Heidegger takes the opposite view.

Death is not an event which happens to man, but an event which he lives through from birth onwards . . . As soon as man lives he is old enough to die . . . Death is a constituent of our being. Day after day we live through death. Man is, in his essence, a being for death. What is the meaning of this death for the individual consciousness? That by interrupting life it makes it complete. Incompletion is a constituent of my being . . . Death teaches us that life is a value, but an incomplete value.

While on the road to Arzamas, Tolstoy was telling himself that life should be pure and free of any death; thirteen years later, nervously yet compulsively, like someone tonguing a jumpy nerve in a tooth, he is exploring Heidegger's notion of life being an incomplete value and forcing Ivan Ilyich to accept that, at forty-five, he was old enough to die and that he was, and always had been, a being for death.

Finally, we must say something about the last illness, which, in Ivan Ilyich's case was also the first illness, for the story is as much a morality of the sickroom as of the grave. In his memoir *Confession*, written the same year as he began *The Death of Ivan Ilyich*, Tolstoy relates an old Easter fable which for him is about a man desperately clinging to life while cancer eats away inside him. It is the allegorical version of Ivan Ilyich's fate.

There is an Easter fable, told a long time ago, about a traveller caught in open country by a wild beast. To escape from the beast the traveller jumps into a dry well, but at the bottom of the well he sees a dragon with its jaws open to devour him. And the unfortunate man, not daring to climb out lest he be destroyed by the wild beast, and not daring to jump to the bottom of the well lest he be devoured by the dragon, seizes hold of a branch of a wild bush growing in a crack in the well and clings to it. His arms grow weaker and weaker, and he feels he will soon have to abandon himself to the destruction which awaits him above or below; but still he clings on and as he clings on he looks around and he sees that two mice, one black and one white, are steadily circling round the branch of the bush he is hanging on, and gnawing at it. Soon it will snap and break off, and he will fall into the dragon's jaws.

The traveller sees this and knows that he will inevitably perish; but while he hangs on he looks around and finds some drops of honey on the leaves of the bush, reaches them with his tongue and licks them.

So I too clung to the branches of life, knowing that the dragon death was inevitably waiting for me, ready to tear me to pieces, and I could not understand why this agony had befallen me. And I tried to lick the honey which had previously consoled me, but the honey no longer gave me pleasure, while the black and white mice, day and night, gnawed the branch I was clinging to . . . I could not tear my gaze from them. No matter how often I was told: 'You cannot understand the meaning of life, so do not think about it, but live,' I could not do it because I had done it for too long. I could not help now seeing that day and night running around bringing me nearer to death. That is all I could see, because only that is the truth. All the rest is lies . . .

For Tolstoy the black and white mice were the scuttling days and nights hastening him to the tomb, for Ivan Ilyich, the disease eating its way through his body. Tolstoy despaired at the time because 'the two drops of honey' which were his family and his writing failed to console him about death. But what of a man who lacked any true sweetness in his life when death preoccupied him, and who thought, not in the manner in which a healthy person thinks, of the years passing and what he can do about it, but as someone incurably ill thinks? The brilliance of the book lies not in yet another of Tolstoy's vivid and many deathbed scenes but in this solitary thinking of its occupant as he is driven by pain and weakness towards – what? It is the tragedy of a man who is a death-illiterate and who has to make his way out of the world through the ranks of other death-illiterates. They degrade his passage and fill it with vulgarities. They do what they understand is necessary, and for Ivan Ilyich it is all play-acting and unnecessary. He sees that when a man is made disgusting through sickness, all those people with whom he has made his life become disgusting as well. And just as he made others suffer and cringe by exercising the law in a professional, obscurantist manner which made them powerless, he sees that the doctors are doing the very same kind of thing to himself. Men make money and reputation by joining one or other of 'the conspiracy of clerks'.

Real help, if not salvation, comes from the lowly. When Tolstoy had been so miserable and frightened at Arzamas his instinct had been to find the optimistic Sergey in the hope that the young servant's joyful nature would blot out his nightmare. But the boy was asleep and Tolstoy had felt vulnerable and forsaken in his Gethsemane. In *The Death of Ivan Ilyich* he makes the reverse happen. A pantry-boy named Gerasim, simple, kind and blooming with health, nurses his master with the most disinterested love for a fellow human being, and carries out the most sordid tasks with complete naturalness. He is neither scared of death nor self-consciously glad to be alive. He finds nothing incongruous in the contact between his own beautiful body and the filth of the sick man. Soon Gerasim becomes for Ivan Ilyich the only decency left. He lies with his legs up on the boy's shoulders, drawing ease from him. In some of Tolstoy's most moving passages we watch this last friendship expand as the judge realises that what Gerasim gives him comes from free-will and selflessness, and lies outside anything he could command from him. Gerasim is loving about life but pragmatic about death, and everything connected with the breakdown of physical functioning which precedes it. 'We all have to die some day,' he says, 'displaying an even row of healthy white peasant teeth'. And yet it was Gerasim who 'was the only one who understood and pitied him'. The dying ache for pity, and the living for some reason find it hard to give real, genuine pity. The idea of

Gerasim the simple man bringing his natural release to the spiritual cripple from a more sophisticated society is an old one. One of his recent appearances was in Pasolini's film *Theorem*, an appearance, one should add, which Tolstoy would have found too explicit, as well as blasphemous. For here it must be said that Tolstoy's dilemma over the problem of death was a Christian one. His preoccupation with the subject eventually becomes rather distasteful to some of his contemporaries, Gorki in particular. Christ-like, he may be, declared Gorki the Marxist, but Christ-like in the sense of vanquishing death he is not, nor ever could be.

'Although I admire him, I do not like him . . . He is exaggeratedly preoccupied, he sees nothing and knows nothing outside himself . . . He lowers himself in my eyes by his fear of death and his pitiful flirtation with it; as a rabid individualist, it gives him a sort of illusion of immortality.' Tolstoy was in his early seventies when this indictment was made. But his recurring death-enquiry was not egotistical; it was made on the battlefield, on the scaffold, in the nursery, in the peasant's hut, in palaces, in gutters, wherever he witnessed the silencing of the marvellous physical machine. It is an enquiry which we all make, one way or another. Death astounds us and the inexorable movement towards it, once it starts, shocks us. Most of us do not see it as a crisis of growth, as did Cardinal Danielou, but as the unmentionable odour of decomposition which the shifty mourners in Ivan Ilyich's house watch Gerasim smothering with carbolic. Though generally, like the sentenced judge, we draw our conclusions from the certainty of the deaths of friends and strangers, and not of ourselves. The latter is too weird an operation, like arranging mirrors to catch our own profile. The dead are bad company and faith has failed to convince us otherwise.

We pray against death, fervently, madly, like the character in Péguy's *Joan of Arc*. 'To pray. To pray that a whole people be spared from falling among the dead souls, the dead peoples, the dead nations. Be spared from falling down dead. Be spared from becoming a dead people, a dead nation. Be spared from mildew. Be spared from going rotten in spiritual death, in the earth, in hell . . .' This was how Tolstoy prayed at Arzamas (though using the Our Father). This was what Ivan Ilyich was praying when he screamed for three whole days. But no man is spared death. Tolstoy's ceaseless toiling after the truth had to involve the dead, and this involvement had to bring him, sensual, thriving, vital seeker after light that he was, to the whirling abyss, and into the fears of those sliding into it. Blind fate (Moira) or that intimate transition of the spirit to the loving Creator? Tolstoy dearly longed to know. In *The Death of Ivan Ilyich* he took a man to the brink of having to leave the world much as he had entered it, kicking and screaming, because he had not taken the trouble to grow up, morally speaking, while he was passing through it, and had then shown how salvation could overtake a slowing pulse-rate, bringing maturity at the last.

Love masters death at the penultimate hour in Tolstoy's story. It could have rescued Ivan Ilyich from all the fright and despair which terrorised him during the final two weeks had he allowed it to. But so rigidly had he repressed love throughout his adult life that anything pointing to its enduring nature, such as certain happy memories of his childhood, upset him. At some early moment in his development he had taken a stand against love and all that emanated from it, which he now saw as 'the real thing', and had opted for other values, although why exactly he could not say. He just had. Though suddenly realising this had given him a moral agony which exceeded his physical agony. Sights and touches, not language, were what were reducing his fashionable way of life to worthless rubble – at first the sight of the goodness in his young servant's face. The lawyer in Ivan Ilyich at once put a case for the defence of the values upon which he had constructed his life, only to discover 'that there was nothing left to defend'. Thus his eyes were opened to a 'dreadful, enormous deception that shut out both life and death'. His wife, whom he now views as the epitome of the unreal situation which has brought him damnation, forces him to admit that taking the Sacrament has made him feel better, but in the next breath he shouts at her to go away, to 'leave me alone'.

Yet belatedly and briefly in their dreary marriage she is offering him sensitivity and love. As with recollections of love when he was a boy, he cannot bear these real feelings of hers. And so, isolated because he believes that the purity of love such as that which Gerasim personifies cannot possibly reach him, and sceptical of there being such reality as love in the false world to which he and his wife subscribe, the sick judge convinces himself that he can neither go forward nor go back in terms of spiritual growth, and that 'he was lost.' It is a ghastly conviction and he screams, first 'No! No!' and then simply – his perpetual hollow 'O'.

It is into this vacuum of horror that love enters without words. A delirious hand comes into chance contact with the head of his son. The boy has stolen into the terrible room and as the hand touches his hair he seizes it and kisses it. The judge's wife is also in the room and he observes unwiped tears on her nose and cheeks. And so, unlike Tolstoy's deathroom at Arzamas, this room in which Ivan Ilyich is about to spend his last hour on earth contains love, 'and suddenly it became clear to him that what had been oppressing him and would not leave him was vanishing all at once – from two sides, ten sides, all sides'. 'So that's it,' he tells himself just before an even greater recognition arrives with his stopped breath.

As one of the major death-explorations in literature, this story has fascinated and influenced many novelists. Its ideas can be felt in I. A. Bunin's *The Gentleman from San Francisco* and Arthur Miller's *Death of a Salesman*, and parallels have been drawn between the fate of Ivan Ilyich and Kafka's Joseph K. in *The Trial*. Gorki too went to this overpowering narrative for the theme of his play *Yegor Bulychov and the Others*. But the bringing together of all its disturbing concepts of vanity, temporary authority, pain, disease and mortality into our own times has been the achievement of Alexander Solzhenitsyn in *Cancer Ward*, where Rusanov the petty official suddenly finds his well-ordered life 'on the *other* side of his tumour'.

Dinner with Dr Stopes

She had been invited to lecture to our literary society – on the sonnet, not sex – and she arrived on the doorstep a little after four o'clock with a huge bag of books from which it was her intention to quote at some length. She appeared to be more embroiled than dressed in quantities of luxurious old russet fur, out of which her head rose, arctic and imperious. Her hair was plentiful and was dyed a rich conker red. In spite of her furs and her jewelled chains, her throat remained emphatically naked. That she was a romantic was obvious, that she was fearless was history, but that her voice should be so far removed from a sounding brass as to recall nothing so much as tinkling teacups was disconcerting.

'Just a raw egg in an ordinary glass,' she said, rejecting the formal thin bread-and-butter, cake and Earl Grey prepared in her honour. 'Take it to my bedroom, if you don't mind, and call me twenty minutes before the lecture.'

Sheathed in her celebrity, cut off from the rest of us by the enormity of her conclusions, she withdrew to have a lie-down.

> No one can go the way I go,
> No one can know the things I know . . .

she had written in one of her poems. There was no doubt that the presence of Dr Marie Stopes, only a wall away as she rested on my bed, did fill the whole house with omniscience.

I left for the lecture hall before the main party to make sure that the carafe wasn't scummy and that the reading-desk was in order. Although there was almost an hour to go, the room was already packed. Such an interest in the sonnet was encouraging. Nervously, I patted my introductory sentences into place, then went outside to stand at the top of the theatrical corporation staircase to receive Dr Stopes. A susurration in the vestibule below heralded her arrival. She still wore the russet fur but beneath it was a trailing frock of some sort of crêpe material which was very lively and animated, so that its hem crawled about all over her velvet shoes even when she was standing still. A bearer followed her, his arms laden with volumes all aflutter with book-markers. The society applauded her enthusiastically as she took her seat on the dais. Accustomed to sensation, she made the slightest of acknowledgements, then slipped the furs from her shoulders and was seen startlingly naked about the shoulders. Her thin arms blazed behind the piled poets. Scrupulously conveyed by the strip of quivering neon high above her flaring red hair was a suggestion of Elizabeth the First.

The voice, however, suggested Cranford. It was soon apparent that the back of the hall could hear next to nothing and was having to make do with watching a huge magnifying-glass hover from sonnet to sonnet. One or two members held out an ear on the palm of a hand and looked pained and cheated. I wrote, 'Please could you speak a little louder?' on the back of an envelope and pushed it gently to Dr Stopes, who read it, tore it up and went on just the same as before. I then wondered how the famous story about Sir Osbert Sitwell would affect her if I scribbled this on an envelope. Pausing during a reading of his work in the States, he had enquired, 'Can you hear me at the back there?' 'Naw,' they said. 'Then pay a little more attention,' he had replied.

Each book which Dr Stopes needed was always at the bottom of the heap and, when she jerked it forth in triumph, its markers always fell out. Once or twice the magnifying glass itself got buried and had to be found. Between Dryden and Pope she drank copiously from the carafe, talking between gulps. 'The octave of the sonnet, in the strict form, is unalterably abba/abba, although Edmund Spenser had gone as far as abab/bcbc,' although she had never gone as far herself. Though before she came to her own sonnets, she must mention those by her dear, late friend Lord Alfred Douglas, who was the greatest sonneteer since William Shakespeare. She read two of Lord Alfred's sonnets and they sounded very beautiful. She said that, of course, they did not mean what they appeared to mean; sonnets rarely did. She said that she could not believe that there was anyone present at this meeting tonight who would give credence to the things said about this noble poet by his jealous detractors. She then concluded by reading some half-dozen of her own poems, swaying, soft-voiced, lost in her own language. The society streamed out into the cold night, baffled and abashed.

This was not the end. A small dinner had been arranged in her honour by the generous, witty soul who bore the brunt of entertaining most of the speakers who came to address our literary society. We sat down, as we always did, at an elaborate table in her dining-room with the shiny green ceiling, Dr Stopes between me and a distinguished gynaecologist. There was also a poet, and her old schoolfriend Kay Gilmour, sister of the composer Gerald Finzi. Looking back, it all seems reasonable enough, though for some reason it was not. Our guest crouched forward on her fragile chair, looked daggers and kept us hesitant. When the wine came round she covered her glass with her hand, but when water was offered as an alternative she looked insulted. The poet courageously retreated to the sonnet as a subject in an attempt to cheer things up, but Dr Stopes was short with him, the inference being that if she had not already exhausted this theme, it had certainly exhausted her. We were very near dessert before contraceptives entered the conversation, and when they did, she talked of them wearily, like a writer who is dogged through an industrious career by his single best-seller. Unfortunately at this stage, in our relief that something was actually being said, we chattered too emancipatedly and were reminded, although not in as many words, that it was Love that made the world go round, not caps.

Coffee was served in the drawing-room and Marie Stopes sank down on one of those little buttoned Victorian nursing-chairs which are so close to being *prie-dieux* that they invest their occupant with a kind of sanctity. A huge honey-coloured cat smouldered at her feet and behind her rose her hostess's steep white bookcase overflowing with novels, Dorothy Richardson, Elizabeth Bowen, Elizabeth Jenkins, Mary Butts. It was dreadfully late but no one dared leave. We discussed education and Marie Stopes, who was waking up, said that no child should be taught a thing until he was ten. Her own son had spent the first ten years of his life being entirely physical in her park, then, under the instruction of private tutors, he had learned to read and write in three weeks, and was soon at work on a play. But when we gently protested that only a handful of people in the land were able to think in terms of tutors and parks, she declined to argue. And so the night dragged on in a miasma of effort and no effort.

Looking back – it was all ages ago – I can faintly see her point. She had made up her mind to fail us because we had quite decidedly failed her. She had been on the defensive for too long and now she found it quite impossible to concede a jot. Her world was sharply divided between midgets and giants, those who feared emotion and had common thoughts, and the throbbing, rapturous, chosen ones. She was sick to death of us all as we tried to insist upon a sensible stance between these poles. She had taught the man in the street to heave overboard the prurience and taboos of centuries so that he could soar up into the ultimate fulfilment of bliss – and what had he done? The oaf had used her gift like an extra gadget in the lavatory.

At last, at last we left, and all talking for a few minutes in the midnight garden. A fig tree creaked against the wall and a late car ground its apologetic way through the sedate residential roads. Marie Stopes stood by the lit front door, signalling to me with a large book as yellow as the moon. I went to her and she pressed it upon me. She took my hand. I grasped the book. It was her poems. By the light of the street lamp I read its title – *We Burn*. Inside she had written, 'Ronald Blythe His Book from the author, Marie C. Stopes' and the date. It was packed with sonnets and rapturous drawings by Gregorio Prieto, packed with burnished hair, partners in joy, fertilised time, encarmined minds, and the more potent, deeper thing. The next day she missed her train and was absolutely furious, and put out magnificent messages on the tannoy system at Liverpool Street Station. I have used her book a lot. In the summer I like to write in the garden and it is the perfect format and weight to support a notebook on my knee. Its title is almost faded away and its hard yellow cover now eaten into by sunshine. But Delamore Press, Alex Moring Ltd of 2a Cork Street, w.1. bound it well and there seems to be no fear that it will not see me out as a reliable portable desk.

Interpreting the Shades

A personal awareness of history seems to arrive much like one or other of the two major factors involved in religious conviction. There is either the sudden blaze on the Damascus road or the slow fuse of inheritance. Stephen Dedalus knew all about the latter and resented it mightily. 'History,' he complained – as every thinking Irishman must – 'is a nightmare from which I am trying to awake.'

Jules Michelet's revelation of history's purpose was of the light transforming, blindingly vivid kind. A young man in search of principles, he was making the customary literary journey when he encountered Vico's *Scienza Nuova*, and was instantly saved. Indeed, so forceful was Michelet's meeting with his fateful interpreter of the meaning of all human endeavour, that Edmund Wilson preferred to call it a collision. At any rate, as the twenty-seven-year-old Michelet confessed, it was from that moment that his path became clearly defined. He wrote down what had happened. '1824. Vico. Effort, infernal shades, grandeur, the Golden Bough. I was seized by a frenzy caught from Vico, an incredible intoxication with his great historical principle.'

But which ever way one comes to it, to accept that a stone thrown into a pond generations ago can set up ripples in the present is to have a committed interest in history. History as a series of achievements and disasters no longer works. There never were any safe periods. Having accepted this, it is only logical to assume that there never will be any – not ever. Whenever we exist, we exist in peril. Uncostumed, so to speak, history is the documentation of a naked predicament. We read in the carefully recorded dates a longing for and even a belief in some moral conclusion, a searching for a harbour where progress – so called – can dock. We also recognise historical situations which seem better than our own and appear worth recovering, though we see that this is dangerous, for, as one historian has said, 'the cult of the past only leads to reaction; the old tyrannies come back with the romance'. This romance is amazing in what it has crammed into its emotional hold-all. Not only idylls and golden ages, but back streets, rural hovels and the blitz. Too much hankering after the good old days is a sure way of preserving some bad old habits. Restoring standards usually means acknowledging decayed totems.

Most people seem to live with some historical consciousness, often with past events being seen as old panoramas running in a kind of personal parallel with current activities and dreams. If they lack the ability to trace the cause and effect of great happenings it is because common sense tells them that their role belongs to the small asides. For them, the historian is an entertainer, a keeper of the past who can pry about in time and unlock exciting ancient rooms inhabited by their earlier selves. On the whole, contemporary man tends to see himself less as a link in history's chain than as a break from history's pattern. History for Computer Man is a fate he has escaped from and a tale he can escape into.

I cannot remember a time when I did not feel history in solid and fairly reliable centennial terms, although it was ages before I learned to feel the history of my own times. Frequently I found myself thinking, talking and writing about events which had actually occurred during my life in quite detached and unfeeling historical terms. It was not so much avoidance as an inability to believe that my being around at the time was of any relevance to what was happening politically or socially. And yet from a child I expected those who had lived during Gallipoli, for example, or through this fashion or tragedy, or that reign or sensation, or just some big change in the village, to be responsible witnesses. To my way of thinking, to be contemporary was to be part of the action and, if it happened to be wicked action, to be guilty of it. I certainly demanded from these survivors of great or notorious epochs a kind of inside information which would not be inside books. And yet, looking back, my own first twenty years remained curiously isolated from what was going on nationally. I realised this quite forcibly when, the other day, during a radio interview, I was asked to recall my boyhood impressions of the launching of the *Queen Mary*. It was a reasonable question and it struck the interviewer as quite unbelievable that, insofar as it is now possible to assess myself at that moment when the beautiful liner slipped down the runway, that I knew nothing whatever about it. Nor of much else that was going on at the time. The implications of this ignorance-cum-innocence are profound.

To have been alive while certain historical changes were taking place, even if one was a child, is to be associated, however tentatively. I was very young when Hitler came to power and a teenager when war was declared, and my personal knowledge of the Fascist decade is so slight as to seem trivial. What I do remember is a general atmosphere of perplexity which, in my subconscious, I have reduced from language to an odour which is pungently sad rather than revolting, like rank pine-needles. And I can also remember the cramp which was brought about by 'holding on'. Entire families held on in those days: if you let go or simply shifted your grip you were lost. Nor, and unlike those families which ranged from the Forsytes to Mr and Mrs Little Man in the radio *Scrapbooks*, did the lives of my parents remotely reflect some modest rural edition of the national will. This chiefly because my mother in particular vigorously excluded the national will – or 'the world', as she called it – for religious reasons.

Mercifully for me, 'the world' did not include historical novels or even (as a rare concession) the occasional historical film, and if anyone really wants to know how those cruel days made so small a dent in so vulnerable a nature, it was most likely because I was early-on headed-off into the gloriously crocketed and cravated territory of imagined history. It was a sprawling territory and superbly sprawling were the writers who lured me through it. Size, as in America still, was the essential concomitant of this fiction, which swelled and swelled all through the 'thirties until it blew up into *Anthony Adverse* and *Gone With the Wind*, tales against whose narrational obesity I still won't hear a word. Their picaresque ramblings merged happily with wanderings in Suffolk, a county full of empty old buildings, churches, ramshackle farms, black-berry-held castles, rivers clogged with sunken barges and cornfields wasted in flowers. Living to oneself, as Hazlitt put it, was what I was doing while Rome, or the Reichstag, burned.

The 'forties altered all this. Poetry, sex and politics arrived together in a tangled rush. It was not what had happened but what was happening. All the same, like all the poets I was reading, my response was private rather than part of the collective reaction. My – our – god was Friedrich Hölderlin, a German poet who had died exactly a hundred years before I first read his name. I – we – were convinced that he had not happened but was happening. From then on poetry escaped being history. A few magazines and books – impossible now to convey their effect to anyone who did not read them at the time – provided the 'civilisation' with which to counter the pain, the general racket and the awful, though now much admired bonhomie, through which we floundered. They made much use of the more civilised patches of history to give us hope and to steady a rocking present.

Towards the end of the 'forties I met Mervyn Peake, and just after having found *Gormenghast* and *Titus Groan* a dazzling progression in the imaginative use of history. Both the drawings and the novels of this extraordinary man reinstated the grotesque as a source of truth after the Belsen photographs had appeared. Mervyn Peake's interior castle, with its battle-course for fantasists, was in fact his own hideout. He was all for escape into this fastness of his imagination. A few years after our talks, about Dickens, I remember, and Thomas Wolfe, he was himself to be tragically captured, a dead intelligence in a still-breathing flesh. His wife Maeve has movingly described his premature senility.

Michelet's definition of a historian was one who, 'taking history as something more than a game, makes the effort in good faith to enter into the life of the past'. He added rather despairingly: 'For where is the life here? Who can say which are the living and which are the dead?' Writing during those years when French absolutism was being restored, Michelet nevertheless believed that the past was as likely a place to find roads to freedom as the future. Because, as Edmund Wilson says, as he considered Vico's breakthrough into history's enlightened classroom,

we see the fogs that obscure the horizons of the remote regions of time recede, the cloudshapes of legend lift. In the shadows there are fewer monsters: the gods and heroes float away. What we see now are men as we know them alone on the earth we know. They will supply us with a record of the adventures of men like ourselves and a record of something more than adventure.

What *we* see now is the immense new audience for history which has been expertly popularised by archaeologist, photographer, tour-master, television producer, novelist and educator. Was there ever a time when times past were so lustfully pursued? Some, like Ezra Pound, who littered his poems, as much as anybody, with ancient sites and excavations, might sigh at all this and repeat his,

> And even I can remember,
> A day when the historians left blanks in their writings,
> I mean for things they didn't know.

The Voyager

It is fitting that the story should begin with tides and destinations, and with humanity adrift from its ancient moorings as rarely before. 'Seafaring men are naive and full of hope,' wrote the poet W. J. Turner, and so were those nineteenth-century multitudes who, having nothing whatever to stay at home for, simply set out – to where? A hopeful land. Sailors observed this huge exodus from their unique vantage point. In the same poem, 'Words and Ideas', Turner continues,

> Landfall now here! Here where a Spirit sitting
> Takes up its skull, looks at its smitten teeth,
> Its barest meaning, here is poetry
> Here where there are no words, wash of flesh-confusion,
> Only the ultimate It . . .

In 1855 the foremast boy of the *Hindoo*, an old East Indiaman returning to the United States from Australia, saw, as still can be seen today, the wash of flesh-confusion as his ship slowly keeled its way up the Hooghly branch of the River Ganges to Calcutta through floating crowds of the dead, and was horrified. Here was none of that grave Lethe-like setting out on the last current, but a merrily bobbing corruption as man, woman and child jostled on the surface of what was sacred. Crows banqueted. Here was the ultimate It with a vengeance. Nothing in either of the two books which the foremast boy had brought from his home in Philadelphia, the Bible and James's *Anxious Enquirer*, provided an answer to this amazing scene, so he drew his own conclusion. This was that most human beings were of no consequence in History. Later he was to write that the majority of men were born 'to find all the best seats at the banquet of life marked "taken" '. It was not only Calcutta which spelled out this black truth, but all the other cities he had glimpsed. Melbourne had been crammed with 'thousands with nothing to do and nothing to eat'. New World, old world, it was the same, the prosperity of a nation did not imply prosperity for most of its citizens, far from it.

Henry George, the foremast boy, was naive and full of hope. So he would be at fifty, some would say. Others, most notably George Bernard Shaw, gave credit where credit was due and admitted that they first saw the socialist path because of the beam of fundamentalist light which Henry George shed upon it. The latter was already formulating his single all-purpose solution to the injustice of life as the *Hindoo* scattered the dead in its wake. Certainly the sea was washing away all sense of parochiality in his vision of a fair life for everybody on a fair earth. The sea had released his grandfather from the limitations of rural Yorkshire and turned him into a dashing shipmaster with clippers in Philadelphia harbour, and Henry George himself, like some character out of Richard Dana or Melville, whose first stories were actually being published during his boyhood, was the very figure of a romantic nineteenth-century ocean drifter. About this time, he sketched the following self-portrait:

[He is] an ardent, devoted, fervent and constant lover . . . who will feel much stronger attachment than he will express. [He is] not very fond of children . . . he chooses as his friends the talented and intellectual and literary. [He is] extremely fond of travelling . . . and has an insatiable desire to roam. [He] will be more likely to make a general than a critical scholar. [He is] qualified to meet difficulties, overcome obstacles, endure hardships, contend for privileges, maintain opinions, resent insults . . . and in cases of danger will be perfectly self-possessed.

If any of the great sea-novelists were applying for a hero Henry George would get the job. If any of the Bentham-Ricardo school of political economists were looking for an evangelist, his would be the last direction. Yet, as the mast dipped to the swell and harbour after harbour in both the latest and most ancient communities alike helplessly exhibited the same polarised picture of the have-alls and the have-nothings, the germ of a single solution crept into George's intelligence. So simple indeed was it, that it was a wonder it had never been thought of before. (It had, of course, but at the wrong time. Also, those who had thought of it had lacked the means to communicate it.) The awakening giant, as the exploited masses were nervously called, had an ear cocked for a rational reversal of the historic situation which condemned them to poverty. They listened for a great non-academic truth, convinced that it must exist. It would be written down, of course, and heard by them as an extension of the sacred word. In Britain, this message of salvation had to pierce its way through the passionate and eloquent concern of poets and priests, philanthropists and politicians, social reformers and revolutionaries, and through the earnest new ethical societies and their debate on the higher consciousness. 'The real history of mankind,' wrote Lord Acton, 'is the slow advance of resolved deed following laboriously just thought.' But need it be? About the same time J. S. Mill was saying that no great improvement in the general lot of mankind was possible until a great change took place in its *mode* of thought. How did one actually precipitate such a change, the traditional revolutionary processes apart, that is?

On a bitter January day in 1855, the same year in which Henry George's ship the *Hindoo* bumped its way through the inconsequential dead of the Hooghly river, John Stuart Mill was standing on the steps of the Capitol in Washington. The freshly gleaming building had inspired him. A new statement was required on Liberty, and he would have to provide it. 'Human development in its richest diversity' could only be achieved by education. Without education men would not be able to challenge 'the despotism of custom'. Without education the majority of people's lives could be used up by trading processes which brought little or nothing to them, and a quite foolish amount of wealth, and thus power, to the comparatively few men who employed them. In a decade in which, not only for Mill but for moralists on both sides of the Atlantic, there was 'scarcely any outlet for energy except business', those who controlled its vast barely-paid work force had to be taught that 'trade was a social act'. By aiming his treatise at the 'ascendant class', as he called it, it would naturally percolate down through the social system and reach every class.

The foremast boy was to think and proceed entirely differently. In his eyes there was no question of the job-seeker trudging the unmetalled Melbourne streets, or of the poorest of poor Indians being a kind of degenerate creature whose long-term fate and privilege it was to 'rise in the world'. When *Progress and Poverty*, his single-solution to what men had always accepted as an intractable condition of society which must necessarily separate the sheep from the goats for ever, burst upon Britain, it was the classlessness of its argument which caused such a sensation. Who was this third-generation Philadelphian who in 1880 was to rival all the popular novelists in the bestseller lists with a book on economics? This converter of Shaw to socialism? This Yankee come to justice who scared the British landed interest more than at any time since the 1820s?

A picture of him at eighteen will show him as mature as ever he will need to be, for it is essential for certain prophets and teachers to develop swiftly, and then not to season. After four years with his family, he is voyaging again, this time to the Californian gold fields. These, since their discovery a decade or so since, have yielded nearly a thousand million dollars' worth of gold and were still attracting armies of mostly young men, not only from the States, but from all over the world. Henry George's motives for joining in the famous trek were mixed. Naturally he hoped to 'soon be scooping treasure out of the earth by the handful' but it was also an acceptable reason for leaving home. Cities such as Philadelphia were experiencing an uncomfortable cracking of their classic Jeffersonian façades. What they stood for could not be adequately discerned by the immigrant hordes funnelled weekly through New York, or to the new kind of expansionist trader, or indeed to the anti-slavery lobby. Mrs George's letters to her gold-seeking son indicate the type of reaction from which he had fled. 'There is nothing stirring or startling in this great city. Religion seems the all-embracing subject. Christians are looking for great results from this outpouring of the Spirit. Look to Jesus, my dear child.'

Shortly before sailing they had argued, as usual, about the slaves, but she had refused to be persuaded. Slaves had biblical sanction and she thought that their troubles were exaggerated. His father, scratching a polite living from Episcopalian publishing, would allow no unorthodoxy of any kind to penetrate the calm of the little brick house near the Senate. Neither could admit that when a child had sailed under canvas to Australia and India he could no longer be a child in their notion of the term. Twenty or so years earlier the artist John Constable had welcomed home his son, aged fifteen, from his first voyage and was shattered by such a clear destruction of what he had been when he set out. 'My son Charlie is returned from the East Indies,' he wrote to a friend. 'His ship is a noble one . . . Yet all the visionary and poetic ideas of the sea and the seaman's life are fled – the reality now only remains, and a dreadful thing that reality is – a huge and hideous floating mass.' This, it should be added, was the reverse to what had happened to Henry George, although no less destructive to his innocence, which was why like some adolescents undergoing a process of emergent brilliance, he let his parents see aspects of his personality which would not worry them and kept his magic for his friends.

These were a group of youngsters who called themselves the Lawrence Literary Society whose activities included ghost stories, boxing gloves, fencing foils, devilry, a drink called Red Eye, singing and cigars. Nearby was the printing works of King and Baird, whose type-setting sheds, full of the odds and ends of learning, were George's real school. His legend remained vivid at the heart of this early centre for many years and the letters from it which pursued him to California are the first indication of the remarkable effect he was to have throughout his life on the individual. For, as with certain religious proselytizers, he obtained his goal by a great many sharply unique solitary convictions, rather than by mass movements. His son was to write how a quality of sympathy was able to carry him directly into another man's place. Henry George himself must have been very aware of this for there was from the start an almost ruthless refusal to become trapped in the intimacy he generated. His mother made no bones of the matter. 'You have passed your nineteenth birthday. Did you think of it, or were you too busy? If you had been at home we would have had a jollification. What a kissing time there would have been, playing Copenhagen and so forth. Hen, kissing is quite out of fashion since you left; no kissing parties at all.' Jeffreys, his best friend at the printing works, but now apparently being shaken off, put a brave face on it.

You are quite right, there never was any affection in speech between us when face to face, and none shall exist now. How do you *know* that we shall never meet again? I should be obliged to you if you would not send such letters to me in the middle of business – letters which are calculated to distract any mind and render me as weak as a child . . . I remember well, how night after night we sat together and alone in your little room, smoking slowly and looking – sometimes at the little bed which was to contain us both and which rested in a corner near the door, at the little case of books on the bureau, at the dim gaslight which could so seldom be induced to burn brightly . . . and then turning from this picture . . . and gazing upon each other, we would talk of the present and the future.

But meanwhile, the voyage to the sun and to the gold. Working his passage as steward of the U.S. lighthouse steamer *Shubrick*, a vessel originally built to control the coastlines of Washington and Oregon, and which was armed with a clever device for squirting scalding water over Indians, should they come too close, as well as with brass guns, Henry George, having already sailed half the world, could afford to be unimpressed by anything California was to offer. Yet it was to provide him with experiences invaluable to a mid-nineteenth-century economist, as Shaw was to acknowledge.

When I was swept into the great Socialist revival of 1883, I found that five-sixths of those who swept in with me had been converted by Henry George. This fact would have been more widely acknowledged had it not been that it was not possible for us to stop where George had stopped. America, in spite of all its horrors of rampant Capitalism and industrial oppression, was, nevertheless, still a place for the individual and the hustler. Every American who came over to London was amazed at the apathy, the cynical acceptance of poverty and servitude as inevitable, the curious shuffling along with as little work as possible, that seemed to the visitor to explain our poverty, and moved him to say, 'Serve us right!' . . . Some of us regretted that Henry George was an American and therefore necessarily about fifty years out of date in his economics and sociology from the viewpoint of the other country; but only an American could have seen in a single lifetime the growth of the whole tragedy of civilisation from the primitive forest clearing.

Thus the saviour arrived at the shore of the land of fulfillable dreams. In 1858 San Francisco was a triple city made up of a little half-forgotten hilltop town where the followers of St Francis witnessed to poverty and regulated the sweet bell of the Mission Dolores through the canonical hours, the new state capital and its architectural pomp, and a vast rags and paper camp flung up by an army of gold prospectors. Western materialism and the west's spiritual response to it held their elementary distance before the youthful traveller's eyes, the adobe city of God and the shanties of mammon. All around he saw the beautiful landscape in its perfect climate being staked out and fought over as each gold-maddened prospector 'fenced in a little oasis from the driving sand', as he was to write. Watching the claims and counter-claims for the earth itself, it struck him how strange it was that a man should actually own so fundamentally a common human inheritance as the actual *ground* and, should such an acre or two happen to eventually become part of a city, that he should be ceaselessly and extravagantly paid for the use of it.

If land was the single basis of wealth and rank, and all that men held dear, then it was only just that land should be the only possession on which man should be taxed. Of course, it was inevitable that such an obviously simple solution to the problem of greed and inequity had been thought of before, but one of the virtues of a scanty education when wedded to an excellent natural prose style is that one is not dragged here, there and everywhere by parenthesis. Also, and here was the crux of the matter, one did not talk up to, or down to, or roundabout to any intelligent man, but directly in his ear. In Henry George's case it was the language as much as the idea which gave his book the status and excitement of a fifth gospel.

For the next eight years 'little Harry George' clung precariously to the spectacular scene which was emerging from the chaos of the San Francisco waterfront, writing his mocked views in a newspaper called *The Journal of the Trades and Workingmen*, and teaching its readers, a great proportion of them new immigrants, not to build into the Californian constitution those same social injustices which had forced them out of Europe. The style which was to revive Britain's comatose radicalism was being developed, along with the West Coast paradise. The hustlers referred to his doctrine as Harry's 'fad'. A slight, shabby but fastidiously clean young man, elegant on his mustang and haunting the gold workings, he is a heretic amidst all the wild, scrambling energy, the insistence that every man has a moral right to a grabbing hand. If he wants to preach, why doesn't he do so from the official preaching place on top of the hill?

When he was twenty-two he met an eighteen-year-old girl, adrift like himself on the restless migrant tide, and married her. She too had been to Australia. On their wedding night he made love to her until five in the morning and then, with a single coin in his pocket, got up and went out to look for a job. Their daughter had her part to play in the great Californian fantasy, for she was to be the wife of Cecil B. de Mille. Odyssey, as ever, was to breed epic. Gradually, Henry George's journalism and quirky personality made the authorities think of him as a possible candidate for a Chair of Political Economy which it was proposed should be founded at the new university, and he was invited to give a trial lecture. It was a disaster, or rather an alarming disclaimer. If society was to be rescued, they heard the sun-tanned, sandy-haired, blue-eyed lecturer tell them, it would not be by academics. They listened aghast as he went on.

'In the study of political economy you need no special knowledge, no extensive library, no costly laboratory. You do not even need textbooks or teaching, *if you do but think for yourselves.*' They were to 'take nobody's opinions for granted' but to look around them and to see for themselves what had happened and what was still happening. And then, perhaps because George believed that scholars had a special guilt in not seeing that the world acted upon their discoveries instead of merely allowing them to be read as nerveless theories, came his famous denunciation of the highly educated theorists who spoke a remote language and whose existence was comfortably walled away from that of most people:

All this array of professors, all this paraphernalia of learning, cannot educate a man. They can but help him to educate himself . . . A monkey with a microscope, a mule packing a library, are fit emblems of the men – and unfortunately they are plenty – who pass through the whole educational machinery, and come out but learned fools, crammed with knowledge they cannot use, all the more pitiable, all the more contemptible, all the more in the way of real progress, because they pass, with themselves and others, as educated men.

The response was predictable. The students clapped and stamped, the faculty sat dumb, the Chair of Political Economy was pulled back. Within weeks of this calculated – and isolated – rudeness, Henry George settled himself down with a ream of sermon paper and a soft gold-nibbed pen to lure Macaulay's dismal science from its arid perch and to set it winging like the paraclete into the understanding of the ordinary reader.

> Wilt thou upon the high and giddy mast,
> Seal up the ship-boy's eyes and rock his brains,
> In cradle of the rude imperious surge,
> And in the visitation of the winds . . .

The economy boomed even as he wrote, but he was not deceived by this.

One of the first times I recollect talking on such a subject was . . . when I was about eighteen and while I was sitting on the deck of a topsail schooner with a lot of miners on the way to the Frazer River. We got talking about the Chinese, and I ventured to ask what harm they were doing here, if, as these miners said, they were only working the cheap diggings? 'No harm now,' said an old miner, 'but wages will not always be as high as they are today in California. As the country grows, as people come in, wages will go down, and some day or another white men will be glad to get those diggings that the Chinamen are now working.' And I well remember how it impressed me, the idea that as the country grew . . . the condition of those who had to work for their living must become, not better, but worse!

All the thought which had accumulated round this and many other similar experiences as he watched and listened to working populations, either still at home and tied to hopeless custom, as in India, or in fresh continents, but trailing all kinds of hopeless custom still, now took literary shape. When he had finished the last page, 'in the dead of night, when I was entirely alone, I flung myself on my knee and wept like a child.' The vow 'made in daylight, and in a city street', had been honoured. This street had actually been in New York, which he had recently visited. He had found wealth and power written on every brownstone front and 'the very air charged with power', and lying just behind all this splendour he had seen an immense human degradation. In comparison, California seemed virtuous and enlightened, and he returned to San Francisco to warn its citizens of the perils in store for them.

He was then part owner of the *Daily Evening Post*, the city's first penny newspaper, and indeed the first such paper west of the Rocky Mountains and which, as the cent had not yet begun to circulate on the West Coast, had been the reason for a shipment of a thousand dollars' worth of pennies from Washington. It was in this newspaper that Henry George denounced the American habit of trying to stifle debate by cries of 'Communism!' 'Socialism!' 'Agrarianism!' etc.,

for it is neither the one nor the other of these, but simply an attempt to set aside the principle of competition upon which society is now based and to substitute for it a system based on the conception of the State as in the main a family, in which the weaker brethren shall not be remorselessly pushed to the wall. It is the exaggeration of individualism of our existing social system that gives free scope to cruel selfishness and monstrous greed.

He sent the book, *Progress and Poverty*, without doubt the best-loved and most popularly understood piece of economic philosophy ever written, to Appleton, the New York publisher, chiefly because the firm had published Herbert Spencer's *Social Statics*. It was promptly rejected. Appleton's were troubled by its clear language and told the author that although it had force it also had aggression. Scribner's and Harper's followed suit. A deputation of Henry George's sympathisers then called on Appleton's, but with no luck. The book wouldn't pay, they were told. After considering publishing it himself, even to setting up the type with his own hands, George had a brainwave. He would try it out in a country which was deep in the throes of a land debate – Great Britain, which, as ever, was plunged into the complications of the Irish Land Question.

The launching of *Progress and Poverty* in Britain in 1879 revealed a very sophisticated author and one who almost might be thought of as an early progenitor of the hype. No fewer than 2,000 free copies were distributed, not only for review but to every possibly helpful celebrity, Dean Stanley, Henry Labouchère – even to Gladstone himself, recently returned from his brilliant Midlothian tour, where he had spoken openly of the 'compulsory expropriation' of land. The moment was ideal for such a book. Not that such moments need be in the past. Replying to Jessica Mitford's questions, George Jackson told her that he had read thousands of books and had been most impressed by Engels' *Anti - Dühring*, Pomeroy's *On Resistance* and Dostoevsky's *Crime and Punishment*, 'And do you know who I was really impressed with, although he isn't a socialist or a communist? I was impressed with Henry George's stuff. His single tax idea is not correct. But I like his presentation.' So did Britain in 1880. By one of those curious coincidences of sympathy, the death of the author of *Soledad Brother* took place exactly a century after *Progress and Poverty* was published and when Jackson, like Henry George at the time, was in his thirtieth year. Such a coincidence is of small consequence beyond the fact that each young writer transcended the actual political content of his book by a personal authority and revelation which took it straight to the reader's heart.

For countless British readers, the effect on them of *Progress and Poverty* was similar to a famous experience of John Stuart Mill. 'When I laid down the last volume of the *Traité de Législation* by Dumont', he wrote in his beautiful *Autobiography*, 'I had become a different being . . . I had a religion . . . the feeling rushed upon me that all the previous moralists were superseded . . . The reading of the *Traité* was an epoch in my life.' George's book arrived during one of those periods when the

British were going in for self-assessment, with contrary conclusions. The *Quarterly Review* said that their examination of society revealed 'a tone of rancour and vindictiveness which, if not absolutely new in this country, is at any rate a more serious phenomenon than ever before.' Whereas *The Times* looked around and declared, 'There is hardly any social envy in the so-called Democratic classes of this country; there is no desire to attack the rich because they are rich, no sense of exclusiveness and no political jealousies. Neither are the desires of the commonality directed to any great or radical measures either of social or political change.'

When Henry George himself arrived in London (and promptly dubbed 'George V') a brilliantly conceived series of events linking his book with the Irish troubles were set in motion. The Irish Land Question ferment now had the support of the noisy American Land League, which was the creation of immigrants who were first-generation escapees from the famine, and who had every reason to hate England. To them George's land nationalisation theory was not so much an hypothesis as a scenario. The huge injustice of classic landlordism in all its cruelty had been acted out in the Irish countryside, and was now repeating itself in the swarming American cities before their very eyes. This Irish indignation and turmoil presented, as he was to admit, a God-given opportunity for the spreading of his cure. By the time he arrived in Dublin in 1882, it only needed a personal brush with the authorities to baptise him, as it were, in the common Irish misery, and for him – much to the fury of the Establishment – to be recognised as saviour. This the Irish police provided by ineptly arresting him and thus guaranteeing him as hero. This occurred in September 1882. A few days later *The Times*, which had managed to ignore it until now, gave *Progress and Poverty* a three-and-a-half column review. It was grandly dismissive and concluded that the book was as impractical as Sir Thomas More's rules for a just society.

But soon something far more interesting and important was happening. Groups of people began to form radical societies up and down the country, and while not for the most part arguing schemes which would eventually implement a land tax or land nationalisation, they were, they felt, in a new politics. In the course of advocating its single save-all doctrine, Henry George's book had, *en passant*, cut across all kinds of class inhibition, popular cant and myth, and the inertia experienced by those who had been taught, and come to believe, that there was no going forward. It was a thrilling work. It took hold of its readers and shook them up, revived them, sharpened their wits, and inspired them.

British landowners, ever realists, and with quite a number of old men among them who had memories of the anxieties which had followed the Napoleonic wars when a French-style revolution seemed not impossible, took practical steps against the popular outcome of *Progress and Poverty*. Calling its author 'the apostle of plunder' and much else, they grouped themselves into the Liberty and Property Defence League. By 1884, when George had stumped some forty-four British cities in the wake of his dazzling tract this League had a dozen branches and a powerful parliamentary committee and, as E. P. Lawrence said, had begun a twenty-year fight with the land tax theory which was to reach its climax in the House of Lords' rejection of Lloyd George's 1909 budget. It has to be remembered that just twenty-one members of this League owned no less than two million acres of Britain between them. It was the Duke of Buccleuch, according to the *New York Tribune*, who sought to avoid the possible effects of what he termed Henry George's 'wild scheme' by contriving a will which arranged for the administration of his estates for the next 1300 years. But it was left to the Duke of Argyll, who, in an article in the *Nineteenth Century* in April 1884, branded George as 'the Preacher of unrighteousness', to debate the whole idea of a land tax in terms which became acceptable to the moderates.

By 1885 the time had arrived to nail Henry George down. Was he just a naive foreign agitator who was running a mad crusade in a country whose real difficulties – including its national myths – were quite outside his American understanding? Or could he be the necessary, even the longed-for, catalyst? Joseph Chamberlain, who in 1882 had been 'electrified' by *Progress and Poverty*, now began to issue dire warnings about it. He told his supporters that 'we may live to see theories as wild as those suggested by the American economist adopted as the creed of no inconsiderable a portion of the electorate'. Both the reactionaries and progressives alike now tried to force George to be what they called 'scientific', meaning statistical, but he would not be drawn. 'His cavalier treatment of statisticians,' wrote E. P. Lawrence, 'was the master-stroke of his campaign.' All that George had to do when facts and figures were demanded of him was to point. The sight was dreadful. The national bookkeeping might show national prosperity, yet it was nakedly obvious that huge numbers of Britain's citizens led lives which, in Thomas Huxley's words, were 'worse than those of any savage tribe'. The rapidly mushrooming reformist societies, not all of them political, and not all of them able to go all the way down such a revolutionary path, were nevertheless awakened to imaginative possibilities of social justice by Henry George's thesis. When the *Daily News* declared that his 'unreasonable demands had taken hold of the imagination of large numbers of our people and the best way of combating them is by reasonable reforms,' his task, in effect, had succeeded.

Alerted and nervous, various reactionaries from both the right and the left now began to attempt to put a halt to what was plainly a dangerous teaching. Lord Fortescue succeeded in getting *Progress and Poverty* withdrawn from the City of London College, and even the socialist H. M. Hyndman complained that the English were always more ready to hear a foreigner than 'one of our people', which was a curious statement coming from a person playing the Baptist to Karl Marx. Press and politicians of all shades joined together in denouncing this 'international busybody' who was prescribing 'arsenic instead of castor oil for the ills of society'. Conventional nineteenth-century philanthropists, smarting from such Georgian accusations as 'It is sad, sad reading, the lives of the men who would have done something for their fellows,' turned on the trim little visitor who had the audacity to criticise them.

None of them needed to panic. Henry George intended no swift change. 'The idea of Socialism is grand and noble; and it is, I am convinced, possible of realisation, but such a state of society cannot be manufactured – it must grow. Society is an organism, not a machine . . .' As if to demonstrate this, George returned to the States and soon, to the bewilderment of his British converts, disappeared into the incomprehensible machinery of New York politics. Now and then they heard of his hardening attitude towards socialism, which, to give him his due, he had never entirely accepted. Just before he left London for good, in 1889, Sidney Webb had written to him. 'I want to implore your forebearance. When you are denounced as a traitor and what not, by Socialist newspapers, and heckled by Socialist questioners, or abused by Socialist orators, it will be difficult not to denounce Socialism in return. But do not do so . . . it will be better for the cause which we both have at heart.'

This letter exemplified what Shaw called the attitude of the 'really knowing' radicals towards Henry George. Edward Pease, the first Fabian secretary, put it succinctly. Britain, he said, had to

insist that a tremendous revolution was to be accomplished by a political method, applicable to a majority of voters, and capable of being drafted as an act of Parliament by any competent lawyer. To Henry George belongs the extra-ordinary merit of recognising the right way of social salvation . . . From him I think it may be taken that the early Fabians learned to associate the new gospel with the old political methods.

Later, another Fabian, J. A. Hobson, journeying about the country,

found in almost every centre a certain little knot of men of the lower-middle or upper working-class, men of grit and character, largely self-educated, mostly nonconformists in religion, to whom Land Nationalisation, taxation of unearned increment, or other radical reforms of land tenure, are doctrines resting on plain moral sanction. Henry George, like other prophets, co-operated with the 'Spirit of the age' and may be considered to have exercised a more directly powerful formative and educative influence over English radicalism of the past eighty-five years than any other man:

> Where lies the land to which the ship would go?
> Far, far ahead, is all her seamen know,
> And where the land she travels from? Away,
> Far, far behind, is all that they can say.

Whilst the *Shubrick* was steaming towards Cape Horn on its immense run via the south Atlantic and Pacific to California and its land grabbers, the assistant engineer became ill with yellow fever. The young man's dying wish, insistent and desperate, was that he should have a land grave. Not even death itself seemed to him so horrific as the thought of his body lying beneath the sea. The captain promised on his honour to bury the boy ashore. However, the Montevideo harbour authority, shocked that anyone could even think of such a thing, know-ing as they must the infectious nature of the disease, ordered the *Shubrick* to take its dreaded corpse several miles out and sink it. Henry George, the steward, who felt himself bound to the collective promise which the crew had made to the dead man, watched guiltily as the body, well ballasted with coal and fixed into a huge rough wooden box with holes pierced into it, was tipped into the depths. No sooner were the engines started and the *Shubrick* on its way, than the coffin sped to the surface and began to bob about on the swell. A boat was launched at once and a macabre contest between the now strangely lively box and the sailors sent to sink it by attaching it to an old anchor and chain took place. Eventually, once again it sank from sight and the *Shubrick*, its superstitions alerted, moved once more up the mouth of the River Plate, which was crowded with all manner of shipping, including the entire Brazilian navy. The *Shubrick*, in order to obtain a clean berth, had to remain in quarantine for a week. Preparations for this kept everybody busy until that evening,

when the quartermaster, sweeping the harbour with his glass, noticed something floating in, which rivetted his attention. Again and again he stared at it and then, with surprise and dismay in his face, called the officer of the deck. The whisper spread through the ship, and in a few minutes all were watching in silence the object that seemed drifting towards us. Onward it came, through all the vessels that lay beyond us . . . turning and tacking as though piloted by life, and steadily holding the course for our steamer. It passed the last ship and came straight for us . . . it was indeed the coffin.

A thrill of awe passed through every heart. Right under the bows came the box; it touched our side; halted a moment as if claiming recognition, and then drifted slowly past us to the shore. There was an excited murmur forward, a whispered consultation, then, 'Man the quarter boat, boys, *take pick and spades*, tow the coffin ashore and bury the body.' It was the work of a moment – the boat shot like an arrow from our side, the ashen oars bending with the energy of the stroke. Reverently and gently they secured the box, and with slow, solemn strokes, towed it to the foot of the desolate looking hill that skirts the bay. There, breaking it open, they bore the corpse, covered with the flag, a little distance up the hillside, and making in the twilight a grave in the chaparral, laid it to rest.

It is a Melville tale. The rules have been made to give for the sake of the individual. An ordinary man had demanded and finally claimed his elemental right and the steward of the *Shubrick* had been involved in a parable and had listened to a sermon. Martin, a man of little consequence, but his shipmate, had cried out of the depths – and had been heard! This is what really haunted Henry George. *He* would be heard. His text would be, 'How wide the limits stand between a splendid and a happy land.'

What's Become of Davidson?

The beginning of the 1880s in Britain struck many people as a possible time for an alternative politics. In order to prepare themselves, some subscribed to declarations, some to mustering in force, and a few to taking vows of regeneration. All were aware that the old strands of radicalism which stretched back through the Utilitarians to the French Revolution were surfacing once again, and all felt a personal urgency to use them to correct, rather than overthrow, a system which was giving a huge part of the population a very rough time indeed. But if not outright revolution, then what? A new ethics, it was suggested, a change of the individual heart which must eventually (no rush, that was the secret) change the world. One of the reasons for this new seeking – 'new' had become the operative word for all that was enlightened and progressive – was because Benthamite thinking had become academic, and thus dusty, to late Victorian liberals and socialists, and they were looking for solutions with much more of a shine to them. Henry George's achievement that decade has been, after all, to rig out a dull old classic, Ricardo's *Law of Rent*, in the freshest of language and so transform it into an exciting manifesto. Could there be other prophets who, by steering a 'new' course past the old radical paths of some economists and churchmen at this very moment, were waiting to lead mankind towards the light?

Percival Chubb, a young clerk from the Local Government Board Department in Whitehall, told his close friend Henry Havelock Ellis, a young medical student from St Thomas's Hospital, that he knew of such a prophet. The couple, both in their early twenties, had met at the Progressive Association, which was a creedless debating society-cum-church, for which Havelock Ellis was writing hymns that were uncontaminated by even the slightest 'theistic tinge'. He was strikingly good-looking and would have had some of the ethereal beauty of a G. F. Watts' Galahad if his eyes had been set a shade or two further apart. Although

94

he had already travelled the world and taught at an elementary school in Australia, and was now studying medicine in London, he was still shy and introverted. He liked Percival Chubb for the qualities he did not himself possess, for his zest and optimism, and for the laughing enthusiasm which he displayed towards all this 'newness' which was being let loose on the cast-iron fabric of official belief in England. Where Havelock Ellis was tentative and fastidiously enquiring, Chubb was a bit reckless to the extent to which he would commit himself to theories and movements, and apparently beamingly happy because of it. Where Havelock Ellis would watch from afar, Chubb would move in. Their contrasting natures reflected the two main strands of reaction to the message which political-philosophical movements were expounding in gas-lit halls up and down the country. Havelock Ellis was later to conclude that Chubb 'was without the originality and force which place a man in conflict with his own time'. Chubb's actual difficulty, if one can call it that, was that he was a kind of natural citizen of the 'higher plane', as the New Lifers called it, and thus had no need to struggle to reach it.

The two friends met daily for lunchtime walks. Increasingly, the shadow of a third presence fell across their conversation, that of a Scottish Socrates named Thomas Davidson. Davidson, it seemed, knew everything, and was a walking university and a peripatetic shrine. He spoke a dozen languages and he knew, more than any other individual, what had to be done to rescue men from the soulless treadmill to which nineteenth-century trading practices had condemned them. He knew too that his own business was to make converts and collect followers. This was not hard to do; matching his enchanter's tongue was a physique so splendid that it alone proved the existence of a different and better way of living on this earth. Every time Percival Chubb mentioned this extraordinary person he shone as though lamps had been lit all round him, and his ordinary cheerfulness spread out into radiance. Even to Havelock Ellis's cautious eyes, it was clear that Davidson, this wandering encyclopedia and disciple-maker, did indeed possess something which all the radical speakers he had heard most decidedly did not. Chubb told him that they had met at a monastery in Italy, and explained that Domodossola was a Rosminian centre which attracted young people from all over Europe, and that it was there that he had been taught how to accept the 'food' or real nourishment of 'all' religions and systems. The teacher who had held out this concentrate was Thomas Davidson. Chubb had immediately accepted his message and revered him for it. But some of the students had not. Adrift from home, their own ideas as yet inchoate, and sheltering behind the usual youthful aggression or exhibitionism, they had led Davidson quite a dance. But he never rejected even the worst of them, and it was this indifference of his to being loved where he himself loved, and his total indifference to money or fame, which gave him a genuine stature. What worried his followers most was his compulsive and unpredictable travelling. He was just like Browning's 'Waring', complained one of them. 'You met him, talked with him, were inspired by him – and the next day you found he had fled.'

Chubb and Havelock Ellis, and some half dozen like-minded radicals were at this time forming a little society in order 'to socialise what we call our physical life in order that we may attain greater freedom in what we call our spiritual life', as Ellis himself put it. They gathered in a suburban house, nine innocent dreamers who were later to look back on themselves as eccentrics, a bit absurd, and as people who intended to give the country an object lesson in simplicity by substituting for the cumbersome intricate fashion in clothes, furniture and almost every manufactured object, a good plain choice, and who intended neither to fight nor defend economic socialism but to prepare the people for the unique changes which would soon be overtaking their existences. Had not Bentham himself said that there should be times when governments themselves should lie low and practice quietism? How much more essential then it was that serious men and women, with signs all around them of the impending challenge to capitalism, should make a retreat and strengthen themselves with this discipline. It would be a return to the anti-revolutionary plans drawn up by the physiocrats. Some wondered how long it would take for this personal purification to affect the teeming millions. Some were a bit brutal. 'The typical Londoner,' said Sidney Webb, 'was a frail and sickly unit, cradled in the gutter, housed in a slum, slaving in a sweater's den and dying in a workhouse infirmary.' What price Davidson's healthy Platonism in these black streets?

Soon, Davidson, strolling and captivating his way across kingdoms and republics, began to very much dislike what he heard about the London movement. He found its first programme 'meagre and indefinite' and he attacked 'the kind of quietism' which it advocated. It was self-indulgent and non-missionary. Worst of all, it had quite misunderstood his teachings. He had come to London especially to tell them what to do and had set them on fire, as he did everybody he met, by his sheer presence, and they had somehow gone out. At the first meeting in October they had read the Pauline epistle-like instructions which he had left behind and, under their spell, had declared themselves worker priests, united in their intention to live the 'higher life' whilst pursuing their present callings in the world. Some sixteen members had been present, including Mrs Hinton, H. H. Champion, Havelock Ellis, Edward Pease and Frank Podmore. But at the second meeting, a terrible hollowness crept over them. All the same, it was on this occasion, in the Modern Press Office, Paternoster Row, that they decided to call themselves the Fellowship of the New Life, complete with a motto from Goethe, '*Im Ganzen, Guten, Schönen resolut zu leben*', and where they passed a resolution 'recognising that the competitive system had broken down'.

Thus an already un-Davidsonian note had entered the proceedings and when the extremely un-Davidsonian Hubert Bland amended this to, 'The members of the Society assert that the Competitive System assumes the happiness and comfort of the few, at the expense and suffering of the many, and that this Society must be reconstructed in such a manner as to secure the general welfare and happiness,' it was plain to all that a rift had come between those who saw salvation in spiritual terms and those who saw it in economics. 'It is in accordance with the irony of human affairs,' Havelock Ellis was to write,

that Fabianism should indirectly have been produced by a man so alien to its spirit as Thomas Davidson. I, who had no political interests, while sympathetic with the Fabians, decided to remain with the parent body, though as I came to realise the inevitable limitations of the movement, my more active participation diminished and ceased . . .

This was contrary to what happened to Thomas Davidson's own interest in the young Havelock Ellis, after their introduction by Chubb in London. Bewildered more than anything else by Havelock Ellis's failure to be overcome by him and mystified rather than put out by a series of letters from the medical student criticising his philosophy,

Davidson demanded to know the reason for what he called this 'perpetual obstinacy'. Surely he must know, wrote the master, 'that I have rarely been attracted to anyone so much as to you.' But Havelock Ellis, his native Suffolk wariness now fully to the fore, was not to be seduced. The little band of those whom Pierre Janet dubbed the 'psychasthenics' was not for him. These were people who 'were instinctively repelled by the ordinary social environment in which they live; they could not adjust themselves to the ordinary routine of life; its banalities crushed and offended them; the 'real world' of their average fellow men seemed to them unreal, and they were conscious of a painful sense of inadequacy in relation to it; they sought for new and stronger stimulants, for new and deeper narcotics, a new Heaven and a new Earth. Like the early Christians, psychasthenics preached a subversive faith and attracted to them abnormal followers of an exalted and romantic type, usually of the finest character and highest intelligence.

With Havelock Ellis there was another factor, the generation rebellion. Just before meeting Davidson he had visited Paris for the first time. France had been his great dream ever since, at the age of fourteen, he had been introduced to his grandmother's copy of Rousseau's *Rêveries*. His companion was a poet named Angus Mackay. In 1887 and 1890 he was to travel to Paris again, the first time to join in the official centenary celebrations of the Revolution, and the second to celebrate the end of his medical training. On this latter journey he was accompanied by Arthur Symonds, who was twenty-five. They had not gone there, said Havelock Ellis, 'to seek out the venerated figures who still survived to enjoy a fame won in a generation before,' but because they themselves 'represented the young generation and were concerned only with its leaders or prominent representatives'. He meant in particular Verlaine, Mallarmé and Rodin. Such people were 'by no means necessarily the kind of men society was likely to count "great"', but it was they alone who could exert a 'miraculous effect on the respiratory activities of the spirit'. Thus the reason for Thomas Davidson's failure with Havelock Ellis is clear. Although he 'was the most intensely alive man I ever met', at the age of forty-three the marks of popular veneration showed all too plain for comfort. And evangelical puffings, however eloquent, were the last thing to attract a young man who was already on an intellectual journey which would lead him from *Rêveries* to *A la Recherche du Temps*

Perdu. Davidson's mistake had been to pick out Havelock Ellis as one of his natural believers. His great service, Havelock Ellis said, was to make me a sceptic – 'and for this I remain thankful to the end of my life.'

Davidson had the kind of face which used to be described as a countenance, or something which created discomfort in those who could not respond to it. It affected one woman 'like a hot stove' which she had to stand back from, and William James the American philosopher went so far as to put this famous display of Davidson's 'inward glory' down to the heroic physical construction of the master's head. Shaw too withdrew from all that this fine head stood for: 'The Tennysonian process of making stepping-stones of our dead selves to higher things is pious in intention, but it sometimes leads downstairs instead of up.'

In 1888 Thomas Davidson forsook the old world for New England, settling first at Farmington, a delightful little riverside town in Maine, and then a year or two later at Glenmore, an exquisite site in the Adirondack Mountains, New York State. Such was the perfection of the Glenmore commune that only those who had not beaten a path to it could afford to mock. Here during the summer months, the followers of Thomas Davidson's cult of the renewal of the self were roused early from their beds of balsam twigs by the blowing of a horn and, after a plunge in the cold mountain stream, were at their desks, so to speak, to hear a series of brilliant 'Lectures and Interpretations' by their guru. In the afternoon there would be swimming, walking and tree-felling, and after supper music and conversations on art and ethics. The followers lived in simple rustic huts made of logs, or in tents, using the old farmhouse of Glenmore as a library and classroom. They dressed as they pleased and shared their homes with friends, Davidson himself sharing his two-roomed cottage – with Percy Chubb. Dominating the lecture-room was a large text: 'Without friends no one would choose to live, even with all other good things.' Davidson's and Chubb's cottage was perched about a hundred feet above the main encampment on the side of Mount Hurricane. All the surrounding landscape had been tamed into groves, winding paths, bathing places, wooden seats for the contemplative and drying-grounds, where middle-class New York ladies in rational clothes could be seen hanging out their laundry. On Sundays, Roman Catholics and Seventh-Day Adventists from the city would arrive to listen to strange songs and free language, whilst cart-loads of the New Lifers themselves would explore the local sights, such as John Brown's grave and the Whiteface Mountains. Sometimes the master himself would be seen taking his disciples for immense hikes, cramming them with Hegel, Goethe, Edward Carpenter and T. H. Green as they swung along, and accompanied always by a bound-ing collie named Dante.

Now and then, William James would arrive and join in these excur-sions. He and Davidson were about the same age and had first met in 1874 at Boston, when James had tried to persuade the penniless young Scot, who did nothing but pursue a naked idyll of sun and seabathing, to become a resident Platonist at Harvard. Longfellow aided and abetted this scheme. The Chair of Greek Philosophy was his for the taking. But with a gesture which had an extraordinary similarity to that of Henry George, when he was offered academic anchorage at a university, and at almost the exact same moment, Davidson too saw that it was pulled from under him by slating the faculty. Davidson's way of doing so was by an article in the *Atlantic Monthly*. This, wrote James, 'with his other uncon-ventionalities', sealed his fate. But it was a pity because 'a few undisci-plinables like Davidson may be infinitely more precious than a faculty full of orderly routinists.' On one of their Adirondack walks, Davidson turned on James for his own particular 'musty and mouldy' academi-cism, and never, wrote James, had the wilderness vibrated more repug-nantly than it did that night to the word 'academicism'.

It was while he was at Glenmore that Davidson had been briefly attracted to socialism by reading a novel called *Looking Backward* by Edward Bellamy. Then, according to a student, he had suddenly thrust the whole thing from him, saying that it was a regression to utilitarian-ism, and a threat to personal liberty. But what he had momentarily sniffed was a brief rank whiff of the authoritarianism to come. As in London, the American New Lifers inevitably attracted early Marxists, and towards these Davidson displayed an American dislike of any kind of collectivism, although wrapping-up his anti-communist arguments in his customary language of the eternal. One such tentatively Marxist visitor was Morris Cohen to whom the master wrote,

I once came near to being a socialist myself; and indeed, in that frame of mind founded what afterwards became the Fabian Society. [This, of course, was not strictly accurate.] But I soon found out the limitations of socialism and I am sure you will . . . We both believe that the present economic and moral condition of society is bad and needs reforming. We both believe that this can be done only through an increase of social sentiment, of brotherly relations . . . Further, I suppose, we both see that mere economic socialism – that is the owning of the means of production by the state – would not necessarily insure economic well-being . . . I am free in a society when it is the expression of my rationality . . . Feudalism was socialism, that is often forgotten . . .

Reforms based on human kindness and ways of restoring human dignity could only have struck Cohen, embroiled as he had been from birth in the horrors attendant on immigrant labour in the New York sweatshops, as pipedream solutions to what was happening. Like hundreds of other seekers, he had travelled up and up to the 166-acre farm, set two thousand feet above sea level, via a sail along the Hudson River, then a beautiful train ride from Albany to Westpoint, and finally by horse and trap through some twenty miles of flowery lanes. The sight which met him was the apotheosis of all nineteenth-century summer camps and reading parties. Sunburnt girls, young men singing German songs, ladies lying in hammocks sewing balsam pillows, plain and plentiful food, music, uninhibited talk, free companionships, books and, at the back of everything, splashing water – this was what he was being asked to personally assimilate and somehow recreate even among the rich grabbers and penniless hordes of New York. 'When society is social enough to adopt socialism,' the master told him, 'it will be ready to adopt something better!' Then 'the afflatus of great ideas' would be carried off by its own windiness and there, positive and actual, would be what these ancient patterns of humanity most needed – a new life which was really a retrieval of the way of life they were meant to have. But, warned Davidson, 'If the New Life [he was referring to the Fellowship of 1883 in London which had so easily succumbed to the heresies of the wily Fabius Cunctator] means the destruction of habits, then I have no desire to live it. My great aim is form habits . . . habits of breaking up habits when they are no longer useful.' This, of course, was what the Fabian Society was doing then, and still does. But it is always a bitter blow to the founder of any institution to have it seized and developed in ways not his own. In 1894, some ten years after the split, Edward Pease, its first secretary, informed the Fabian Society that its 'pious founder' was in

London, and an invitation was at once sent to Davidson asking him to give a lecture. He declined.

Back at Glenmore, the New Life flourished in the pellucid air. Its master had now completely reverted from being a world wanderer to an extremely businesslike principal of a well-run educational establishment. Although Davidson himself, as William James noted, remained outside its regulations –

He avoided stated hours for work . . . Individualist *à outrance,* Davidson felt that every hour was a unique entity to whose claim on one's spontaneity one should always lie open. Thus he was never abstracted or preoccupied, but always seemed when with you as if you were the one person whom it was right to attend to. It was this individualistic religion that made Davidson so indifferent to socialism and general administrative panaceas.

James never saw him work with his hands in any way, and observed him accepting 'material services of all kinds without apology, as if he were a born patrician'. Nor was he in any way interested in rainy days. There was no insurance when part of Glenmore burnt down – and no particular grief either. Trees were everywhere, so were healthy New Lifers. It could be rebuilt – and soon was.

He was writing an important book when death came for him, but everyone knew that his being unable to finish it meant nothing to him. Thrift and caution, time-saving and investing for the future were all aspects of a mean streak where he was concerned – 'If you believe in a protective tariff you're in hell already.' Just before he died, the superb body suddenly and agonisingly wrecked by prostate trouble, he had told the young workmen who attended the night school which he had founded in a New York slum, that industrial politics also meant nothing to him and that they were fools if they imagined that trade unionism alone could rescue them. On the briefest outing which toil allowed from their tenements and factories, they heard him telling them to first find the invincibility of their separate selves, and then step out and inherit the earth. For an hour or two they were spellbound; for the rest of their lives, secretly ruminative about what would have happened had they tried to do what he said.

As the master approached the grave which he was so certain would not contain him, and the Adirondackians sang from Mount Hurricane, Herbert Casson, the founder of the American Labor

Church, offered a comparative trans-Atlantic analysis of the progress of the new politics:

In America, Socialism is in ferment: in England it is a growth. In America it is caused by the aggressions of the few; in England by the enlightenment of the many. In America it is rushing ahead like a train that has lost its driver; in England it is jogging along like a stage-coach that stops at every wayside inn. The sturdy army of English Socialists is laying the foundation stones of its campaign as patiently and as thoroughly as if they expected to live forever, while we in America rush to the newspaper bulletin-boards every morning to see if Judgment Day has arrived.

Back in London, Havelock Ellis, the chosen one who, to Davidson's not wholly vain expectations, had turned down an invitation to discipleship, was helping to celebrate the bicentenary of the birth of Jean-Jacques Rousseau in 1712. The world, thought Havelock Ellis, became a stranger mystery than ever when we contemplated its 'saviours'. 'Sometimes it seems doubtful whether they ever existed at all, and when we know their lives intimately how vague and dubious and complex they are apt to appear.'

Thomas Hardy's Courtship Novel

On Monday, 7 March 1870 Thomas Hardy, who was then staying with his parents at Bockhampton, rose very early in the morning and set out while it was still starlight for Cornwall. It was to be the most significant journey he was ever to make. He was twenty-nine. A few days before he had finished his second novel, *Desperate Remedies,* and sent it off to Alexander Macmillan, who was to reject it. His first novel, *The Poor Man and the Lady*, also turned down, lay in a drawer. Apart from these creations his writings to date consisted of poems which would not be published until many years later and a light-hearted essay in *Chambers's Journal* entitled 'How I Built Myself a House'. Yet in spite of the tenuous nature of such a claim at such a time, and in spite of a common sense which resigned him to architecture as a livelihood, he had inwardly moved to a position which committed him to literature. Thus it was the manuscript of a poem, and not the plan for restoring the parish church, which was observed jutting from his pocket when he arrived at St Juliot Rectory, Boscastle, between six and seven that evening.

A woman of his own age dressed in brown welcomed him, and from that moment there proceeded emotions, events and imaginings which were to culminate in one of the major sequences of love poetry in the English language, and in *A Pair of Blue Eyes*, the first novel by Hardy to carry his name. It was a book whose autobiographical element was to provide much intrigue and speculation, and was greater than he cared to admit. Unlike the magnificent love-remembered poems of 1912, the transmuting forces of time are absent in this story. It was written while the experiences and thoughts which suggested it were happening to him in the most intimate personal sense. His method of artistically coping with his own courtship, his spiritual universe from which a benign creator had been deposed and the invasion of rural insularity by disturbing new elements, belonged more to the sphere of the poet than to that of the novelist, and his early readers were swift to see it. Coventry Patmore, reading the newly published *A Pair of Blue Eyes*, 'regretted at almost every page that such unequalled beauty and power should not have assured themselves the immortality which would have been impressed upon them by the form of verse,' and Tennyson was enthralled by its poetic conception and, later, confessed to Hardy that he liked it the best of all his novels.

In 1877 Hardy wrote in his notebook, 'The ultimate aim of the poet should be to touch our hearts by showing his own,' and this final personal intention pervades the sad story of Elfride. It is a fragile work but not a slight one. In many ways it is surprisingly advanced, for, although all its characters announce themselves in stereotyped 1860s fashion, they soon break through the convention of mid-Victorian fiction and emerge as moderns, with their uncomfortable semi-awareness of confused genders. A further fascination is felt when it is perceived that these characters and their landscape – one of 'those sequestered spots outside the Gates of the World' – both belong to the most important experiences of Hardy's youth. The novel attracted a special kind of attention and admiration from the start. Forty years later Hardy was still defensive about it. In 1913 he informed a correspondent, 'It is very strange that you should have been attracted by *A Pair of Blue Eyes*. The character of the heroine is somewhat – indeed, rather largely – that of my late wife, and the background of the tale the place where she lived. But of course the adventures, loves etc., are fictitious entirely, though people used sometimes to ask her why she did this and that.'*

Proust, a great reader of Hardy, said of *A Pair of Blue Eyes* that it was 'of all books the one I would myself most gladly have written'. Its picture of individuals nervously exploring private emotional thresholds which they either cannot wholly comprehend or accept allows the reader an uncommon amount of personal interpretation. Although it is constructed with the characteristic mesh of plot and sub-plot which typifies all of Hardy's fiction, there is in this fresh morning work only a suggestion of the imperious tragic philosophy which was to dominate future novels. What occurs at Endelstow is poignant to an unforgettable degree, yet it is but a lead up to those 'dramas of grandeur and unity truly Sophoclean [which] are enacted in the real, by virtue of the concen-

* Michael Millgate, *Thomas Hardy: his career as a novelist* (1971).

trated passions and closely-knit interdependence on the lives therein,' as Hardy described the subjects of his mature period. The celebrated irony, however, is immediately recognisable. Humanity as time's laughing stock has made its entrance. Human order is derisively measured against some hollow cosmic disorder. The fate of lovers is made infinitely more melancholy when its trivial connection with the vast unfeeling forces called Nature is exposed. These forces are given a precise geographical location in the shape of the immense, beautiful and frightening north Cornish seaboard, so that the heroine is seen on both an actual and a symbolic cliff edge. The pounding Atlantic mocks her heartbeat. 'At Beeny Cliff . . .' wrote Hardy in his notebook in 1872, 'green towards the land, blue-black towards the sea. Every ledge has a little, starred, green grass upon it: all vertical parts bare . . . The sea is full of motion internally, but still as a whole. Quiet and silent in the distance, noisy and restless close at hand.'

Forty years later, after his wife's death, the cliff's edge balances an old happiness –

> The woman now is – elsewhere – whom the ambling pony bore,
> And nor knows nor cares for Beeny, and will laugh there nevermore.

Elfride and the boy architect who makes his descent upon her father's parish are a decade younger than Hardy and Emma Gifford when they first met at St Juliot. This immaturity is the key to the novel. Elfride knows little about herself and nothing about men, but she has no reason to think that intelligence and instinct will not tell her plenty about both in due time. She is not ambitious and she lacks the type of self-dramatisation which sees herself as a storm centre. Such fantasies are reserved for her pen, for, like Emma Gifford, she is writing a romance.* Elfride, in fact, is rather ordinary and a bit gauche, easily impressed, and has 'special facilities for getting rid of trouble after a decent interval and is shocked when she finds out how many people cling to their misery'. Suitors besiege her. She expects them to know what they are about. But their movements are tentative and unsure, and they push her into making bad mistakes. In spite of their essential weakness, the egotism of these very different young men involves them in a great deal more action

* See Emma Hardy, *Some Recollections*, ed. Evelyn Hardy and Robert Gittings (1961), p. 90, for details of Emma Hardy's unpublished novel 'The Maid on the Shore'.

than the circumstances really warrant and none of them stops to ask himself if his violence or self-concern is endangering the girl.

Unsuspecting and entirely vulnerable, Elfride has gradually to learn that hers is not a happy destiny. She tells a friend that she asks very little of life and that she is 'content to build happiness on any accidental basis that may lie near at hand', but the irony remains that there is not one single accidental factor pointing to happiness connected with her existence. All things work together for ill. For what purpose? No one can say. She is 'unlucky', that is all. Some people are. Instead of her successes and mistakes merging into a tolerable if flawed entity, which is the common lot, bit by bit everything goes wrong for her and she is left with nothing to cling to. The stars are not to blame. They and the huge seas, rocks and winds among which she has always lived know nothing about her. It is vanity to imagine that she is even the lowly component of a vast creation which needs her and is aware of her. Others as well as Hardy had at this moment arrived at a state of black disbelief in the benign intentions of the cosmos. Richard Jefferies continued to worship terrestrial glory and to give himself up to the ecstasies of the physical world but, in *The Story of My Heart*, he admitted

there is nothing human in nature. The earth, though loved so dearly, would let me perish on the ground, and neither bring forth food nor water. Burning in the sky the great sun, of whose company I have been so fond, would merely burn on and make no motion to assist me . . . The trees care nothing for us; the hill I visited so often in days gone by has not missed me . . . If the entire human race perished at this hour, what difference would it make to the earth?

If a man falls from a cliff 'the air parts: the earth beneath dashes him to pieces'. Nature has no special concern for humanity. Worse. Science has destroyed the old protection. The safety net of the Everlasting Arms is no longer trustworthy. Elfride Swancourt slips towards the abyss, her fate entirely unseen by those who insist that they love her.

These are Felix Jethway, Stephen Smith, Henry Knight and Spenser Luxellian. The first, after a single attempt to kiss her, dies because he seems to have convinced himself that Elfride is beyond his reach. The second is direct, attractive and able to delight her – until the realities of life demonstrate that he is as much a child as she is and in no position to become her husband. The third, who is the eldest of the suitors by several years, has a problem where women are concerned. Elfride is dazzled by his intellectual qualities but is bothered by him in other respects and complains, 'I almost wish you were of a grosser nature, Harry.' The fourth lover, Lord Luxellian, her kinsman and a young widower still in his twenties, marries her and makes her pregnant. She dies of a miscarriage only five months after her wedding-day. The inexorable progress from the time when she was free as a bird and, like Emma Gifford, Hardy's own rectory girl, 'scampering up and down the hills on my beloved mare alone, wanting no protection, the rain going down my back often, and my hair floating on the wind,'* to her Shakespearian descent into the Luxellian family vault occupies less than five years. The four lovers – each in his own unwitting way – have driven her into the dark. Or have they?

The plot of *A Pair of Blue Eyes* is really the basis of a poem. It is composed of symbols and metaphor, and even where it is luridly invaded by melodrama it retains the power of poetry. Hardy has had to invent a special kind of story-telling to carry the multiplicity of his private experience which has not as yet provided the moral philosophy which he used to control his later novels. It is a book which contains many of the impulses and much of the emotion of a tragic ballad.

An exceedingly handsome boy arrives at a dull country rectory with instructions from his employer, a London architect, to draw up plans for 'restoring' the parish church. He stays at the rectory with the latitudinarian Mr Swancourt and falls in love with his daughter Elfride. The rector allows the friendship, believing that Stephen and Elfride are too young for seriousness, and then finds out that this person is not at all the well-bred, educated man which everything about him implies, but the son of one of his humble parishioners, Smith the mason. More nonplussed than angry, Mr Swancourt forbids further contact between the pair. Thrillingly caught up in first love, they elope to Plymouth, intending to get married, but an inefficiency on Stephen's part concerning the licence forces them to travel on to London for the ceremony. There they panic; 'I don't like it here – nor myself – nor you!' says Elfride on Paddington Station, her faith in Stephen as protector quite vanished. They scramble back to Cornwall on the very next train. The entire escapade has been muddled and innocent, but Elfride is terrified that somebody from Endelstow will have seen her and conclude otherwise.

* *Some Recollections*, pp. 50–1.

She has indeed been observed (village cognisance) and by none other than Mrs Jethway, the vengeance-seeking mother of her first admirer.

When Elfride reaches the rectory it is to find that her father has chosen that very time for his secret marriage to their neighbour, the rich Mrs Troyton. The new Mrs Swancourt launches the girl upon the London Season and for a few weeks the parochial matters of Endelstow seem of small account. When her stepmother's famous relative, the essayist and critic Henry Knight, accepts an invitation to Cornwall, life seems to be opening up for Elfride. Knight is in his early thirties and highly sophisticated. Elfride is first awed by him, then dazzled. He has had a long and influential friendship with a lad from the very village he is now visiting, but only once, in a generalised way, does he make reference to him. This is in striking contrast to the hero-worshipping outpourings which Elfride has had to endure when Stephen tells her about Knight, and which ironically lay the foundations of her own admiration for the writer. Class partly prevents Knight from discussing someone like Stephen with a lady. From the first, instinct tells Elfride that Knight will either despise or forsake her if she tells him about the youth. Knight, however, will not allow Elfride any kind of reticence and demands to know all about her life before he entered it. Profoundly in love with the writer by now, she is alerted to the danger of her situation. For she has learned an unpleasant but unalterable fact about Knight – that he must have, in his own morbid phrase, 'untried lips'. His questioning of her on her sexual experience exposes far more of his own pathology than Elfride's guilt. The only lull in this questioning occurs when the pair of them are involved in a life-or-death struggle on the Cliff-without-a-Name, when Elfride strips herself in order to save this virgin male from destruction. The scene, one of Hardy's greatest, magnificently combines thought and action.

After the rescue it seems that Knight must accept Elfride for what she is, and not force her to measure up to the fantasy he has about women. But he cannot. Grateful though he is, he cannot even bring himself to kiss her after she has saved his life. His 'peculiarity of nature' prevents him from doing so. There is a curious justice in his not doing so because, unknown to him, Elfride had gone to the cliff in the first place to watch a ship arrive carrying Stephen back from India. After the elopement débâcle, the boy had fled abroad to become the man, and to prove himself capable of supporting a wife. Part of the proof, a banker's receipt for £200, is concealed in Elfride's dress. But it is all of no avail, for Stephen has shrunk into insignificance in comparison with Knight. And so, a few days later, the young architect discovers that the girl whom he has been addressing as 'wife' in confident letters, and for whose sake he has worked so hard, is deeply in love with none other than his adored friend.

Soon afterwards, the three meet during one of the funeral episodes which are strung out like dark pendants along the whole length of the story. Stephen's father is preparing the vault to receive Lady Luxellian, and Stephen himself is in the tomb writing in a notebook when Elfride and Knight suddenly appear. Knight is patronising and doesn't at first introduce 'a lady betrothed to himself' to the mason's son; and Stephen, though bewildered and hurt, tactfully says little. He is shortly returning to India, he informs them. 'The scene was remembered by all three as an indelible mark in their history.' Each has been privately lacerated because 'the deed of deception was complete'.

Immediately afterwards, Knight renews his probing into Elfride's history – 'You don't tell me anything but what I wring out of you.' She breaks under his interrogation, her strength undermined by threatening letters from Mrs Jethway. Elfride and Knight are actually resting on Felix Jethway's grave when the truth is dragged out of her. While the reader knows how essentially innocent she is, it is possible to understand something of both Mrs Jethway's and Knight's point of view. It is also plain that Knight rejects her more out of terror of having to cope, as he thinks, with an experienced woman than because she might be scandalous. Disturbed by her openly loving nature – it permeates the novel with an irresistible sweetness – and more scared than shocked that she can compare his response to it with that of previous lovers, he abandons her, though not before offering prim advice. Desperately in love, Elfride rushes to London after him and pours out her pent-up criticism of his sexual timidity – 'O, could *I* but be the man and *you* the woman. How I wish you could have run away with twenty women before you knew me . . .' Knight flees from such emotional involvement to the Continent. His 'was a robust intellect, which would escape outside the atmosphere of heart . . .' The psychological insight into the nature of an intellectual is a memorable feature of the novel.

Some considerable time later Stephen and Knight accidentally run into each other in London. The former has done meteorically well in India and has become an architect of fame and promise. He is also no longer a boy but a man, and Knight's cool attitude towards him reflects the development. It is as if maturity puts an end to any type of relationship which he can accept. He only displays an unflattering relief upon hearing who was Elfride's earlier lover. It was 'only Stephen'. What kind of rival was that! Immediately, and with no sense of how he has insulted her, Knight sets off for Cornwall to make her his wife, the meeting with Stephen having revived his masculinity. The young architect catches the same train with the same intent. Master and pupil are now simply predatory males in competition, each with his self-esteem in ribbons and his desire heightened. Unbeknown to either of them, Elfride herself joins the train at Chippenham in a special dark, strange carriage – in her coffin, in fact.

The full story emerges when the two suitors take shelter from the thudding Cornish rain in an inn called The Welcome Home on the road to Endelstow. They learn that Elfride had wed Lord Luxellian, her widowed kinsman, and had perished soon after. 'False,' whispers Knight to Smith, though he withdraws this accusation later. But his prying interest in the girl persists. Was her husband 'very fond of her?' he asks her maid. '*Very* fond of her?' he repeats.

The tragedy is played out against a background of rural violation and resurgence. Throughout its telling the railway creeps nearer and nearer to the village, and will soon not only bring crowds of visitors to it, but also make it easier for bright countrymen like Stephen Smith to escape from it. Its church, bastion of its defunct mysteries, is actually made to crash down upon its local Vengeance – Mrs Jethway. Two kinds of old village power are destroyed at a stroke. All the ancient certainties are in flux. New people are coming in, the old are dying out. Faith is the casualty of improvement. Neither Stephen nor his parents show much feeling for Endelstow, while the talk of their neighbours is marked with village cynicism. What energy the place still possesses is taking a new direction. Dissenters are active; Mr Swancourt would not have rebuilt his church had it not been for their enthusiasm. Stephen's mother reveals both her agnosticism and her unsentimentality in remarks about snapdragons, which 'are more like Christians than flowers', and Jacob's

Ladders, whose persistence she despises – 'I don't care for things that neglect won't kill.' The Smiths, like the Hardys, are 'liviers', that part of the village workforce which has become superior and independent of the gentry and farmers. Mrs Smith is also proud, talkative and down-right, and for these reasons alone Stephen's deception at the Rectory could not in the ordinary way have occurred, village gossip being what it is. Considering his looks and his career, and his being an only child, who would not have heard of him in this tiny place? Even the Swancourts, surely, although they had only been at the Rectory for a year. Yet Lickpan and Worm, his father's intimates, wait on him without recognition. Stephen, then, must be accorded some of the licence of romance. He is Elfride's girlish dream of a lover come true; his arrival which a thousand clergymen's daughters, languishing behind the ivy, must have prayed for.

Hardy's apparent indifference to certain realities (he revised the book more than once) must have been deliberate. He doesn't even allow Stephen to show emotion when he has to preside over the destruction of a church with which his family has been associated for generations. There has been a funeral on the day of the young architect's arrival but Hardy does not mention it until Chapter 8, so that when Stephen goes to the churchyard early the following morning to begin work he sees 'nothing horrible . . . in the shape of tight mounds bonded with sticks . . . or wheelmarks'. He should have seen Felix Jethway's new grave and, the evening before, some sign from Elfride that someone she knew had just been buried. A funeral had taken place the day after Hardy himself had arrived to restore St Juliot Church. 'To Mr Holder's room,' states his diary. 'Returned downstairs. Music . . . A funeral . . . Staying there [at the church] drawing measuring all day, with intervals for meals at the rectory.' This is an exact synopsis of what happened when Stephen came to Endelstow, except that news of the funeral is deferred. Stephen talks to the rector in his bedroom, has high tea prepared for him by Elfride, who is noticeably excited, and hears her sing a setting of Shelley's 'When the Lamp is Shattered'. Originally, Hardy made her sing 'The Banks of Allan Water' because he intended to use one of its lines. 'A winning tongue had he', as the title for the novel.

His livier background and arrival in Cornwall apart, Stephen Smith is decidedly not the young Thomas Hardy. Many critics have tended to dismiss Stephen as a nebulous creation, attractive but hazy, forgetting that he exists to shed light on the far more important character of Henry Knight. While Hardy remains almost indifferent to the verisimilitude of Stephen's feelings for his native village he is precise about the boy's feelings for his guide and mentor. He had 'adored' Knight 'as a man is very rarely adored by another in modern times'. The adoration stemmed for the most part from a young man's recognition of a higher being, someone from the university and the recipient of real education and taste. It is in this aspect of Stephen that we discover references to Hardy, for Henry Knight is now generally accepted as a portrait of Horace Moule, the young novelist's confidant and teacher, and his greatest friend.

Eight years his senior, Moule was the central figure in Hardy's early literary development. As a Cambridge graduate and a poet-reviewer-essayist, his was a profound influence on the boy working in the Dorchester architect's office and, later, the young writer encountering London publishers. It was Moule who told Hardy what to read and who introduced him to the Greek dramatists who were to influence his outlook on life and authorship so tremendously. Moule also gave him the copy of Palgrave's *Golden Treasury*, which supplied so many of the quotations for *A Pair of Blue Eyes*, and provided the perfect kind of intellectual male companionship for early genius. On 21 June 1873, three weeks or so after the novel, which he was to review, had been published, Moule was with Hardy in Cambridge. On 'a never to be forgotten morning', wrote Hardy, the two of them stood on the roof of King's College Chapel and watched 'Ely Cathedral gleaming in the distant sunlight'. A little later that year, while Hardy was working on *Far from the Madding Crowd* at his parents' Bockhampton home, he received the appalling news that Moule had killed himself at Cambridge by cutting his throat. Five days later Hardy attended the funeral and wrote against the passage in *In Memoriam* which describes a rare spirit at the university, 'Cambridge. H.M.M.' In a poem called 'Standing by the Mantelpiece' he attempted to enter Moule's mind just before the suicide and makes this clergyman's son say,

> . . . all's lost, and nothing really lies
> Above but shade, and shadier shade below . . .

Elfride, the clergyman's daughter, is driven to the same conclusion.

No small part of her disaster lay in the coincidence of her falling in love with two men whose long and considerable friendship carried the seeds of her destruction. It is they, and not she, who are guilty when circumstances force them to adopt crude postures of male rivalry for which the older man in particular is quite unsuited. Knight had become acquainted with Stephen when he was still a child, had helped him with books and eventually formed a sympathetic 'but no great intellectual fellowship' with the boy. 'He somehow was his friend. Circumstances, as usual, did it all.'

The gentleman is not democratic and tells the village lad that, 'much to his regret', he sees a time coming 'when every man will pronounce even the common words of his own tongue as seems right in his own ears, and be thought none the worse for it.' Perhaps it should be mentioned here that William Barnes was living next door to the office in which Hardy served his architect's apprenticeship. Stephen not only learns to speak like a gentleman, but to lace his talk with the Latin tags which indicated a gentleman's education. Yet Knight's interest in him was not so as to change his class by superficial means but to admit him to taste and culture. The Swancourts smelled a rat almost from the start but, having made fools of themselves over Stephen's beauty – the rector reads breeding into it and his daughter is simply dazzled – they are obliged to bite back a great many questions. Now and then a remark slips out, making the amiable impostor quake. 'Fancy a man not being able to ride,' says Elfride. Hardy goes to extreme lengths to give Stephen the kind of looks which disturb the judgement. He was, he said, the idealisation of a pupil who had followed him as a trainee in the office of his Dorchester employer John Hicks. Stephen's looks, like Tess's, were a kind of blood challenge. Fallen blue blood now having to make a professional living is how the snobbish rector sums it up. Had not his own family 'been coming to nothing for centuries'? We learn that Stephen looked 'patrician' and that he had a 'mouth like Pitt's'. And, 'though gentle, ambition was visible in his kindling eyes'. His complexion was 'as fine as Elfride's own', but because he has reversed the fairy-tale convention by arriving as prince and departing as peasant he is never permitted to be entirely satisfactory even before this bewildering transformation. 'His face is – well – *pretty*, just like mine,' Elfride complains.

Stephen's quandary in the country is all about roots. His roots should claim him but they do not. His friend Knight has grafted him on to a broader culture which he rightly believes supersedes Endelstow's claims to him. But, at twenty, everything is still formative and village pressures on one side and London freedom on the other make him feel like an impostor. 'I have a trouble,' he tells Elfride, 'though some might think it less a trouble than a dilemma.' He confides it to her and she, unlike her father, takes it in her stride. 'That sort of origin is getting so respected that it is acquiring some of the odour of Norman ancestry.' But the rector, about to marry a widow whose ancestral claims he knows are as 'raked-up' as the Indian provenance of Birmingham brass, treats Stephen like a confidence trickster. Marrying for money outside Society's magic circle is respectable, marrying for love is not. Stephen's mother is more realistic. She tells Stephen, 'You might go higher than a bankrupt Pa'son's girl.'

Hardy, who was to remain enthralled by the psychology of class throughout his life, takes stock of Stephen's situation at this point:

his brain had extraordinary receptive powers, and no great creativeness. Quickly acquiring any kind of knowledge he saw around him, and having a plastic adaptability more common in woman than in man, he changed colour like a chameleon as the society he found himself in assumed a higher and more artificial tone . . . Yet to a dispassionate observer his pretensions to Elfride, though rather premature, were far from absurd as marriages go, unless the proximity of simple but honest parents could be said to make them so.

Stephen's dilemma, a common one at the time, was how to pick up an education and the improved circumstances which went with it without looking like an adventurer. Hardy is not concerned with his morality in the sense with which Jane Austen is concerned with that of Frank Churchill in *Emma*. What fascinates him is the effect of opportunity on innocence.

Elfride's poise both attracts and upsets Stephen. She always comments when his standards differ from her own. His occasional odd ways of talking and behaving are among the things which make him so attractive to her. She knows, too, how to get under his skin, although sometimes her little digs are evidence of how certain aspects of his existence worry and irritate her. One of these is his obsessive talk and praise of someone who changed his life. When Elfride begins to call this man 'Mr Clever', the reader knows that she is referring to a rival. Ironically, she will only destroy Stephen's love for Knight by attempting to destroy Stephen's love for herself. This is galling for Stephen but lethal for Elfride. She had made a huge mistake. Unconscious of the fact that Stephen's worship of Knight could indicate that the latter 'was not shaped by Nature for a marrying man' or that 'his lifelong constraint towards women, which he had attributed to accident, was not chance after all, but the natural result of instinctive acts so minute as to be indiscernible even by himself', she forsakes Stephen for a different type of immaturity. Stephen's greenness at twenty is temporary; Knight's virginity at thirty-two is permanent. Stephen's love feeds on absence, whereas Elfride's is starved by it, so there can be no waiting game. Knight can never know what love is yet he attracts adoration. In the ordinary way he should have benefited by the excited girl whom Stephen has left behind, but the truth is that this aspect of her is repellent to him.

In what strikes one as a direct reference to his own experience in Cornwall, Hardy wrote of Elfride, 'Every woman who makes a permanent impression on a man is usually recalled in his mind's eye as she appeared in one particular scene, which seems ordained to be her special form of manifestation throughout the pages of his memory.' This is certainly how the reader thinks of the parson's daughter. Reminded by her father that, whatever the outsider might think of their provincialism, 'It is all the world to us', we see Elfride cheerfully enduring 'the monotony of life we associate with people of small incomes in districts out of the sound of the railway whistle', scribbling romances as she rides through the valley on her pony, or 'running with a boy's velocity'. When she says that she is 'content to build happiness on any accidental basis that may lie near at hand', she doesn't imply a dull contentment but an inner gaiety. The lopping-off of this gaiety, piecemeal and apparently without reason, is very shocking. Elfride cannot avoid this pointless destruction, nor can others recognise what is happening to her. When Knight was alone on the cliff-face she could restore him to the advanced, intellectual creation (staring at fossils in the black rock, he was humiliated to think that he was to be 'with the small in his death'). When the Luxellian children became motherless she could provide a loving substitution. When Stephen looked like being forsaken as an impostor, she never left his side. She even sees the pathetic solitary aspects of her father's situation, absurd though they are to her way of thinking, and supports his *amour propre*. But no one independently observes *her* desperate need for help, and Knight, the person who owes her most, turns away in distaste when she pleads for his assistance. Yet it is a vanity in any one of them to believe that it was their selfishness or evil which destroyed her, and their final remorse is as futile as their initial hope. A few months after his first visit to St Juliot, the geographical centre of his own heart and of *A Pair of Blue Eyes* –

> Why go to Saint-Juliot? What's Juliot to me?
> Some strange necromancy
> But charmed me to fancy
> That much of my life claims the spot as its key.

– Hardy wrote in his notebook, 'Mother's notion (and also mine) – that a figure stands in our van with an arm uplifted, to knock us back from any pleasant prospect we indulge in as probable.' Why me? Elfride in effect cries as the arm descends. Why anyone?

Elfride is the first of Hardy's lost women, pliant, suggestible and at her most enchanting when an arbitrary fate moves in and casually obliterates her joy. Except for Felix, the non-starter, she tries to please the love-led men who pursue her by trying to be the kind of girl they have in mind, while at the same time not quite comprehending to what extent these various emotional friendships are hastening her maturity. Because hers is all the movement in a vast, static landscape, she at first believes that hers is all the life too. Then comes the chastening truth: she is no more and no less than the rocks or the momentary spray. Hardy said that a later novel would explore this theme more fully. He meant *Tess*.

Much has been written about Hardy's fatalism. It stemmed partly from his direct contact with what was still a brutal countryside whose customs were more Georgian than mid-nineteenth-century, and in which was rooted his strong interest in pain; and partly from the scientific upheaval of the 1860s, which overturned all the old certainties. Divine caring – and vengeance – gave way to natural causality. For Hardy, as for others, there was a new view of life but no new order. Man had become simply another facet of matter and not the pinnacle of a creation which existed for his comfort and honour. As if this were not sad enough, Hardy has to inject this fresh situation with the personal morbidity which is so notable an aspect of his genius. He dramatically exploits the randomness of things, and when some mindless force checks Elfride's average expectations of happiness and spins her into the dark Hardy makes sure that Nature is sufficiently ruthless and thorough. What does it all mean? It *means* nothing. It is. It was. As Guildenstern told Hamlet, 'On fortune's cap we are not the very button.' The most intriguing thing about *A Pair of Blue Eyes*, however, is not its picture of a delightful girl receiving no more consideration from Nature than a blade of grass on the headland, but of a heroine being harried along to oblivion by her creator. She is even confined to a limited field like a coursed hare, and her escape made impossible. For, although she appears occasionally in London and three of her lovers, Stephen, Knight and Lord Luxellian, travel extensively, the pursuit takes place within the boundaries of a village and, in spite of its moor and ocean, Endelstow, like all villages, can close in without mercy upon those who belong to it. Visiting the same rocks, lanes, meadows and scenes with different men fills Elfride's mind with guilt and comparisons, and the reader's with a strong sense of her treachery. Hardy evokes the humus-like aspect of rural life by letting both Stephen and Knight hear of the existence of poor young Felix Jethway while sitting on his grave. The hyper-sensitive Knight has no doubt at all that someone else has accompanied Elfride along these paths before him and he questions her as though she were in the dock. She is evasive, muddled, angry and frightened. But she is also thrilled. Knight's raised voice soon becomes preferable to Stephen's soft talk. Mr Swancourt had disliked the latter – 'Uniform pleasantness is rather a defect than a faculty. It shows that a man hasn't sense enough to know whom to despise.' Knight often comes close to despising Elfride. He is smart and epigrammatic at her expense, and he insults her by making literary notes about her character. She gets her own back with her clumsy little references to his sexual timidity. Eventually, excited by his depths and contrasts, and awed by the way in which he dominates her, she begins to love him. She was to discover that 'It was infinitely more to be even the slave of the greater than the queen of the less.' She even attempts to rejoice in Knight's 'spare love-making' and his 'piquant snubbings', associating these with 'somebody further on in manhood' than Stephen. Male and female concepts, manhood, friendship, reliability, maturity, etc., all form part of the misunderstanding. Every now and then Hardy sets off down still-uncharted psychological paths and points to feelings and behaviour which are decades away from popular recognition. We learn, for example, that 'the emotional side of [Stephen's] constitution was built rather after a feminine than a male model', which illuminates why both Knight and Elfride were so successful in their friendships with him. But to the girl 'Stephen was hardly enough of a man'.

... Stephen's failure to make his hold on her heart a permanent one was his too timid habit of dispraising himself to her – a peculiarity which, exercised towards sensible men, stirs a kindly chord of attachment that a marked assertiveness would leave untouched, but inevitably leads the most sensible woman in the world to undervalue him who practises it. Directly domineering ceases in the man, snubbing begins in the woman . . . [ch. 27]

While Elfride shows some astuteness where Stephen is concerned – though this doesn't excuse her for treating him so treacherously – she is quite mistaken about Knight's chilly, abrasive manner. She thinks it is male purposefulness when, in fact, it is the armour-plating which covers a fear of women. Hardy, brilliantly and melodramatically, puts Knight to the ordeal so that Elfride – and the reader – can see him stripped of every guard and protection. He stays brave and intelligent, but imminent death itself cannot make him declare much heart.

The literal cliff-hanger in which intellectual pride is questioned and humbled, and physical courage extolled, is a wonderful piece of descriptive writing, and one of the first indications of Hardy's genius. In it, the metaphorical and the actual are perfectly fused. Even the double sensations of physical and spiritual vertigo are made to reel against each other in sickening succession. The man-of-letters clings feebly to existence by his fingertips, his whole ethos challenged, while the steamship *Puffin* with the 'fortune's favourite' Stephen aboard casually passes by. Before the accident the two men had actually been staring at one another through telescopes, but without recognition. Each lens registered the basic outline of a male, no more. Then the shale gives way, and one figure, who has never been 'inconveniently in love', slips out of focus. Hanging there above the boiling sea, Knight should have changed, should have given love its pre-eminence over mind, but he doesn't. He cannot. It is Elfride's love which saves him. Knight knows it and is more astonished than grateful. Eventually, the lengths to which she went to rescue him do no more than stimulate his conjectures about what sort of lengths such a loving nature might have gone to before he arrived on the scene. Her capability to love upsets him; it was something which he believes that he should have taught her. If he did not, who did? Cruelly and remorselessly, he prises some of the past out of her, driving her foot by foot towards an abyss from which there can be no salvation. Oblivion.

Although *A Pair of Blue Eyes* appraises some of the claustrophobic pressures of village life, the ordinary village people are treated with small affection and considerable detachment. At best, they are poetically quaint, and talk and act like Shakespeare's bucolic mechanicals. They never approach the far more real picture of 'Endelstow' and its neighbourhood which Emma Hardy drew in her little memoir *Some Recollections*. She writes of the sullen congregation at Lanivet and the superstition and evil-speaking of St Juliot, 'where hard labour upon the stony soil made a cold mostly ill-natured working class, yet with some good traits and fine exceptions'. And although she never liked 'the Cornish working orders' and found 'their so-called independence of character . . . mostly disagreeable to live with' she did occasionally discover 'a dear heart-whole person' among a populace of 'dull, aggressive workers'. The same account also reveals that, as with Elfride, Emma's love for the young architect who penetrated this not entirely happy scene was preceded by her being aware that she had attracted the interest of a farmer, 'a man gentle of nature, musical, christlike in guilelessness, handsome of face and figure, David-like farming his own land: he never married, and told after I had left of his disappointment, and attraction on first seeing me on the stairs'.

A Pair of Blue Eyes is, among much else, the story of escapes from a social class in the English countryside which perfectly understood its position between that of the brutalised field-workers and their gentry or yeoman employers. It was a position of unique village independence and Hardy himself derived from it. A lady such as Elfride would know little or nothing about this, and even as she was waiting, somewhat fatalistically, for Stephen to marry her she faced the prospect of her future in-laws with something verging on horror. Their 'deflecting influence' itself was almost enough to make her change her mind. Was not Mr Smith 'a decidedly common man' and his wife 'vulgar'? The novel's concentration on this particular social gap, that between the liviers and the aristocracy (for the parson and his daughter were connections of the local peer), puts everyone below it – virtually the entire community – out of court, so to speak. When the ordinary village men, mocked with names like Lickpan and Worm, make their entrance, it is mainly a comically picturesque one. It is the place and not its people which receives Hardy's most profound attention. It surges wildly and over-whelmingly across the tentative passions of the characters, providing great imagery and metaphor, symbolism and yardstick. There a rather ordinary, conventional female innocence is made to shatter under the blows of male ambivalence, vanity and ignorance; and humanity in general is shown as temporary scratchers on the covering soil which thinly hides the barren rock.

Thomas Hardy's Marriage Novel

Far from the Madding Crowd was the novel which announced Hardy's arrival as a great writer. It is also the peak of his literary innocence. The imaginative writer, in common with the rest of mankind, sheds innocence as he gathers experience, even though, as with most good novelists and poets, the shedding is only a matter of degree. Yet there is often a wonderful moment towards the beginning of a literary career after the pump has been substantially primed with 'early works' when a book appears which is all morning brightness, inspiration and possibility, and no English novel so completely fulfils these fresh conditions than does this one. In it the big recurring themes of mortal existence, love, power, treachery, happiness, toil and transcendence, are played out on the farm. The rural scene isn't limited and hedged; on the contrary it is sumptuous. We are not looking into a midden or even to the stretching headlands, but at a landscape which satisfies every stir of the imagination and which ravishes the senses. Not Arcadia or Goshen by themselves but a compromise of the two, and not the author's native Dorsetshire, even if these homely chapters were written in the little room under the thatch at Bockhampton, but a more spacious reality and a new set of bucolic verities. On the first page of Chapter 50 of *Far from the Madding Crowd*, Hardy writes the name of this place for the first time – Wessex. Eventually it would stretch to Cornwall. Later it would cloud and grow dark. But here, for the most part, it is bathed in an absurdly glorious light. Things go wrong but they are righted, there are hurts but there is healing, there is melodrama but the steady farming cycle, superbly described, manages to give it an edge. For Hardy this novel stood at his life's divide between the years of his architectural career, courtship and apprenticeship as a writer, and the years of his marriage and celebrity. Its tone among his works is unique, there was to be nothing in the future quite like it.

The comedy lies in the assumptions made by both the characters and the reader. Here are spread a few fields, a few houses, a few short journeys in this humdrum direction or that and a few men and women in stances which have been partly laid down by workaday village tradition and partly by classical poetry. That such ordinariness should tempt fate or folly is not in the reckoning of the inhabitants of Weatherbury or in those about to be entertained by their simple annals. But Hardy troubles this pastoral rather as one imagines the angel troubled the water, lightly and magically, so that it no longer reflects just the conventional things in its vicinity but them – and something extra. This something extra was new to fiction in the 1870s and it has remained new and unsurpassable to this day, no subsequent writer ever having been able to succeed it in its penetratingly original view of the English countryside. We read Hardy to share the inimitable vision of his 'bilberry' eye. In *Far from the Madding Crowd* the vision is enchanting and ultimately benign. Wander into it, invites the young novelist – he was thirty-three when he wrote it – explore it night and day, winter us and summer us (for these were his own people pressed into a comic drama), take your fill, luxuriate in Eden, primordial love, opulence, temptation, flaming sword and all. See cooped up in the parish boundary sights which, as the Americans say, stretch from Dan to Beersheba, from hell to breakfast. Although litera-ture has many examples of a little confined territory being put to use for the widest philosophical purpose, not to mention entertainment, only Shakespeare compares with Hardy in his rich and inspired manipula-tion of its simple assets. As in Shakespeare, the lanes and meadows are full of wise fools, upright heroes, vulnerable ladies, Greek-chorus gossips, ill-starred amorists and representatives of the local authority, all criss-crossing each other's paths, helping, hindering and raising the temperature. Although Hardy was profoundly indebted to Gray and once said, in answer to an inquiry, 'Stinsford *is* Stoke Poges', his optimistic masterpiece *Far from the Madding Crowd* is a Victorian journey to Shakespeare's pastoral with its vigour and joy, spills and recoveries.

All the Weatherburians have a double dimension, one part of which is familiar to themselves and the other symbolic and fate-ridden, and seen only by the reader. They work incessantly and time for other things such as love-making, visits, etc., has to be snatched. Talk goes on throughout the work but if you want to do something odd, such as reading or learning a new card game, you hope for a brief illness. ''Twas a bad leg allowed me to read the *Pilgrim's Progress*, and Mark Clark learnt All-Fours in a whitlow,' says Joseph Poorgrass, hearing that Cain Ball had managed a few days in Bath on the weakness of having 'that felon upon his fingers'. The plot is so tied in to the implacable demands of rural toil that a good part of the comedy is caused by the notion that by rights there should neither be the time nor energy for these fanciful passions, and that leisure breeds disaster. Village custom and the common law are supposed to provide these busy people with cover from the worst of the arrows of adversity and there is a wide range of shocks which stem from the psychological necessity of occasionally shattering the rural peace. As with Bathsheba's mock valentine, no one is supposed to suffer any great injury by these antics, though they do. There cannot, in fact, be the jog-along serenity of the accepted countryside until this disturbing girl farmer submits to the stolidly acceptable Oak. It is plain from the very beginning that Gabriel is the man for her but given Bathsheba Everdene's combination of looks, economic independence and ignorance, who is she to fall for plainness? She is instead excitedly aware of her uniqueness in the village. Hardy calls her decrepit hall turned farmhouse her 'bower', suggesting a woman's intimate abode. It soon preoccupies the sensuous speculation of the neighbourhood. From the middle-aged Boldwood, who is nearly a squire, down to her own labourers, her presence is challenging and unsettling, and the reader knows that as tumult is antithetical to the principles of the pastoral tradition, something must be done about her. Elfride Swancourt in *A Pair of Blue Eyes* and Tess created similar tumults and were destroyed. Bathsheba in her flightier moments is herself a destroyer but ceases to be when she comes down to earth.

'Souls alive, what news! It makes my heart go quite bumpity-bump!' says Liddy,

when she hears that her mistress has accepted Farmer Oak.

'It makes mine rather furious, too,' said Bathsheba. 'However, there's no getting out of it now!'

And so, on 'a damp disagreeable morning' . . . 'two sensible persons' walked to church, she in a cloak that reached her clogs. Joseph Poorgrass, the ditch philosopher, quotes Hosea, '"Ephraim is joined to idols: let him alone." But since 'tis as 'tis, why, it might have been worse, and I feel my thanks accordingly.'

All the nymphs and shepherds have been routed, so has the lurid village melodrama which fed Hardy's darkest imagination. The novel's comic dénouement is Dorset on a dull day and the obliteration of fancy by sound common sense. We are warned not to despise it, this partnership which arises through similarity of pursuits and which 'is unfortunately seldom superadded to love between the sexes, because men and women associate, not in their labours, but in their pleasures merely'. As we read this, all the magnificently described scenes of Weatherbury's skill and toil during the farming year are recalled with a far from prosaic reality. Here, Hardy is saying, is the poetry of life for lovers such as Bathsheba and Gabriel, here is the courtship which they failed to see was happening, here in the shearing shed, barn, cornfield and stackyard is a seasonable drama to satisfy them forever. In order to substantiate his story's claim to be in direct descent from Theocritus, Virgil, Spenser, Shakespeare, Herrick, Gray – and the Psalmist – Hardy saturated all the common knowledge and experience he possessed about his birthplace with literature. His object was a stylised actuality, the style being that of the richest classical pastoral, the actuality being ordinary farming practice in the West Country on the eve of the long agricultural depression. It was a justification of his being of this society by blood and of being apart from it due to genius. He said he meant to finish it 'within a walk of the district in which the incidents are supposed to occur' and that he found it 'a great advantage to be actually among the people described at the time of describing them'. All beyond anything they could comprehend, Hardy left them in their rut where their tasks were concerned and lifted them out of it for his own higher purposes. As with Gray, the routine, effacement and calm incuriosity of such lives, not to mention the grimness, would have made them an awkward subject for a work outside an established literary convention, although Crabbe and Clare had tackled it, the former deliberately, the latter with his own starkly sweet rural candour. Hardy chose Gray's method and then went far beyond any work known to the English pastoral tradition. But the readers of its most popular poem, 'Elegy Written in a Country Churchyard', had their bearings and could follow.

> Far from the madding crowd's ignoble strife
>   Their sober wishes never learn'd to stray;
> Along the cool sequester'd vale of life
>   They kept the noiseless tenor of their way.

A few years after writing *Far from the Madding Crowd*, Hardy explained what he believed was the purpose of fiction. It was, he said, to give pleasure by gratifying the love of the uncommon in human experience, mental or physical, and that this succeeded most when the reader was made to feel that the characters had as much reality as he had himself. The writer's problem, he added, was 'how to strike the balance between the uncommon and the ordinary so as on the one hand to give interest, on the other to give reality. In working out this problem, human nature must never be made abnormal and . . . the uncommonness must be in the events, not in the characters; and the writer's art lies in shaping this uncommonness while disguising its unlikelihood.'

Such statements were influenced by the requirements of the monthly magazines in which so many great Victorian novels made their début. Some of the period's finest literary artistry and invention exists because writers were forced to circumnavigate plots and ideas forbidden them by the 'polite' rules of these touchy publications. Hardy was to suffer more than most, even going to such lengths as omitting controversial matter in the serialised version of a novel and reinstating it when it came out in hardback. But on the whole he got what he wanted to say past the Grundies and the hypocrites, and from his first attempt at serialisation, *A Pair of Blue Eyes*, he showed a workmanlike attitude towards the demands of the serial and its vast readership. In *Far from the Madding Crowd* he was obliged to treat Troy's seduction of Fanny Robin in the words of his editor, Leslie Stephen, 'in a very gingerly fashion', but, as Hardy told Stephen's daughter Virginia Woolf at the very end of his life, her father had been a great support to him and 'we stood shoulder to shoulder against the British public about certain matters dealt with in that novel'. In 1871 Leslie Stephen had succeeded Thackeray as editor of the *Cornhill Magazine*, an illustrated monthly which set brilliant new standards for serialisation, and he immediately began looking around for up-and-coming novelists to fill it. Very soon after his appointment, Stephen read *Under the Greenwood Tree*, particularly admired its rural descriptions and invited its young author to write something in a similar vein for the *Cornhill*. It was, said Hardy, only by the merest chance that the letter ever reached him, the Dorset postal arrangements being so primitive. A labourer had found it lying in the mud where some school-children from the next village had dropped it. Other than the newly born, it may be added, children make few appearances in a Hardy novel. But another, less distinguished journal had claimed him. Even so, while writing at enormous speed the beautiful, poetic *A Pair of Blue Eyes* for *Tinsley's Magazine,* Hardy told Leslie Stephen that he would send him a tale called *Far from the Madding Crowd* in which 'the chief characters would probably be a young woman-farmer, a shepherd, and a sergeant of cavalry'. Much later, when he had done with novel-writing, he recognised it as one of those creations which are one with the springtime of their creator and said that 'perhaps there is something in it that I could not have put there if I had been older'.

As with so many good writers at the threshold of their careers, Hardy was at this time both flexible and suggestible, and obdurate, doing what was asked of him but doing it as he wished it done. When his first novel *The Poor Man and the Lady* was turned down, 'the tendency of the writing being socialistic, not to say revolutionary', and the publisher's reader, who was none other than George Meredith himself, advised him to 'put it away altogether for the present' and write something with a more complicated plot, Hardy did exactly this. The result was the over-complicated *Desperate Remedies* which, although slated for its sensationalism, was praised for its vision of the countryside. The Hardy villagers, seen for the first time on the page, astonished the critics. 'The scenes allowed to these humble actors', wrote one of them,

are few and slight but they indicate powers that might and ought to be extended largely in this direction . . . This nameless author has, too, one other talent of a remarkable kind – sensitiveness to scenic and atmospheric effects, and to their influence on the mind, and the power of rousing similar sensitiveness in his readers.

The response by Hardy to this was the serene *Under the Greenwood Tree* in which, via a hero based upon the carrier who brought his father's timber, he produced a story of exquisite minor eventfulness. The critics too commended him for so clearly staying on his own ground. Hardy eventually grew to resent that his readers would not allow him the authority to depict the upper classes or London, or to be other than autobiographical when he wrote about the farming community, but during these rich early days of his art there is plenty of evidence to show that he accepted guidance from two mentors in particular on where his genius would best thrive.

The first of these helpers was his old friend Horace Moule. While still in his teens and studying architecture in Dorchester, Hardy came under the influence of this charming intellectual young man, who was already establishing himself as a literary critic. It was Moule who had deflected Hardy from studying the classics with a view to entering the university and it had been Moule who had given him the most useful advice and backing when he had turned to literature. His brother, Bishop Handley Moule, in his *Memories of a Vicarage*, reiterates Horace's 'magical' gift for teaching and how he would walk through the springing corn with his pupils 'shedding an indefinable glamour over all we read'. Hardy was such a pupil and when in due time their friendship began to move towards intellectual equality, the magic aspect of Moule remained undiminished. During the early 1870s Moule combined authorship and reviewing with the job of HM Inspector of Workhouses in East Anglia. It was in September 1873, when Hardy had written about a third of *Far from the Madding Crowd*, that Moule killed himself. The horror burst in on Hardy and on the idyll he was constructing. Although Leslie Stephen had already shown indications of extending to Hardy a more influential version of Moule's philosophical guidance, the latter's suicide plunged him into a loss and isolation of a kind from which he was never entirely to recover. It deepened the texture of the novel which was to establish him among the greatest English story-tellers, although there is no single point in the narrative at which this tragedy can be seen at work, nor did it deflect Hardy from his original concept of a natural bucolic happiness and sanity. The book carried him along; it was a *tour de force* sweeping him past the dangerous nervelessness threatened by grief. Death, it has to be admitted, can stimulate the senses to a fresh appreciation of touch and sound. In *Far from the Madding Crowd* Hardy is glad to be alive and eager to show off to their very best advantage all the rural activities and beliefs which fed his imagination and created his vigorous inner life.

He wrote in and out of doors at Bockhampton. 'He would occasionally find himself without a scrap of paper at the very moment when he felt volumes. In such circumstances he would use large dead leaves, white chips left by the wood-cutters, or pieces of stone or slate that came to hand', he recalled later on in the concealed autobiography which was issued under the name of his second wife. Anxious that the *Cornhill*'s illustrator might make his characters appear cloddish he offered to send

Stephen some sketches he had made of 'smockfrocks, gaiters, sheep-crooks, rick-staddles, a sheep-washing pool, one of the old-fashioned malthouses, and some other out-of-the-way things'. The first instalment, unsigned, came out in January 1874 and, to Hardy's delight, was the first story in the magazine. He had bought a copy at Plymouth station on New Year's Eve on his way back from seeing his fiancée in Cornwall. Before the year was out it would be reprinted seven times. The critical response was tremendous, the *Spectator* insisting that if it was not the work of George Eliot then her equal had entered the literary scene, and the *Westminster Review* said that it stood to all contemporary novels precisely as *Adam Bede* did to all other novels some sixteen years before. But the highly individual Hardy style and tone, met with in all its power and glory for the first time, 'threw' most of the reviewers, who possessed no yardstick for measuring it or key to understanding it. Not comprehending his art, they attacked him for unreality. The gist of their blindness can be seen in the following extract from the *Saturday Review*.

Mr Hardy, whether by force of circumstances or by fortunate selection, has in this story hit upon a new vein of rich metal for his fictitious scenes. The English Boeotian has never been so idealised before. Ordinary men's notions of the farm-labourer of the southern counties have all been blurred and confused. It has been the habit of an ignorant and unwisely philanthropic age to look upon him as an untaught, unreflecting, badly paid, and badly fed animal, ground down by hard and avaricious farmers, and very little, if at all, raised by intelligence above the brutes and beasts to whom he ministers. These notions are ruthlessly overturned by Mr Hardy's novels. Under his hand Boeotians became Athenians in acuteness, Germans in capacity for philosophic speculation, and Parisians in polish. Walter Scott has left many sketches and some highly finished portraits of the humbler class of Scotch peasants, and has brought out the national shrewdness and humour, and the moral and intellectual 'pawkiness' for which that class of Scotch society is justly celebrated. But he had good material to work on and two out of three of his characters were in all probability drawn from life. George Eliot . . . has drawn specimens of the illiterate class who talk theology like the Bench of Bishops – except that they are all Dissenters – and politics like the young Radicals who sit below the gangway. But the reader felt that the author had seen these rustic theologians and politicians and heard their conversations. Shakespeare also has his metaphysical clowns . . . but neither these clowns, nor George Eliot's rustics, nor Scott's peasants, rise to anything like the flights of abstract reasoning with which Mr Hardy credits his cider-drinking boors . . . We feel that we have misjudged the unfranchised agricultural classes, or that Mr Hardy has put his thoughts and words into their mouths. And this suspicion necessarily shakes our confidence in the truthfulness of many of the idyllic incidents of rustic life which are so plentifully narrated here ... Are they a faithful rendering of real events taking place from time to time in the south-western counties, or are they not imaginary creations with possibly some small ground work of reality?

The answer is, of course, that the events are imaginary creations of the most inspired kind which have been constructed upon the huge ground-work of all that Hardy inherited and understood at Bockhampton. His nativity was his validity. It licensed his genius. Certainly one will not find a documentation of the wretchedness and gropings towards political and economic freedom of the period, and which were to be called the 'Revolt of the Field' in his novels, but neither does one see the enclosure riots and misery in Constable's pictures of the Stour Valley. Yet this writer and this painter are now accepted as saying something permanent about rural England and saying it in a unique language which everybody understands but which no one has surpassed.

Far from the Madding Crowd, like 'The Hay Wain', is a celebration of the old rural certainties. It is the everlasting circle of springtime and harvest shrugging off the trivial disorderliness of human misconduct, and a homily on the rewards that accrue when life's drama is not divorced from the seasonal round. Throughout the novel things go wrong and people get hurt when they forget or neglect the laws and commands of the everlasting circle, and they go dreadfully wrong when, as Troy did after his marriage, these laws are despised and dismissed. The farm is seen as the part of nature which allows men to control it, though only whilst they acknowledge that they too belong to the cyclic pattern. When life turns in time with the herds and crops, as it does in the pastoral ideal, all is perfect, all is harmonic. It involves an important matter of duties and roles. These are not fixed as in the eighteenth-century doctrine of subordination. One of the things which fascinated Hardy was what might be called the snakes-and-ladders fate of village families, well on the way up one generation, back to base the next. Gabriel Oak's advances and retreats are an extremely realistic history of many a superior countryman, even to his decision to cut his village losses and emigrate, which at this time thousands like him were doing. But, of course, the laws of Arcady do not permit this final abandonment. Gabriel is Dorset's Corydon, its sound and faithful heart, and he cannot leave. Shepherds have since ancient times been our foremost image of faithfulness and Gabriel's last-page wedding to Bathsheba settles not only her future security but that of Weatherbury as well. And it is pertinent at this point to remind ourselves that Theocritus, the Sicilian poet who invented Corydon and the pastoral idyll which descended to Hardy via Virgil and Shakespeare, was much criticised in his day for allowing his ignorant rustics to speak on high and exalted subjects, and for their explicit sexuality. The idyll was not a rarefied meadow starred with innocents; it was a combination of natural labour, natural argument and natural bliss.

There is a passage in Milton's 'L'Allegro' which has a striking similarity to Weatherbury, with Bathsheba in her bower, Gabriel in his cottage and all the farm work and village movement in a kind of dancing action.

> While the Plowman neer at hand,
> Whistles ore the Furrow'd Land,
> And the Milkmaid singeth blithe,
> And the Mower whets his sithe,
> And every Shepherd tells his tale
> Under the Hawthorn in the dale.
> Streit mine eye hath caught new pleasures
> Whilst the Lantskip round it measures,
> Russet Lawns, and Fallows Gray,
> Where the nibling flocks do stray . . .
> Towers, and Battlements it sees
> Boosom'd high in tufted Trees,
> Where perhaps som beauty lies,
> The Cynosure of neighbouring eyes.
> Hard by, a Cottage chimney smokes,
> From betwixt two aged Okes,
> Where *Corydon* and *Thyrsis* met,
> Are at their savory dinner set
> Of Hearbs, and other Country Messes,
> Which the neat-handed *Phillis* dresses;
> And then in haste her Bowré she leaves,
> With *Thestylis* to bind the Sheaves;
> Or if the earlier season lead
> To the tann'd Haycock in the Mead . . .

Far from the Madding Crowd is really a questioning title for a novel which is about disturbance in a context traditionally accepted for its passivity. The period in which the story is set, although frequently designated as a 'golden' one in the history of English agriculture because it drew breath, as it were, between two stretches of farming depression, was nonetheless one of unsettlement and change. But these changes have not filtered through to Weatherbury to an extent which is strong enough to endanger its ancient footings or to destroy its contentment with suggestions of improvement. Later on, Hardy would be accused of darkening the countryside for his own dramatic purposes, although the truth of the matter was that towards the turn of the century the lives of many farmworkers and their families had become so brutalised that the Norfolk novelist Mary Mann, herself a farmer's wife, could look at their lot and presume that only some purpose known to God could justify it. Hardy's essay 'The Dorsetshire Labourer', written in 1883, is a direct piece of rural sociology which shows his deep factual knowledge of the society from which he drew the Chorus for his novels and although the study reveals a grim state of affairs, there are moments in it that are nostalgic for a lost village innocence. One of them points to the composed, unfragmented farming scenes of *Far from the Madding Crowd*, although he doesn't mention his novel. But it is among the old farm workers' communities, he says, 'that happiness will find her last refuge on earth, since it is among them that a perfect insight into the conditions of existence will be longest postponed'.

Weatherbury's insight into the conditions of existence is not so much imperfect as stigmatic, or inimitable. The village gazes at life through a sheltering barrier made up of all kinds of inherited squints and customs, and handed-on ways of looking at things, few of which have as yet been corrected or warped by popular notions racing down from London along the railway track. As a post-Darwinian, it suited Hardy to depict Christianity as a once potent faith which was now on its last legs and the profundities of the Bible and the *Book of Common Prayer* are rusticated to make a kind of parish-pump high language in which Weatherbury can philosophise, and thus blind itself still further on the meaning of life. But if thought is static, the natural year is not. Its turning is inexorable and the entire prosperity of the place is geared to a skilled and harmonious attempt to turn with it. Even so in this naturally turning year there is no guarantee of bliss. People get tossed aside, or up into the seats of the mighty, or down on their uppers; they get hurt, they change for better or worse; they grow up or they don't grow up, and still the seasons grind on to the sound of shibboleths and incantations, and the very motion of them makes questioning a sacrilege, and without questions there can be no answers, so that all that remains is a lively instinct for what is least painful and most endurable.

The life of the clod? This slur on the villager Hardy wiped out from the start. It was too near home. But the problems of animating what had either been ignored as below the level of literary interest, or merely lumpen, would have seemed insuperable had he spent time trying to work them out. But he did not. He wrote his rural novels with a magnificence which made it useless to ask 'Why these poor toilers?' He had more than Gray's pensive stanzas to tell him that the realities of country life were worth a glance – even a gasp! He had the harsh facts of his mother's girlhood and a mass of inherited material which all too eloquently proved that such lives were as rich as any other life. In his poem 'Spectres That Grieve', Hardy causes the dead who have been denied a history to protest from their graves:

> 'We are stript of rights; our shames lie unredressed,
> Our deeds in full anatomy are not shown,
> Our words in morsels merely are expressed
> On the scriptured page, our motives blurred, unknown.'

His work is an articulation of the society which produced him. Being what he was he could not be what he had come from – this is the dilemma of a great creative talent – but he never hesitated to explore the ancestral territory and make what he wished of it. This intimacy provided a paradox. The more he used his background, the less he was of it. His novels, and none more than this one, accurately depict this background in its full working order, while at the same time providing the kind of comment on the action which lies beyond the imagination of those causing it. This thought never accommodates itself to the general view of the village, whether informed or romanticised, but pursues its own direction with such magnetism that the reader is drawn after it and into it. Hardy, he finds, is not a height offering a fresh sweep of the English landscape and those toiling there, but an intricate coppice where sharp facts engage with fancy and the deep blood experience of a place is made to keep his mind within its boundaries. Hardy does not offer country drama as a quaint and simple synopsis of the drama taking place in the 'great world', as so many writers do. Instead, while we are reading him, the densely rich texture of his parochial vision makes it impossible for us to take a world view of anything. His enclosure of us in everything that is his by birthright is total. Strange, too. No one before or since has given the full village picture with such original authority, no writer conceded less to what it was generally held to contain, either socially or spiritually.

Far from the Madding Crowd is also a searching title about disturbance in an area which is traditionally calm and passive. Further emphasis on the ancient quiet is maintained by Hardy setting his novel in the 1840s. This was on the brink of a so-called 'golden' period of British agriculture, following the troubled post-Waterloo years of enclosure, riot and famine. The terrible farming depression which was to begin in the late 1870s and continue right up to the Second World War was not suspected. Except for such telling vignettes as the description of the Benthamite workhouse which was to claim poor Fanny Robin, and its being steeped in the confused Christian sentiment peculiar to mid-Victorian England, there is much in the story to make its setting timeless. Weatherbury is the village of Hardy's reading of English poetry as well as that of his roots. Its inhabitants are a mixture of the indigenous and the Johnny-come-latelies. The 'old people', as the long-settled labourers are sometimes called in the countryside, keep up a stream of philosophical talk, whilst the newcomers are all action – with calamitous results. As in *A Pair of Blue Eyes*, the novel he was in the midst of writing when he was invited to contribute a rural tale to the *Cornhill*, we have a desirable girl challenging a group of suitors. Although, apart from this, Elfride Swancourt and Bathsheba Everdene have nothing much in common. Elfride, one of literature's most enchanting heroines, is too fine a clay for the various male egos she attracts and is driven, like Tess, over the brink. Bathsheba, on the other hand, convincing woman-farmer as she is, lacks such fragility, and, after causing much emotional havoc, not all of it her own fault, marries her virtuous shepherd Gabriel Oak, who, as Henry James remarked, 'is, in our opinion, much too good for her.' But this is the essence of Hardy, the entanglement of the naturally good with the worthless, and the lure of both.

Bathsheba is neither. She is all potential. That is how Weatherbury sees her. She is sex, she is a good marriage, she is property, she is authority, but only as male Weatherbury decides. Refuting this, she goes her own way. She has inherited the village's big house and although it has long been reduced to a farm it still carries with it overtones of the old style and power, and these reflect upon Bathsheba like the glimmerings of a worn-out faith towards which gestures of respect are still made. But as everybody knows where she came from, this crumbling grandeur does not protect her. It simply makes her conspicuous. Hardy has a way of deftly and ecomomically touching in the backgrounds and antecedents of his characters which allows the reader, like some village gossip, to draw reckless conclusions. The divinity who is mistress of the old mansion is the daughter of Levi Everdene, gentleman-tailor 'and a very celebrated bankrupt'. Mr Everdene pretended that he and his wife were not married when they made love; it made him more excited and thus kept him faithful to her. He also found her so beautiful that he lit the candle several times a night to take a look at her. This brief information about her parents tells us about Bathsheba herself.

Against Elfride's four lovers, Bathsheba has three, a young shepherd, a young soldier and a middle-aged yeoman farmer who is not quite a squire. They are each handsome, although the farmer, like the man of letters in *A Pair of Blue Eyes*, is sexually timid and uncertain. The soldier is sexually sure and direct, whilst the shepherd's powerful control and earthy sense of union cuts him off from the excitements of sexual speculation where the girl is concerned. Looking at Gabriel, his very permanency is a staggering notion to her. 'Why, he'd always be there . . . whenever I looked up, there he'd be.' The list of what he'll give her if she'll give him her hand abruptly cancels itself out when it comes to the final item. She'll have a piano, his flute-playing, a little ten-pound gig for the market, nice flowers and cocks and hens, a cucumber-frame and the babies announced in the newspaper – 'every man jack of 'em! And at home by the fire, whenever you look up, there I shall be – and whenever I look up, there will be you.'

Events precipitated by the swift ups and down of farming fortune in the nineteenth century, when the liviers, or independent villagers, could soon be toppled into servitude by a little disaster, swiftly reverse their positions. Bathsheba becomes a woman of property and Gabriel a man with no other possession than his craft. Her being his mistress as an employer has a piquancy which does not escape either of them. Their trial of strength, he with the masterful farming ability which she must have to make her new position a success, she with the orders and dismissals he can afford inwardly to ignore, is not an unequal one, however. Were it so, one or the other's weakness would ensure an ultimate closeness. Not the least of the shepherd's assets is his rural understanding of time, his ability to wait.

Sergeant Troy lacks all understanding of time. He exists in a brilliant immediacy which either dazzles those caught up in the inexorable time patterns of agriculture or makes them suspicious of him. He seizes upon Fanny's unpunctuality as an excuse to abandon her at the altar and his arrival into Bathsheba's life is so instantaneously bright as to overthrow the black country night with 'the effect of a fairy transformation'. Troy 'was to darkness what the sound of a trumpet is to silence'. Some critics attribute his name to Troy Town, a village which lay between Puddle-town and Dorchester, but in *A Pair of Blue Eyes* 'Elfride was startled to find that her harmonies had fired a small Troy, in the shape of Stephen's heart', and so it is likely that Hardy called his military destroyer of the jogging rural time-scale after a scene of confusion and conquest.

The third person whose passion has to reckon with the country clock is Farmer Boldwood, a tragic figure. Both by temperament and middle age, he takes too leisurely a view of time, lagging behind the season for love and offering Bathsheba such a protracted engagement that even to someone as wedded to the unhurried nature of things as herself, his patience itself is off-putting.

Hardy's picture of the classic rural time-scale in which he makes the temporal chime with the eternal is at its most glorious in *Far from the Madding Crowd*. He creates it around the central figure of the true pastoral, that of the faithful shepherd. Gabriel Oak may rise to a farming tenancy and to being the master of men, and ultimately to being the consort of the local goddess, but never for a moment can he escape his role as bellwether to the village flock. He is the unconscious leader. He stands in the novel in simple but somewhat overpowering moral and physical dimensions, like a shepherd in a Blake painting, glowing and archetypal. Although he is never ponderous and Hardy even goes so far as to bring him down to Dorset earthiness by revealing the sort of limitations which would make Bathsheba justified in looking around for a better match, Gabriel stays stolidly within the parish limitations. It is there that he shines. It is there that he presides over such unmatched scenes as the sheep-washing, the shearing, the stackyard and all the inescapable set-pieces of farming toil and skill, risk and salvation, profit and loss. Hardy allows inferior dramas to intrude upon these sacred agrarian moments, distracting courtships and feastings that are irrelevant to their higher celebrations, and then uses Gabriel Oak, his good shepherd, as an indicator by which we can steer our way into farming's centre of gravity.

The richest instance of this is Chapter 22, 'The Great Barn and the Sheep-shearers'. Critics had praised what they called the subsidiary scenes in Hardy's earlier fiction and Leslie Stephen had commissioned him to write *Far from the Madding Crowd* on account of them, but there had not been – nor would there be in quite this sense – anything to equal this. It is a form of sumptuous reality. It challenges every view of the quaint and simple task, as Chardin did, and directs us towards a vision of fundamental labour that contains within it satisfactions that are usually searched for in poetry and religion. Scenes such as this are the permanent cliffs in his writing, stalwart headlands against which melodrama and suspense can fret and dash without any danger of their becoming a merely sensational movement. They steady his story-telling and fill it with meditation. In such episodes we are made to share in his strangely divided intelligence, on the one hand seeing life as the countryman himself sees it and, on the other, through a private imagination which depends upon certain basic rural everyday matters to fuel it for its flights. The scene is set in the medieval tithe barn at Cerne Abbas and Hardy the architect and Hardy the apostate Anglican, as well as Hardy the new great novelist, are all present.

Here at least the spirit of the ancient builders was at one with the spirit of the modern beholder. Standing before this abraded pile, the eye regarded its present usage, the mind dwelt upon its past history, with a satisfied sense of functional continuity throughout – a feeling almost of gratitude, and quite of pride, at the permanence of the idea which had heaped it up. The fact that four centuries had neither proved it to be founded on a mistake, inspired any hatred of its purpose, nor given rise to any reaction that had battered it down, invested this simple grey effort of old minds with a repose, if not a grandeur, which a too curious reflection was apt to disturb in its ecclesiastical and military compeers. For once mediaevalism and modernism had a common standpoint. The lanceolate windows, the time-eaten arch-stones and chamfers, the orientation of the axis, the misty chestnut work of the rafters, referred to no exploded fortifying art or worn-out religious creed. The defence and salvation of the body by daily bread is still a study, a religion and a desire . . . Here the shearers knelt, the sun slanting in upon their bleached shirts, tanned arms, and the polished shears they flourished . . . Beneath them a captive sheep lay panting, quickening its pants as misgiving merged in terror, till it quivered like the hot landscape outside . . .

Joseph Poorgrass sums up the activity in this temple, and the whole business of growing things, whether it be wool or wheat, when he remarks, at the end of the chapter, ''Tis the gospel of the body, without which we perish, so to speak.' Another aspect of the gospel of the body and equally well known, one suspects, in such a warm and gloomy and sweet-smelling place during the tumbling generations, is personified by Bathsheba, who, as mistress, steps among the lyrical drudgery 'in her new riding-habit of myrtle-green, which fitted her to the waist as a rind fits its fruit'. A few minutes earlier she had stood over Gabriel as he sheared, and he had felt a 'dim and temperate bliss' because he and the girl and the ewe made an isolated group in the animated barn. Bathsheba times him as he strips the fleece away until the sheep is as naked as Aphrodite. She chatters, he is silent as he flings 'the ewe over upon her other side, covering her head with his knee, gradually running the shears line after line round her dewlap, thence about her flank and back, and finishing over the tail'. The never before exposed inner surface of the fleece is flawless. The incident is both workaday and erotic.

The narrative saunters along in a climate which is created by the parallel desirabilities of farming regularity and non-extreme human affection. A natural wisdom in the Weatherbury air tirelessly promotes such activities as the best union in the local circumstances but, Gabriel excepted, such advice is disregarded. Thus the sacred rhythm is disturbed and the impious get hurt. And not only the disturbers, but their victims too. Pretty Fanny Robin, the paradigm of the wronged village girl, and the skilfully conceived Farmer Boldwood, a man standing uncertainly betwixt ages and betwixt classes, whose innocence is real enough, if of another sort. Gabriel saves the harvest from fire and storm, Bathsheba from innuendo, her flock from disease and much less, but he cannot save them. He himself is redeemed by the modesty of his expectations – even when he wrathfully tells the lordly Bathsheba, 'I was made for better things.' Hardy makes him fascinatingly dull in order to complement characters that are fascinatingly bright, and his rewards for not struggling to discover something more ecstatic than 'a dim and temperate bliss' are a beautiful, hard-headed wife, the best farm in the place and masculine respect all round. Who, in an English village, could ask for more?

Two chapters in the novel, 'The Hollow amid the Ferns' and 'Fanny's Revenge', are startling and unforgettable. Their quite different kinds of brilliance halt the reader in his tracks. They are virtuoso performances by a young hand and, like the mesmerised Bathsheba caught in the light of 'Troy's reflecting blade', we are brought up stock-still by such a dazzling display of Hardy's literary prowess. Our post-Freudian intelligence makes it impossible to read 'The Hollow amid the Ferns' without swiftly interpreting symbolism which not only the Victorians but Hardy himself would have found anything but obvious. They would, however, have recognised in 'Fanny's Revenge' aspects of melodrama which had been rescued from the purely sensational and given new depths. But it would be crude thinking to believe that Hardy was some accidental precursor of D. H. Lawrence or that he purposely set out to deepen the popular story-telling vein of his own day. His mind did not work like this. What is absorbed, whether it was about human psychology or the rites and customs which had grown up around it, is processed in a guise which was quite unlike anything that was to come or anything that had been. It grasped all that was most rare and all that was most ordinary with the same leaping interest.

Although we can't escape them, Freud and Lawrence will not be able to make us see more than Hardy intends us to see below the perimeter of the saucer-shaped pit where Bathsheba is transfixed by Sergeant Troy's sword-play. It is one of the greatest seduction scenes in the history of the English novel. One of the many keys to an understanding of Hardy is to know that seduction is used in his novels as an irresistible force to deflect the direction in which not only a woman but her village is moving. Hurrying, colourful men seduce, patiently waiting men court. Troy is good at seduction but no good at all at extricating himself from its result. Nothing less than callousness saves him from marriage to the pregnant Fanny and little more than greed attracts him to Bathsheba. But one feels that he would never have been cruel or mercenary were it not that women connected marriage with seduction. He did not. Hardy was intrigued with the erotic idea of what, in a very early poem* he called 'Red shapes amid the corn' and the country girl's double longing for a reliable husband at the plough and a gallant from the neighbouring barracks. In his poem 'The Dance at the Phoenix', he describes with wit and pathos the lasting effects of 'scarlet fever', as the nineteenth-century's passion for soldiers was called, when an old village woman creeps from her beloved husband's bed and goes to a military ball and returns to die from her exertions. One of his favourite ballads was 'The Banks of Allan Water', with its theme of brief joy being pursued by retribution – the popular morality of many folk-songs, and of rural life itself. These warrior-intruders are eloquent and beautiful.

> For his bride a soldier sought her,
> And a winning tongue had he:
> On the banks of Allan Water
> None was gay as she!

'A Winning Tongue Had He' was Hardy's first choice as a title for *A Pair of Blue Eyes* and in this novel he contrasts Stephen's lively chatter with the bloodless conversation of an intellectual lover, so that Elfride is deceived into thinking that heavy, charmless talk denotes the worthier suitor. Troy's too is a winning tongue. When we compare his approach with that of Gabriel we see that it is not so much a case of how things are put as the contrasts between too much sound and overmuch silence. At the end of the story Gabriel says to Bathsheba,

'If I only knew one thing – whether you would allow me to love you and win you, and marry you after all – If I only knew that!'
'But you will never know,' she murmured.
'Why?'
'Because you never ask.'

He has asked, of course – only it was the minute after meeting her, so to speak. The shepherd's understanding of the country clock may be correct but he is ignorant when it comes to women and timing. Troy can judge their reactions to the second. There is a scene in which he overwhelms Bathsheba by the spontaneous gift of his most valued possession, a gold watch, and then takes it back again without her – or

---

* 'The Harvest Supper' (1850).

the reader – being absolutely sure that he intended her to keep it in the first place. But the emotion of the act of giving survives what comes close to being the prattle of the huckster. But as we know that he is a young man who is 'vulnerable only in the present' we recognise that much of his talk is a defence. He speaks 'fluently and unceasingly' and Bathsheba is distressed by hearing what he says and yet wants to hear more. In the famous sword-play chapter he puts action to his words where, after raising his sword in the evening sunlight and making it gleam 'a sort of greeting, like a living thing' and making a few introductory thrusts, he decides to be 'more interesting, and let you see some loose play – giving all the cuts and points, infantry and cavalry, quicker than lightning, and as promiscuously – with just enough rule to regulate instinct and yet not to fetter it'. Being assured that his sword is blunt and cannot pierce her, Bathsheba endures the marvellous performance, even when Troy's sword-arm 'spread in a scarlet haze over the space covered by its motions'. But when he enacts the rape of the lock and severs a curl, then spits a caterpillar which is crawling on her breast, she loses her self-command and bursts into tears, the final assault not being the blade but 'the gentle dip of Troy's mouth downwards upon her own'. The miracle of this superb piece of writing is that Troy acts and talks simply as an artist in swordsmanship throughout who is enchanted by his own skill, and that the liberties of a lock of hair and a kiss which make Bathsheba feel that she has 'sinned a great sin' could have been to the show-off soldier the harmless trophies of a flirtation. Yet we as much as the girl are shaken by what has occurred. We have been swept along in these few pages into the disarray caused by physical attraction to an extent we could scarcely have imagined.

'Fanny's Revenge', the other chapter in this novel to show Hardy's genius in a special manner, sees Troy cruelly ridding himself of the encumbrance of Bathsheba's passion for his person in a macabre scene around the coffin of the only woman he loved, and their child. The ingredients are the stock ones of sensational Victorian fiction: a wronged woman and her baby come home to her own parish in a pauper's coffin from the workhouse; society's forgiveness of her, since she has paid the great penalty; the father's remorse and a livid illumination of the deathliness at the heart of things. Female intuition has convinced Bathsheba of the truth even before she forces the lid of the coffin and it is for herself that she is bound to weep as she sees that, in death, Fanny's failure is turned to success, 'her humiliation to triumph, her lucklessness to ascendancy'. For she has retained what Bathsheba was never able to grasp, Troy's love. His arrival in the room is a lurid *coup de théâtre*. Wildly and uselessly, Bathsheba begs him to share the kiss he gives to his dead sweetheart but he tells her that 'This woman is more to me, dead as she is, than ever you were, or are, or can be.' Hardy never lets Bathsheba escape the thrall of Troy's body; after he has been murdered, she tenderly undresses him and lays him out, before she magnanimously buries him in Fanny's grave. He is twenty-six.

These and other startling events ricochet through the Weatherbury acres like shot on a placid day, setting up alarm and frenzy at first, then fading away to become the common stuff of village gossip. But while Hardy perfectly comprehends a little community's need occasionally to ruffle its own orderly texture, his drama is never confined to the upheaval alone. His vision incorporates the entire action of the place, both natural and metaphysical and he never breaks off into the pleasantly descriptive passage which is designed to create a foil for excitement. An enormous part of the satisfaction which we increasingly derive from his writing is due to the authority with which he treats of so many different and often conflicting subjects. In *Far from the Madding Crowd* he offers us, as well as the adventures of a rustic beauty engaged in a sentimental education, his country-bred self, and with all that this implies. His meditative commentary on all that occurs in Wessex is not something which he applies to it, but which he draws from it. Subject after subject, its scenery, its animals, its buildings, its paths, its hardness and its delicacy, its manners and its limited horizon, is displayed from Hardy's private vantage point, which is deep down in the interior. Everything is witnessed by his own eye, which is knowing and independent. Conventional history and sociology inform his vision but play little part in its literary expression. Nor does he belong to the category of novelists whose work invites the reader to expand his own imagination. The fecundity and predominance of Hardy's thought makes this impossible. When we read him we are entirely restricted to his version of existence. Tracing its spiritual and social roots is not difficult and was practised, much to his dislike, in his own day. But what remains bastioned and mysterious, and still immeasurable, is the element in his writing which removes it from all the usual analysis. This special voice is heard in the smallest matters – the chat in Warren's Malthouse, the practising of the new hymn 'Lead, Kindly Light' by the church choir, the purity of scores of landscape descriptions such as the following,

> Winter, in coming to the country hereabout, advanced in well-marked stages, wherein might have been successively observed the retreat of the snakes, the transformation of the ferns, the filling of the pools, a rising of fogs, the embrowning by frost, the collapse of the fungi, and an obliteration by snow. This climax of the series had been reached to-night on the aforesaid moor, and for the first time in the season its irregularities were forms without features; suggestive of anything, proclaiming nothing, and without more character than that of being the limit of something else – the lowest layer of a firmament of snow.

In Joseph Poorgrass we have the Malaprop of the Church of England, the religion which Hardy gave up but from which he never emotionally escaped. It permeates the novel with its sunset glow, a faith on its last legs, its meaning tottering in the mouth of a labourer. Hardy is perhaps less emancipated from rural Anglicanism than from any other aspect of his background, actual belief apart. Weatherbury echoes with its moral and aesthetic resonance: it remains the ultimate language for the acceptance of things. But creeping into it with a comfortless and destructive force is his recognition of there being no everlasting arms to check the fall, whether of man or sparrow. These Christian and post-Christian attitudes, however, never really cloud a countryside where so many classical rural values prevail. This village is as much the territory of Hardy's readings in classical mythology as his boyhood involvement in church services. 'Ovey, ovey, ovey!' (from the Latin *ovi*, sheep) calls Gabriel to his flock. 'Yes,' says Joseph in a later crisis,

> 'and I was sitting at home looking for Ephesians, and says I to myself, "'Tis nothing but Corinthians and Thessalonians in this danged Testament", when who should come in but Henery there: "Joseph," he said, "the sheep have blasted theirselves –"'

These two sources of Hardy's literary version of Wessex cross and re-cross each other to the end of the novel, and with perfect euphony. Against them we encounter, for the first time in a major key in *Far from the Madding Crowd*, his own creed, his own commentary.

The Dangerous Idyll

Extreme though it may sound, any literary undertaking by an English villager has until quite recently, by which I mean the late nineteenth century, been received with much the same suspicion as novels and poetry written by English women. Each, by daring to produce literature, had broken through ancient orderly concepts of their functions. So at best they were odd and ingenious, and at worst unnatural. John Clare didn't object to being called a peasant and was great enough not to demand that he should always be referred to as a poet. What helped to cripple him was the term 'peasant-poet', with its freakish implications. But this is what he was called and the terrible conflict between his 'condition' and his genius raged until it exploded into that vast, silencing affirmation, I AM. Twice he made this huge nameless statement, perhaps an imitation of the profound claim he had heard Yahveh make during the First Lesson in the village church, though each time there was never a hint of pride or blasphemy. Just the fact of John Clare. The first I AM poem is such a perfect expression of a man's discovery of himself as superfluous, unneeded and abandoned, that it speaks for every ignored man. The second I AM poem, a sonnet, is different. It is Clare's apology for being a poet:

> I feel I am, I only know I am,
> And plod upon the earth as dull and void;
> Earth's prison chilled my body with its dram
> Of dullness, and my soaring thoughts destroyed.
> I fled to solitude from passion's dream
> But strife pursued: I only know I am.
> I was a being created in the race
> Of men, disdaining bounds of place and time;
> A spirit that could travel o'er the space
> Of earth and heaven – like a thought sublime,
> Tracing creation, like my Maker, free –
> A soul unshackled like eternity:

Spurning earth's vain and soul-debasing thrall –
But now I only know I am, that's all.

What is a man's identity? Of what does it actually consist? That self which only he can feel and see? Or the conglomerate of job, address, appearance, class, and inherited name by which society recognises him? How many a man, harnessed for life to what Geoffrey Grigson once called 'the penal labour of farm work', must have told himself I AM during the eighteenth and nineteenth centuries. And where such trapped lives were concerned, the nineteenth century ended during the 1940s.

Here I shall be mostly concerned with those who broke the harmonious rules of rural England by freeing themselves from such permissible literary expressions as ballads, folk-songs, saws and tales, eloquent and genuine though such things can be, and, by accepting themselves as very special 'beings created in the race of men', soared far beyond the words and music popularly associated with the fields. I shall also try to show how the great classic vision of the English countryside which the Augustans created, and which writers such as Clare, Bloomfield, Hardy and Burns challenged, which John Constable celebrated and which Jane Austen satirised, is not at all the same country vision which more and more occupies the conservationists of our own day.

The face of England, as thousands of sunny modern guidebooks like to describe it, has remained wonderfully serene and unmarked in spite of the polluters. Neither its contemporary environmental problems nor its past tragedies – the Industrial Revolution, Micheldever, Tolpuddle, the clearances and enclosures, the squalid cottages which it upset John Constable to enter, the signs of greed and pride in the park – have marked it in such a way that its central beauty and inspiration have been defaced. In fact, we are at the beginning of a new cycle of reverence towards the countryside and its far from simple conditions. These we intuitively recognise as the result of a practical compromise made between the claims of neo-classical pastorals and intensive farming. The result of this combination has never been a particularly happy one for the ordinary countryman. It has had a way of limiting him in the eyes of the sophisticated, who see him as admirable but quaint. Quaintness was one of the things which Clare rejected when he cried, 'I am!' His father could sing ballads by the fireside and not make those who heard him feel uncomfortable. But when Clare read his first poems to his parents, or to the neighbours, he pretended that they were by someone else – an educated person – so that they did not have to feel that they were living with a kind of monster. And people still like village folk to 'fit', to stand upright and reassuring in the little innocent niches sentiment has carved out for them. They like to imagine village life as one of lasting and unchanging verities. To view it intellectually is thought vaguely treacherous.

Clare, when writing his autobiography, says that he was born in 'a gloomy village in Northamptonshire'. Gloomy or not, the sight of a single violet on Primrose Hill in London once caused him to hurry home to it. The incident illustrates the key factor in village experience: the fatal involvement, the need to remain. Robert Bloomfield wrote his enormously successful *The Farmer's Boy* – 20,000 copies published – while he was working as a shoemaker in London. The poem was an act of nostalgia, for himself and for all his readers. Its appalling effect was to cut him off from his own village involvement for ever.

John Clare did the harder thing. He stayed in 'gloomy' Helpston although from childhood on his isolation was to be intense. 'I live here among the ignorant like a lost man.' Charles Lamb advised him in his kindly fashion to do what all sensible poets did and 'transport Arcadia to Helpston'. It was civilised advice inasmuch as it made clear to Clare that Lamb, by suggesting that the young ploughman was quite capable of using classical allusions and imagery, did not think of him as a peasant-poet. Yet Lamb had not understood. 'Gloomy' Helpston – how the ecstatic nature poems refute the adjective! – *was* Arcady where Clare was concerned. When they forced him to live in a cottage only three miles away from this village which was part of him, he became mentally ill. And when they carried him to Northampton Asylum he eventually had to find a new persona to inhabit and chose, among others, Lord Byron's.

'That is where learning get's you!' his old mother believed. She thought learning 'the blackest arts of witchcraft' and Helpston itself thought reading was synonymous with sloth. From about twelve years onward, Clare lived a furtive, aberrant existence, hiding in woods with his books, hoarding old sugar-bags to write on, muttering behind the plough. The village verses which, a century later, collectors like Cecil Sharp and Sabine Baring-Gould were to rescue from oblivion for the English Folk-Song Society, were, for Clare, so much trash. For him they merely reflected the ignorance from which he was determined to escape.

When he was thirteen, a young weaver showed him a scrap of Thomson's *The Seasons*. Now, if ever there was a single poem which moulded, sensitised, sentimentalised, elevated, and generally formed the British character during the eighteenth century it was *The Seasons*. It has been credited with being one of the chief agents to bring a spirit of tenderness and humanity to brutal Georgian England. For all that, the young weaver had no time for it because he was a Methodist. But he showed the scrap of it he possessed to this strange boy, who read these four lines, and was saved. Or lost. It all depends upon the value one places upon restless spiritual inquiry at the cost of contentment. These are the four lines:

> Come, gentle Spring, ethereal mildness, come,
> And from the bosom of yon dropping cloud,
> While music wakes around, veil'd in a shower
> Of shadowing roses, on our plains descend . . .

It isn't much, is it? And it is even less when we recall several hundred lines like it. But the fact is that for the path-seeking Clare the fragment hung in the workaday air of Helpston, changing everything. His experience had something in common with that of James Northcote, the artist, who told Hazlitt that he had been life-long affected by an actor singing Shakespeare's 'Come unto these yellow sands, and then take hands', and that he felt it to be a kind of weakness or folly on his part. Hazlitt's reply was, 'There is no danger of that sort – all the real taste and feeling in the world is made up of what people take in their heads in this manner.'

There was precious little taste or feeling connected with what next happened at Helpston. Unable to find time or even sufficient smoothed-out sugar-bags to establish the stream of poetry which Thomson's four lines had set flowing, Clare began what he called his 'muttering'. In other words, he spoke his poems softly into the Northamptonshire air, repeating the words many times until they no longer disappeared on the wind, but remained with him as whole and recognisable acts of creation. It was about this period, 1812, that poor Robert Bloomfield was reversing this process. His descent from the unsettling fame which the best-selling *The Farmer's Boy* had brought him now included an attempt to make money by selling Aeolian harps. So, while he heard that Murray the publisher had given 'Parson Crabbe £3,000 for his Tales', Bloomfield had nothing more to offer *his* readers but simple home-made instruments to whine wordlessly in a gale. There is no evidence that they sold. And so we have this curious pen-less moment in the lives of the two poets, the once lionised Bloomfield hawking his wind-harps and the still unknown Clare entrusting the Northamptonshire air with his poetry because there was no other place for it.

As one can imagine, Helpston did not take kindly to this muttering boy. Nor did the Marquess of Exeter's Master of the Kitchen Garden, who employed him. The persecution proper began at this point. So superb a creature had the master gardener seemed to Clare that, when applying for a job, he had sunk on his knees before him. The mockery being more than he could stand, he fled to the open fields. The fields to any village are its sea. The rancour and glances, the creeds and criticisms of the village centre, cannot be contained there. Solitude and the elemental processes of the growing year take over. People were always suggesting that the more refined task of gardening would suit such a delicate person but Clare found, throughout his working life, that labouring in a great field provided the best conditions for his happiness and his art. Eventually, it was his inability to do this work, as much as anything else, which hurried him towards madness.

Poets like Shelley might attempt to rouse his rural workers with,

> Men of England, wherefore plough
> – For the lords who lay ye low?
> The seed ye sow, another reaps,
> The wealth ye find, another keeps . . .

but John Clare, England's most articulate village voice, remained untouched by such revolutionary ideas. He ploughed in order to perfect what he called his 'descriptive rhyming'. Each night he wrote these spoken poems down and each day some of them vanished, as though mice had got hold of them – though it was only his mother stealing them 'for her own use as occasion called for them'. She thought he was only practising pothooks. But the realisation that the ploughboy was up to something, with his mutterings and hidings, his starings at flowers and his traipsing after books to Stamford, soon leaked out, and the laughing began. When we read Clare's frequent references to it we at once appreciate that this was no ordinary touchiness but a flinching from what George Herbert once described as 'the mockery of murderers'.

The unnaturalness of Clare offended like the unnaturalness of writers such as Lady Winchilsea, the Duchess of Newcastle, Currer, Ellis and Acton Bell, and George Eliot when they claimed the same author's rights as men. In fact, when Lady Winchilsea scathingly attacked the system which allowed only males access to full literary expression, her words are curiously relevant to writers such as Clare whose 'condition' barred them from normal consideration as artists.

> How are we fallen! [she wrote]
> Fallen by mistaken rules,
> And Education's more than Nature's fools;
> Debarred from all improvements of the mind,
> And to be dull, expected and resigned;
> And if someone would soar above the rest,
> With warmer fancy, and ambition pressed,
> So strong the opposing faction still appears,
> The hopes to thrive can ne'er outweigh the fears.

Nothing finally outweighed the fears of Clare, as we know. We also know that he routed the picturesque pastoral and returned the landscape to its natural contours in the English imagination. The most overwhelming thing in his life was the revelation that he was no versifying rustic but a total poet. This knowledge was both terrible and wonderful. And Helpston's laughter was probably generated as much by fear as by amusement.

For most of the eighteenth century a policy of moral and aesthetic containment had concealed a good deal of the pressures which were drastically altering the lives of the village people, still at this period the nation's largest labouring force. Because this containment was not imposed entirely from the top but possessed many deep cultural and religious elements springing from the people themselves, there were periods of classic harmony which, particularly during the famine which followed Napoleon's defeat in 1815, were looked back on by all classes as the golden years. Lord Ernle in his *History* says that the 1750s were the Golden Age of English agriculture. This euphoric memory seems to have resulted from the elegant propaganda disseminated by various painters, poets, landscape-gardeners and architects during the golden age itself, for in 1769 we have Oliver Goldsmith sending his new poem *The Deserted Village* to Sir Joshua Reynolds with the following letter attached:

How far you may be pleased with the versification and mere mechanical parts of this attempt, I do not pretend to enquire: but I *know* you will object (and indeed several of our best and wisest friends concur in the opinion) that the depopulation it deplores is *no where to be seen,* and the disorders it laments are only to be found in the poet's imagination. To this I can scarce make any other answer, than that I sincerely believe what I have written, that I have taken all possible pains in country excursions for these past four or five years to be certain of what I allege, and that all my views and enquiries have led me to believe those miseries real . . . In regretting the depopulation of the countryside, I inveigh against the increase of our luxuries, and here also I expect the shout of modern politicians against me.

What had happened, of course, was that the unsightly inhabitants of Auburn had been tidied away to make a park. They had been resettled, as a matter of fact, though this was not the point. Like many a native in our own day, their ancestral homes and fields had to make way for 'civilisation'. *The Deserted Village* can be read as a lasting indictment of white Africans at any time and in any place. For generations, on the principle that it couldn't happen here, the English liked to believe that Goldsmith's 'country excursions' must have taken place in his native Ireland, where things were different. But, as we know, Sweet Auburn was Nuneham Courtenay, Oxfordshire. And what Goldsmith was witnessing was a scene which, for a very different reason than the beautifying of a peer's new house, was soon to be familiar all over Britain. For the cruel if logical process by which the small independent farming units created by the manorial system were rationalised by 'enclosure' was soon to affect the country people. The enclosure of Helpston runs as a disturbing counterpoint to the lyricism of Clare's poetry. Few villagers, however, were to describe these profound changes for, as Crabbe said,

Few, amid the rural tribe, have time
To number syllables, and play with rhyme.

George Crabbe, however, was the exception to every statement made about the peasant-poet for, having been born into the labouring classes and having heard, seen and experienced all their emotions, he totally and absolutely severed the connection when he became an established writer. The impetus behind his verse-tales is neither nostalgia nor enlightenment but a fastidious disenchantment with provincial life. He gazed at the individuals in the harsh little Suffolk community which he had abandoned with much the same dissecting accuracy as when his eye searched out the minute flora of the bitter shingle beach and the lonely marsh, except that he was apt to save his lyricism for the latter. He made no bones about his 'having fled from those shores'. 'Few men who have succeeded in breaking through the obscurity of their birth have retained so little trace of their origin,' remarked his son. Crabbe certainly made no bones about presenting his grimly brilliant anti-idyll in the same poetic form, the heroic couplet, in which Pope and other eighteenth-century writers had manufactured the idyll itself. These rhymed novels were packed with the sights and sounds which one was not supposed to see or hear on an excursion to the coast or to the fields. Worst of all, Crabbe had the audacity to examine the *mores* of his own tribe as though he were some visiting inspector. It was as if Margaret Mead had been a South Sea Islander. Yet, as E. M. Forster said,

To talk about Crabbe is to talk about England . . . He grew up among poor people, and he has been called their poet. But he did not like the poor. When he started writing, it was the fashion to pretend that they were happy shepherds and shepherdesses, who were always dancing, or anyhow had hearts of gold . . . but Crabbe's verdict on the working classes is unfavourable. And when he comes to the richer and more respectable . . . he remains sardonic, and sees them as poor people who haven't been found out . . . To all of them, and to their weaknesses, he extends a little pity, a little contempt, a little cynicism, and a much larger portion of reproof. The bitternesses of his early experiences had eaten into his soul . . .

During the summer of 1787, soon after Crabbe had published *The Village*, another country poet, William Cowper, for whom this had been a miserable, worrying year and who, to keep the Black Dog at bay, was reading anything and everybody, read at last the poems by Robert Burns which for months had been astonishing the literary world. Burns was twenty-eight and a ploughman, albeit on his brother's farm. Working a little Scottish farm was as penurious then as it was to be in the 1920s, when many a younger brother, tired of being the unpaid family hired-hand, emigrated to East Anglia, to fall upon those stagnant but promising acres and make his fortune. Robert Burns's object in publishing his poems was not to celebrate his oneness with the village of Mossgiel but to make enough money to get off the land altogether and sail to Jamaica and work on a plantation. Cowper read these now famous poems with bewilderment. In fact . . .

I have read them *twice*; and though they be written in a language that is new to me . . . I think them, on the whole, a very extraordinary production. He is, I believe, the only poet these kingdoms have produced in the lower rank of life, since Shakespeare . . . who need not be indebted for any part of his praise to a charitable consideration of his origin, and the disadvantages under which he has laboured. It will be a pity hereafter if he should not divest himself of barbarism, and content himself with writing pure English. . . . *He who can command admiration dishonours himself if he aims no higher than to raise a laugh*. . . .

William Cowper, that gentlest, kindest of men and one who lived in the deep Buckinghamshire countryside with all the charity, simplicity and good taste of a Mr Knightley, and is as far from being a Sweet Auburn tyrant as could be imagined, remains none the less a devotee of the Augustan doctrine of rural harmony and neo-classical order. Although he cannot avoid the fact that Robert Burns is a genius, neither can he avoid the implications of that wild free language. And so, with a terribly similar reflex action to that of the Helpston villagers when confronted by John Clare, Cowper laughs.

Cowper's feeling for the countryside was the purest distillation of the old conservative attitudes – those same attitudes which still flow through so much of the vast literature we annually produce to congratulate ourselves on our rural basis. A writer can let himself go on the iniquities of the city but the village remains critically sacrosanct.

Cowper's *Letters*, in which village joy and sorrow are so perfectly conveyed, was John Constable's favourite book, and he died with it in his hand. The greatest painter of the English romantic movement was a revolutionary on canvas only, and the superb series of Suffolk riverside paintings which he created during the years immediately following

Waterloo, and which have since been called 'the landscape of every English mind', were, in effect, a marvellous apologia for Tory-Augustan 'order', as well as being 'true to Nature'. Looking at them now, it is impossible to believe that while they were being produced, labourers rioted and were lighting bonfires on the hills, that on one occasion at least things had got so out of hand that both the squire and rector had fled, and that Captain Swing was in the neighbourhood. Constable himself travelled constantly from Soho to East Bergholt to refresh himself at the 'fountain-head', as he called it, of all he worshipped and understood. To him, the pattern of life in the Stour Valley, an eighteenth-century creation so far as he could appreciate it, was a divine one.

Post-war famine, Enclosure, and the strange, unknown pressures brought about by the industrial revolution were behind the disorders of East Bergholt. The 1817 map of the village on which its inhabitants stated their claims before Enclosure shows that all John Constable claimed was the cottage he bought, while still a boy, to turn into a studio. But many, as elsewhere, were unable to claim anything because of illiteracy or ignorance, and were made paupers. When Constable heard of the sufferings of these villagers, he sent blankets from London, that basic charitable gesture. But when he heard that the Suffolk and Essex labourers were forming protective unions – those little men who carry on with their quiet tasks in his great pictures – he was shocked and angry. Archdeacon Fisher, his friend, had a more sympathetic attitude. He and his family were virtually isolated by thousands of starving country people. He saw their desperate attempts to band themselves together as a natural reaction to the disaster which was engulfing them; Constable, on the other hand, saw them only as an evil menace to the God-ordained pattern of rural life. His warnings to Archdeacon Fisher were harsh and to the point. 'Remember that I know these people well. There are no such corrupt hordes as any set of mechanics who work in a shop together as a party . . .' A century and a half later the Agricultural Workers' Union is still looked at by some as a development which the beautiful British countryside could well do without.

Meanwhile, as the 'union' workhouses went up, to the best Benthamite designs, to shelter large numbers of displaced peasants, the scenery Constable worshipped intensified its spiritual hold over him.

'Nothing can exceed the beauty of the country', he wrote. 'It makes pictures seem trumpery.'

When the long peace between the gentlemen and the peasants was broken by the rationalisation of what remained of the manorial system, the contrast between the two rural cultures was often so extreme that the baronet in his park could feel that he was surrounded, not so much by his countrymen as by savages. The work forces were moving towards the time when they no longer possessed faces, only 'hands'. 'Osbert', remarked Sir George Sitwell, staring across Sheffield, 'do you realise that there is nobody between us and the Locker-Lampsons?' Even good Archdeacon Fisher told Constable that it wasn't because he and his wife had to run a private welfare state for a great tract of Berkshire that he was so depressed, it was because 'there is nobody we can meet'. Both he and Constable continued to revel in the new concepts of Nature as described by Wordsworth. 'Every step I take, and to whatever object I turn my eye,' said the artist, 'that sublime expression in the Scriptures, "I am the resurrection and the life", seems verified about me,' – except, that is, when he caught sight of the inhabitants of this beautiful country, when he was obliged to add, 'The poor people are dirty and to approach one of the cottages is almost insufferable.'

The threat to the idyll flutters nervously – though usually so slightly that it escapes ordinary detection – in the novels of Jane Austen. And, of course being Jane Austen, she puts it to good comic use, no more so than when, in *Emma*, she allows that peerless girl to wed Mr Knightley because his presence in the house will be an added protection against someone who is stealing hens from the hen-run. Why, it may be asked, is Mr Woodhouse so jumpy? Why did 'poor Miss Taylor', by marrying Mr Weston and going off to live in a house only *half a mile* from Hartfield, create such difficulties? Emma, who is only nineteen and in flourishing health, had once walked to the Westons, 'but it was not pleasant'. *Why* wasn't it pleasant? When Harriet Smith and her school-friend, two other excessively healthy teenage ladies, had taken a walk and encountered a gypsy family, they behaved as hysterically as though they had run into cannibals. Why? When Jane Fairfax is seen strolling by herself across the meadows to the post office, the consequent consternation concerning her safety could not have been greater had she been making off for 'Swisserland'. Critics have dwelt upon the hermetic quality of Jane Austen's country society, 'Two or three families', etc., being her ideal recipe for fiction, but what really lies behind all this witty terror of the ordinary agricultural background? Jane Austen's inter-pretation of Augustanism is to present the park as paradise. It is unnatural or unwise to wish to leave, or to leave, paradise.

The novel's climaxes are created by the author's allowing this deli-cious country paradise to make moral collisions with the sane heart of the English countryside as she recognised it. The scene in which a young working farmer is thought 'too low' for silly Harriet by proud Emma, and then turns out to be the *friend* of Mr Knightley himself, is one of many which steady the comic impulse in this, the wittiest novel in the language. The laughter in Jane Austen's villages is always at the expense of dishonesty and affectation, the tears at the threat of destruc-tion of any part of a unique rural civilisation.

But if Harriet's young farmer is so low that Emma has to include him in the yeomanry, which is 'precisely the order of people with whom I feel I can have nothing to do', what hope of salvation is there for Hodge himself? None – in the literary sense – beyond those utilitarian appearances when either he or his wife clump by on the way to toil. No wonder that the poor creature bursts out laughing at the charades which are supposed to be going on above his head, so to speak. Now and then they go on a bit more than he can bear, and then he lets fly. William Hazlitt heard such an outburst with shock and disbelief at the extra-ordinary effect it had on him. He was used to mockery – but he hardly expected it from this quarter.

His favourite hide-out was Winterslowe, the Wiltshire village intro-duced to him by Sarah Stoddart, his uncomfortable wife, and the proto-New Woman. There Hazlitt's own special concept of rural bliss – lying on his back on a sunny hillside, doing absolutely nothing – could be indulged while Sarah hiked. But one fatal day he read a book while drinking in the village pub and something was said, and then somebody laughed. For an ugly moment the lettered and the unlettered out-stared each other from their incommunicable solitudes. Then Hazlitt the radical, the eloquent defender of the village people of England against the horrible proposals of the Reverend Mr Malthus, unleashed such a tirade against country loutishness as no squarson could even have imagined:

All country people hate each other! They have so little comfort, that they envy their neighbours the small pleasures or advantage, and nearly grudge themselves the necessities of life. From not being accustomed to enjoyment, they become hardened and averse to it – stupid, for want of thought, selfish for want of society. There is nothing good to be had in the country, or if there is, they will not let you have it. They had rather injure themselves than oblige anyone else. Their common mode of life is a system of wretchedness and self-denial, like what we read of among barbarous tribes. You live out of the world . . . You cannot do a single thing you like; you cannot walk out or sit at home, or write or read, or think or look as if you did, without being subject to impertinent curiosity. The apothecary annoys you with his complaisance, the parson with his superciliousness. If you are poor you are despised; if you are rich you are feared and hated. If you do anyone a favour, the whole neighbourhood is up in arms; the clamour is that of a rookery . . . There is a perpetual round of mischiefmaking and backbiting for want of any better amusement . . . There are no shops, no taverns, no theatres, no opera, no concerts, no pictures . . . no books or know-ledge of books. Vanity and luxury are the civilisers of the world, and sweeteners of human life. Without objects either of pleasure or action, it grows harsh and crabbed. The mind becomes stagnant, the affections callous . . . Man left to himself soon degenerates into a very disagreeable person. Ignorance is always bad enough, but *rustic* ignorance is intolerable . . . The benefits of knowledge are never so well understood as from seeing the effects of ignorance, *in their naked, undisguised state,* upon the common country people. Their selfishness and insensibility are perhaps less owing to the hardships and privations, which make them, like people out at sea in a boat, ready to devour one another, than to their having no idea of anything beyond themselves and their immediate sphere of action . . . Persons who are in the habit of reading novels . . . are compelled to take a deep interest in . . . the thoughts and feelings of people they never saw . . . Books, in Lord Bacon's phrase, 'are a discipline of humanity'. Country people have none of these advantages . . . and so they amuse themselves by fancying the disasters and disgraces of their particular acquaintance. Having no hump-backed Richard to excite their wonder and abhorrence, they make themselves a bugbear . . . out of the first obnoxious person they can lay their hands on . . . All their spare time is spent in manufacturing the lie for the day . . . The common people in civilised countries are a kind of domesticated savage. They have not the wild imagination, the passions, the fierce energies, or dreadful vicissitudes of the savage tribes, nor have they the leisure, the indolent enjoyments and romantic superstitions which belong to the pastoral life in milder climates. *They are taken out of a state of nature, without being put in possession of the refinements of art.*

Invective aside, there was plenty of truth in Hazlitt's rage. Lost, that was what the country people of England were in 1817, when this censure of them appeared. The condemnation was published just a few months after *Emma* and at the very moment when John Constable had begun the marvellous series of Stour Valley landscapes, each with its sprinkling of minuscule boatmen and field-workers, with which he hoped to establish himself in the eyes of the Royal Academy. And also during the period which saw the publication of Crabbe's last poems. Byron thought Crabbe's subject-matter 'coarse and impractical', and the majority of people found the workaday village life of Constable's paintings 'too low' to hang in their drawing-rooms. As for John Clare, those whose taste for rural life had been conditioned by schoolroom immersions in Virgil and Homer, and later lessons from *The Seasons*, or even by William Wordsworth, saw in this great poet little more than a clumsy kind of precocity.

In 1871 – the beginning of the decade in which there was a disastrous combination of great rains and efficient grain-ships from the Canadian and American ports through which poured the harvests from fabulous prairie farms – rural England slipped once more into depression. Its agriculture was literally washed out and, except for brief government protection during the First World War, was to remain so until the 1940s. Country people fled in their hundreds of thousands from the stagnant scene. They went into the railways, into service, into factories, to the colonies and into limbo. All this while the land itself began to receive a new veneration, this time from the tycoons of the Industrial Revolution who needed a great many acres of it in order to support the titles which began to come their way during the 1880s. Their efforts to assimilate the rural-based culture of the old landed families created much of the drama in late Victorian fiction.

It was in 1871 that Tinsley the publisher put out a mystifying novel called *Desperate Remedies*. The reviews were mixed, as they say. The story was anonymous but contained such expert descriptions of girls getting dressed that the general opinion was that the author was a woman. The novel was also found to be 'disagreeable' and 'full of crimes', although some critics were able to trace in it a new kind of 'awe' and noticed that the 'humble actors' exhibited powers which had 'previously been ignored in peasant society'. Thomas Hardy, who was thirty-one, read the worst of these reviews, that in the *Spectator*, while perched on a Dorset stile, and the bitterness remained with him until the end of his life. The decision to forsake architecture for literature had been hard, and immediately after posting off *Desperate Remedies* to the publisher he had gloomily underlined in his copy of *Hamlet* the words: 'Thou would'st not think how ill all's here about my heart: but it is no matter!' It was certainly a more tentative summing-up of his literary temerity than Clare's, who at the end was able to say,

> A silent man in life's affairs
> A thinker from a boy,
> A peasant in his daily cares,
> A poet in his joy.

A few weeks later, this time while reading Smith and Son's remainder list on Exeter station, Thomas Hardy found *Desperate Remedies* offered at 2*s*. 6*d*. and was so upset that he wrote to Macmillan's, to whom he had sent another novel, *Under the Greenwood Tree*, demanding the return of his manuscript. He would, he told his sweetheart in Cornwall, 'banish novel-writing for ever'.

Then, pragmatically for one who was to be such a key figure in the unification of the lettered and the unlettered cultures of England, Hardy set about earning his living designing buildings for the London School Board. All the same, *Under the Greenwood Tree*, with its hero based upon the man who brought the author's father his building materials, was published a year later; and now both critics and readers began what was to be the slow, touchy, self-examining process of allowing ordinary village people access to the passion, imagination, feeling and eloquence previously reserved for the parks and rectories. For a short period these disconcerting country forces revealed by Hardy managed to entertain the public with their quaint customs and displays of rustic love; but soon, as with George Crabbe, less bearable sights began to intrude. Extraordinary crimes, sex, fatal pressures, pagan strengths which showed no sign of ever having been conquered by Christian ethics. The style, too, was upsetting – 'Like sand in honey', Richard le Gallienne called it. And reviewer after reviewer began to echo Cowper's stricture on Burns – 'It will be a pity hereafter if he should not divest himself of barbarism and content himself with writing pure English.'

Many years later, when Hardy's genius was recognised, Havelock Ellis made an interesting comment on his success. He said that 'the real and permanent interest in Hardy's books is not his claim to be an exponent of Wessex – i.e. the rural workers – but his intense preoccupation with the mysteries of women's hearts.' And Havelock Ellis goes on to say that what Hardy was finally engaged in, most completely and impermissibly in *Jude the Obscure*, was bringing the instinctive, spontaneous and unregarded aspects of Nature even closer to the rigid routines of human life, making it *more* human (or inhuman); *more* moral (or immoral). Hardy was also emphasising the unconsciousness in Nature of everything except her essential law, and he was not in sympathy with a society which believed that it could live according to rules which did not take this law into account. It was the clash between Nature and 'society' which made the necessary conflict in Hardy the writer.

'This conflict', continues Havelock Ellis,

reaches its highest point around women. Truly or falsely, for good or for evil, woman has always been for man the supreme priestess, or the supreme devil, of Nature. 'A woman', says Proudhon – himself the incarnation of the revolt of Nature in the heart of man – 'even the most charming and virtuous woman, always contains an element of cunning, the wild beast element. She is a tamed animal that sometimes returns to her natural instinct. This cannot be said in the same degree of man.' The loving student of the elemental in Nature so becomes the loving student of women, the sensitive historian of her conflicts with 'sin' and with 'repentance' – the creations of man. Not, indeed, that any woman who has 'sinned', if her sin was love, ever really 'repents'. It is probable that a true experience of the one emotional state as of the other remains a little foreign to her, '*Sin* having probably been the invention of men who never really knew what love is'.

You will see that we have come a long way from *The Seasons*. You will also see that John Clare and Angel Clare have shares in the same profound rural consciousness.

In 1883 Richard Jefferies published that strange essay *The Story of My Heart* which Elizabeth Jennings rightly sees as a non-Christian equivalent of the mystic abstractions of Traherne. As with Hardy, Jefferies repudiates the notion that a countryside shares the opinions of the human beings who happen to be living in it. By one of those strange coincidences, *The Story of My Heart* appeared at the very same time as John Constable's paintings, which might sound odd. But Constable had died in 1837 leaving some eight hundred unsold, unwanted pictures; and these had remained, hidden and more or less ignored, until half a century later the best of them were given to the nation by his daughter.

Thus Constable's superb apology for Augustan harmony, whose claims he had so brilliantly strengthened by his scientific approach to Nature and his revolutionary impressionistic brushwork, burst its way into the country-worshipping hearts of the British at the same moment as the villages had found their native voice. For John Constable, the trees, fields, flowers, rivers and, most of all, the skies lived and moved in concord with the noblest human motives. For Jefferies and Hardy, such things were 'a force without a mind'.

'There is nothing human in Nature', said Jefferies.

The earth would let me perish on the ground . . . Burning in the sky the great sun, of whose company I have been so fond, would merely burn on and make no motion to assist me. The trees care nothing for us: the hill I visited so often in days gone by has not missed me. This very thyme which scents my fingers did not grow for that purpose, but its own . . . By night it is the same as day: the stars care not, and we are nothing to them . . . *If the entire human race perished at this hour, what difference would it make to the earth?*

Such statements wrung much of the contentment out of the simple life and helped to suggest a threatening amoral landscape which Edwardian Hellenists – including E. M. Forster, Saki, and Forrest Reid – peopled with forsaken Pans and other brooding and resentful stream and woodland deities.

Thomas Hardy himself became angry when his anti-euphoric view of country life was constantly put down to his pessimism. 'All this talk about my pessimism! What does it matter what an author's view of life is? If he finally succeeds in conveying a completely satisfying artistic expression, that is what counts.'

All the same, it *was* the cosmic brutality in his work which, among other things, caused the twentieth-century 'country writer' to try and avoid the excesses of both too much moral illumination and too much pounding darkness. Such avoidances have, of course, led to a stream of innocuous rural *belle-lettrism* unequalled throughout the world and to new versions of the idyll. But they have also led to many of the most serious statements of modern literature. When I think of village literature I think of *Four Quartets* as well as of *Lark Rise to Candleford*.

All post-Hardy writing needs to be assessed against a remarkable work published in 1902, *Rural England*, by Sir Henry Rider Haggard, a Norfolk farmer who usually wrote novels. This is a brilliant, factual, statistical, and apolitical account of the social effects of the last great agricultural depression at, more or less, its midway mark. The author chose a text from the Book of Judges with which to introduce his county-by-county analysis: 'The highways were unoccupied . . . the inhabitants of the villages ceased.' Reading *Rural England* now it seems scarcely sane that Britain, then able to command an almost inexhaustible wealth, could have permitted such a disaster to have run its course, blighting both the land and those who lived on it. The indifference and callousness shown towards the agricultural workers in particular, many of whom were starving, was appalling. The legacy of this neglect haunts the shires to this day.

Curiously, it was from this wretched scene that the conservationists feverishly began to retrieve a culture which was no longer regarded as belonging to boors but to the essential heart of Britain itself. The Folk-Lore and Folk-Song and Folk-Dance societies copied tirelessly. Dialect experts listened with respect to accents which they knew to be those of Beowulf, Caedmon, Langland, Chaucer, Shakespeare, Johnson and Tennyson. Now conservation of rural culture has grown until it includes conservation of the entire country scene itself. The cottage which Constable found too disgusting to enter in 1820, and which Rider Haggard found deserted and in ruins in 1902, is now 'desirable'. The poor crooked spade hangs safely in the Rural Industries Museum. Everything belonging to the village now belongs to our higher nature. Those who threaten thatch, hedge or peace are now the barbarians. And it is John Clare's village, not Thomson's, which provides the standards for this idyll. The village of the villagers. It is often said that the conservationists of this village are the middle-classes but they are, in most instances, the grandchildren.

Country Christmas

This year appears to be an exceptional 'season' where I am concerned. A season, says the dictionary, is a proper time and a favourable opportunity. I have been, for the only time in my life, on a retreat and, nervous about exposing my general theological ignorance, have given a public talk about George Herbert and T. S. Eliot, and some private chat about our synod. The retreat was held in the parlour of a Georgian farmhouse which, with an eye to the east wind, had been built right in the middle of the roofless nave belonging to a vast ruined fourteenth-century abbey near the Suffolk coast. When M. R. James came to this place to collect information for the quirky history he was writing, and maybe about ghosts, he found pigs in the sanctuary, hay in the lady chapel, sheep in the frater, a horse in the chapter house and muck everywhere. He had found, in fact, a temple turned farm, and it disturbed him greatly. Although why it should have done, I don't know. It strikes me that animals and corn may as well fill an abandoned shrine as some worldly rich local family and its descendants, which was frequently the case.

But now, after four hundred years, there was reversal, which was why we were there. Mop-headed scaffolders from the Department of the Environment were at the stage of restituting all that could be restituted. We talked about the Quietists whilst they rode past the windows on their motorised trollies, trundling along with child-like glee from cloister to dorter over the official grass. Creating, destroying, shoring-up, restoring, it was all employment. That is what they said in the nearby villages when the government decided to site a nuclear reactor at Sizewell – it was all work. When Henry ordered the abbey's destruction, their ancestors would have said, yes, well, but there will be plenty of jobs. For a season, for this proper time.

The abbey had been built by the Premonstratensians, a tough, white-robed brotherhood whose name means 'a meadow shown'. Watching all the activity outside the cosy farmhouse room, I consider the paradox of an efficient government department showing a perfectly mown little 'meadow' in each of the roofless interiors of the Premonstratensians' old home. Later, there is the drive back through the sun-dried lanes bordered with remnant blooms, muddy yarrow and mats of chickweed. The little towns I pass through are as bright as June and the sun contradicts their tinsel. I try not to remember too exactly what I had been saying in the abbey. Too much? Too little? The next morning having read with care – 'dilligence', as the old instruction puts it – the entire sequence of devotions which Cranmer and others set in solemn motion for Advent, I decide that I may have done fairly well. The style of these words about the Coming is brilliant and their meaning quite devastatingly plain.

The atmosphere of this waiting-for-something-to-happen time runs parallel with the low-ebbed life outside, though the winter corn is up and in front of the house there is quite a blaze of charlock and gold-of-pleasure. Down the hill, holly wreaths are being laid in the churchyard. There will be one on Peter's grave, to contain him in the Christmas. He was only about thirty when he died, although it was 'natural', they said. He had made me a sawing-horse only a month before and it didn't seem a bit natural still to see his boot-prints in the earth where it stood. As he was buried on the twenty-fourth, when the church had been decorated, his coffin had to share space in the chancel with a Christmas-tree. 'I've got a cold coming on,' he had said.

People have grown secretive about the holly trees because of the town 'sharks', but generous boughs always appear in the church about six hours before the midnight communion. Hollies take a long time to grow and there is an old forest a few miles away where they are as huge as oaks, and where the part-petrified oaks themselves are as old as the Reformation. The forest is called a thick, and it is one of the traditional sites where King Edmund was said to have been murdered, shot full of arrows, at exactly the same age as Peter was when he died, to become England's St Sebastian. In this ancient thick the low ebb has extended itself until it now covers the entire year. Apart from a pheasant shout or two, the only sound is of cracking limbs as the vast half-perished trees shift and settle. We take our holly from the field hedges around the village, where it was usually planted to make a ploughing marker or to indicate a drain. When the farmers do their drastic modern hedging, if you can call it by a name which used to mean a great craft, it is rare for them to demolish a holly tree.

Nearly everybody is frantically busy and there is no sign at all of that other preparedness which all the Advent poets and liturgists so urgently insist upon. We may all be getting ready for a birthday, but not for the Coming. The enchantment of what is about to happen is what preoccupies us, not the awesomeness. Food is what is on everybody's mind. 'Button sprouts' are eyed in the garden, turkeys are picked up from farms and butchers. But Suffolk ham, once ordinary enough if delicious beyond compare, seems to be all in Fortnum's and not here for the likes of us, who invented it. There are boasts of almost flourlessly rich cakes and puddings. Most of the smart new recipe books have been thrust aside and the old basic kitchen lore restored to its trustworthy place. As to Christmas Day itself, it bridles with the old family feeling.

How often I have walked 'the street' at that most sated hour of the year, four p.m. on December the 25th, and marvelled why some family-packed cottage did not explode from all this compressed blood-relationship and ritualised duty and food. The flocking home of the brood from distant estates, schools, colleges, jobs, regiments and vague addresses. All these returns create a curious and distinctive atmosphere in the village which is very noticeable at the pub, in church, at the meet and Boxing Day football, and local parties. The custom of walking it off seems to have vanished, and it makes me feel virtuous and adventurous to be alone, outside, cold; beyond the feast, as it were. When I was a boy, dozens of complete families walked it off, flaunting their kinship and strength. There are frozen stains on the lane made by discreet lorries which weekly deliver straw soaked in horse urine from Knightsbridge Barracks to our mushroom factory on the old World War Two aerodrome.

Back at the house I walk into a scene which has little to date it. Small, typical East Suffolk fields screened by elms, and icy here and there with spreading ponds. It is what I see every early morning from my upstairs desk. Daily, I observe it all emerging from the night, moving phosphorescent islands which are my neighbours' sheep, rooks like squawking rags high in the trees and all facing the same direction, lapwings and gulls. There are roses in bloom. Lear said, 'At Christmas I no more desire a rose than wish a snow in May', but he would have to put up with them at Debach, where it is probable that there is never a week in the year when they are wholly absent. I visit the toppling bramley in whose seamy bark I tucked last Christmas's mistletoe seeds. Nothing. Mistletoe is usually unisexual and so could be capricious. Its name means 'missel-twig', but as basil was also called missel at one time, one soon comes to a philological halt. Suffice to say that it was once the village custom to call all the festival plants simply 'the Christmas'.

Working as a writer in the depths of the country is popularly imagined a protected existence. In fact, it is the opposite. The cruelties and idiocies of the world are neither held off by virtue of some kind of impregnable natural innocence, nor does the immutable process of the agricultural year create a fatalism which prevents one struggling along the common, non-seasonal track of the age. But the myth remains and is nourished by poet and advertiser. *O fortunatos nimium, sua si bona norint, Agricolas! Quibus ipsa procul discordibus armis* – 'How blest beyond all blessings are farmers, if they but knew their happiness! Far from the clash of arms!' – wrote Virgil.

Not so any more. Not so most decidedly in tiny, ancient Debach with its ghostly nineteen-forties aerodrome only a minute or so away from a nuclear base. Already, this fragment of Bomber Harris's empire is as remote as a landau is from a Peugeot in comparison. FitzGerald painted some water colours of the lanes and cottages which our old aerodrome flattened off the map, and since he composed on the hoof, as it were, as did so many English poets in the nineteenth century, I have easily imagined him tramping across these table-level fields which are now ruled by buckled runways when the brave Music of a *distant* Drum occurred to him. Virgil's clash of arms or Fitz's faraway drum-roll – what toy sounds these are when set against that ultimate in military din with which farm and farmer will vanish for evermore.

Some of those who are in charge of this final enormity attended our carol service at the beginning of the week, Christmassy-eyed Americans accompanied by their families. Young people from 'all round' have come in carloads to sing medieval lyrics to settings by Ord and Willcocks. The music has been brought back from the dead, as it were, in folk song and archival rescue operations, although this is not a modern triumph. Luther himself preserved the life of *In Dulci Jubilo*. There is an equality about the songs of Christmas. Berlioz's sumptuous

'Shepherds' Farewell' makes no attempt to outdo some banal guitar-led ditty but lends it place. 'Once in Royal David's City' defies all criticism and shakes the collective emotion. Cecil Alexander wrote it in 1848, when she was twenty-five, and it presides as ballad-hymn extraordinary. It pours through the architecture like a river and out over the frosty hummocks in the churchyard and the path which has become such a climb because centuries of those fortunate farmers have been dug into it, their dust raising it up.

Roads to Debach

Living at the conjunction of the Suffolk light and heavy lands gives everything an extra edge. To the north-west stretches 'the old clay' itself, life-providing and death-reminding. To the south-east lie the sandlings and the sea. The soils do not mix to form some kind of moderate intermediate territory but remain sharply defined. It is one land or the other. You know where you are. What you can do is to journey to what is virtually another country in thirty minutes. In this brief time every ecological thing changes, oak to pine, hawthorn to broom, arable to marsh, hills to flats. The sandlings are a subtle shading-off of all that is emphatic in landscape, a series of earth and water abstractions which, just beyond those walled villages which border The Wash, reach some ultimate of geographical indefinition.

The old clay, on the other hand, never ceases to shout its hard-line reality. It is the ancient forest bed over whose bumpy surface the first ploughs rode after the defeat of the trees. The farms were once locked in scrubby woods or approached through glades; now they lie exposed for miles. To confound matters further, since the 1920s the Forestry Commission has roofed in huge tracts of the old open country with conifers, so that acres of the sandlings have lost their wild candour and have grown dark and secretive.

Mercifully, the Suffolk and Norfolk heaths are still such a complex mixture of social and physical forces that the larch and pine regiments will never be able to march all over them. So one can relax in the sand gardens of Snape and feel comparatively safe. And even pit-props must hesitate when they come up against the peach orchards of Iken. But the marvellous Breckland can never be the same again, and it is moving to recall that East Anglia's unique moor survived unchanged and unchecked from prehistoric days to just after the First World War. An order nominating a similarly ancient landscape all along the Suffolk coast arrived just in time a decade or so ago to save the sandlings from such a fate. Science farming, block afforestation, NATO installations and now a proposed second nuclear reactor at lonely Sizewell, like the hosts of Gideon, are on the prowl all the same.

Winter reveals vivid contrasts between the water patterns of the two lands. On the sandlings they are anarchic, spilling over for miles beyond the estuarial limits and flooding the shallow valleys of the Stour, Orwell, Deben, Alde and Blyth. Thin bright lakes spread themselves with colourless deliberation round the traditional defences. On the heavy land the water is disciplined by medieval utility measures. Few in these days of mains could guess at the number of splendid moats, wells and ponds which still exist in fine working order the county over. There is not a hamlet which cannot boast something extraordinary by way of catchment. Such a variety of quiet, trapped waters, few of them to be seen until one has almost tumbled into them, has multiplied the mallard population. The field ditches alone still remain workaday, churning incredible amounts of Tiber-yellow liquid along icy cuts a few feet below the corn. The sound of all this half-hidden water is the voice of our arable winter. No babbling brook but 'a cry of Absence, Absence, in the heart, and in the wood the furious winter blowing . . .' Except that in East Anglia the blowing tends to arrive with the spring. It is no wonder that the oldest man-made structure in Suffolk – according to M. R. James – is a wind shelter near Ipswich. Who could argue this?

One road from my house near Woodbridge begins with surprisingly Persian references. It is the land which Edward FitzGerald walked every time he went to sea, which was as often as he could. It drifts along pleasantly past his family's Home Farm, their park, their coverts and past the poet's grave, which is lush in summer with quaking grass, ox-eyed daisies and the roses which the late Shah sent all the way from Omar's tomb. Past too, on the left, the rectory once inhabited by George Crabbe's son and the path which Fitz took many an evening to smoke a pipe with him. And so, in a matter of four miles, one encompasses Suffolk: the Plain Facts and Suffolk: the Transcendental. Then comes the Deben and a quite different climate.

Sparseness, freedom, the view running away to the palest of land markings and then into the illimitable. To the south a few small humps can be seen. These are Sutton Hoo, the graveyard of the Anglo-Saxon kings. This is where they pulled their funeral ships out of the river and buried them shallowly among the faint evidence of an Iron Age settlement. Domestic hearths and princely ashes. The hole left by that tremendous haul of gold and garnets, harp, mystic standard and banqueting silver is now the merest ghost of a boat and could be taken for a gravel scratching. But for years after it had been archeologically looted it held the full imprint of sand prow, sand ribs, sand keel and a profound impression of its sandy destination.

Arrow-straight roads lead to the sea from here. In summer the unhedged fields dry to dust and drift across the lanes. In January their sheer featurelessness establishes a great calm. Here is a country which specialises in renewal; there is space in it for action. Anyway, it is far too cold to sit about. Old Suffolk people say 'I fare to be all right if I keep on the goo.' Soon the North Sea strikes across our consciousness from just below a natural flint barrier called Shingle Street. It is intriguing to come to Shingle Street in the hot weather and to find it apparently deserted, and then to plunge along this huge shifting stone wall and stare down on the holiday-makers, each bare shape fitted into its flint matrix and each face turned to the horizon and the precise departures of the Harwich-Hook line.

Stones in such quantities and diversity are mesmerising. The sea-pea which so curiously thrives on them is said to have saved the local people from starvation during a famine long ago. They pay it respect. Apart from the beautiful grey-stemmed sea-poppy, the most delightful flower on this spartan coast is the rare *Vicia lutea*, the vetch whose pale yellow petals light the beach just where it begins to gather soil. Bracken and wild mignonette spread along the sea path. Marsh harriers and gulls swoop across military litter left over from old scares, Martello towers and concrete machine-gun nests. FitzGerald liked to hug his boat, the *Scandal*, along the shore here and was certainly happier than he has since been imagined. But another poet, Alun Lewis, stationed here during the last war, found its bleakness more than he could bear:

> From Orford Ness to Shingle Street
> The grey disturbance lifts its head
> And one by one, reluctantly,
> The living come back slowly from the dead.

There is another subtly indefinite area of Suffolk which I sporadically attempt to explore, and this is the one which lurks among the more comprehensible wonders of the famous local architecture. Not perp and dec but the all but rubbed from history creatures, human and divine, which they housed. A holy romance world, in its way, in which Felix, Gobban, Dicuil, Fursey, Foillan, Mindred (whose well at Newmarket is now in the possession of the Jockey Club), the Pied, White, Grey and Black friars, Tobias, Sir John Shorne (a medieval Dr Scholl who conjured the devil from a boot), Edmund, of course, Apollonia, cherubyn, sarafyn, potestate, principatus, Michael Arkeangelus *et al*, still faintly crowd. And a prevalence of painted St Christophers on north walls, with carp and pike gliding around their naked legs, could indicate that wateriness was a common feature met with by generations of travellers crossing England's driest county.

Reading
Other People's Diaries

There was once a group of poets which William Aytoun dubbed the 'Spasmodic School' on account of its intermittent bursts of creativity, and if there happened to be a similar school for a certain type of diarist, then I should belong to it. My diary-keeping comes into the New Year's resolution, brief Lenten resolve, temporary cutting-down on this or that class of activity, and is no more than a sincere but short-lived attempt to do what I feel I should do. The true diarist never writes against the grain of his own inclination, but rushes along with it. He is pulled to the daily page, however late the hour. The one thing of which I have never had any doubt is that when I am reading a diary I am able to feel the relief of the diarist as he settles to his task. Anyone reading my broken fragments would feel at once that I had been driven to write them by forces that were a compound of duty and experiment. No pleasure there in my own dailiness, only a pronounced struggle to set it all down. All the same, I am addicted to what the natural diarist sets down and have, over the years, read an enormous quantity of, 'January 7th. Took Edward to the station. Returned home the back way and saw the sea through the bare wood . . .' and so on for thirty or forty years. Sometimes it is the full works and no holds barred, sometimes it is nothing very much at all, yet still I read on. It is April 1878 and there is late snow and Mr Williams has called . . . It is enough.

All-out or discreet, natural diarists exhibit the pathetic principle to a naked degree, and even Parson Woodforde isn't quite hidden behind his food mountain. The only diaries I can't read are those by British and American politicians and militarists. So much consciously and artfully putting the record straight puts me off, this and the sound of man-oeuvres for outsize publishers' advances. Although the natural diarist would seem to write for himself alone, and even in some instances – Pepys, Beatrix Potter – invents codes to ensure that posterity will not alter this personal condition, there is something very strange in telling oneself everything that one did and is. Vanity? Taken all in all, vanity is at a low ebb in diaries. Natural diarists are compulsively self-staring, self-prying, self-explaining and self-presenting, but without being actually narcissistic. Self-bragging occasionally (Boswell) but rarely self-enamoured. The opposite, in fact. Evelyn Waugh's diary is thick with self-disgust. But whether a diarist is in the 'dead secret' category or simply a person who is compelled to put his day down before he sleeps, oblivious to such considerations as for whose eyes or for what purpose, there is little doubt that diary writing has much to do with turning what is transitory into what is permanent. Without a diary, our talk and actions, and our dreams and current notions, slide down a shute into a vague experience labelled 'last Summer' or 'when I was twenty-four' or 'in the office' or an address or 'work'. *In* a diary everything is held – the verb reflects a safekeeping and a security – in place and in sequence. It is holding in place of the detail of life which makes diaries so riveting.

Here are a few favourite diarists. First that of the boy King Edward VI, which he kept from March 1549 to his death at sixteen. I never read this without feeling as though the Reformation air is raising the leaves in the garden below. Among English monarchs, only Edward and Victoria kept diaries which have been published. Hers is a masterpiece of its kind, his stiff, bright and sharp, like a pennon. All in his own hand, it proclaims most eloquently the precocious education which he, his sister Elizabeth, Lady Jane Grey and similarly learned high-born children received in the sixteenth century. The tone of Edward's diary is part innocent and part rather overwhelming. The King's Highnesse in these edgy pages is never the sickly majesty of history. A contemporary commenting on a poem which Edward had written said, 'This young Prince became a perfect schoole-maister unto old erroneous men,' and after reading the diary one can believe it. It is not the work of a runtish interruption of the succession list. *I* was here, *I* was king, it proclaims, as intelligently and promisingly as Elizabeth herself. A child of his time, he describes with equanimity a hideous glimpse of the festivities surround-ing the nuptials of Robert Dudley, his sister's future lover, and Amy Robsart. A goose has been strung-up to make a fluttering, difficult target. It is June 1550 and the diarist is thirteen.

Sir Robert Dudley, third sonne to th'erle of Warwic, maried sir John Robsartes daughter, after wich mariage there were certain gentlemen that did strive who shuld take away a gose's heade, which was hanged alive on two crose postes. Ther was tilt and tornay on foot with as great staves as they run withal on horsbake.

When it comes to the execution of his uncles, Edward is as casual as the White Queen, and glacial in his account of how the members of his first council grabbed great titles for themselves.

I think that the first youthful diary I read was Denton Welch's. Although thirty-three when he died, there is a fretful quality in Welch's *Journals*, due to illness and pain, and a kind of thudding reality which was constantly informing the writer of a death sentence, which has always made him seem perpetually late-adolescent. Or as if time had stopped for him, as with a fine watch crushed by a car, on the day of his accident, 7 June 1935. A woman driver had knocked him off his bicycle and there had been a terrible fracturing of his lower spine, with subsequent constant bleeding, tuberculosis and agony. It was not that he projected himself back to the years before this disaster, when his body was perfect, but that, by some inner strength of will, and by using art and literature as preserving agents, he was able to bring forward much of the poise of his healthy, uninjured being of the pre-1935 period to enable him to lead what was a remarkable literary and social life by any standards, crippled though he was. And then there was the war, and Welch's unique position as a badly wounded young writer whose injuries had nothing to do with the fighting or the bombing, and yet whose work became a correct part of the anti-heroic literature of the hour. Thus it was that Maurice Denton Welch, born in Shanghai in 1915, the year of the Battle of Mons, became an authentic voice of the Second World War and indeed became a cult almost during the late 1940s.

Everything about him focussed an extreme attention. He in his turn seemed to understand this and to accept its implications, although he occasionally defended himself with a kind of malice, or appeared ingenuously incapable of knowing what it was that made people write to him or to try and seek him out. 'I keep on wondering if I'm producing semi-demi AE Housman', he wrote in his *Journal*. Certainly the two generations which had responded to Housman (and Forster) would be practised in reading between the lines. The peculiarly English climate which raises art and moral courage from such disparate ingredients as hyper-sensitivity, bourgeois cultural standards and homosexual love was familiar enough, but Welch added an irresistible – at the time – quality to it.

Perhaps the best-known photograph of him can partly explain his fascination. It shows a young man seated at a chequer-board on which are arranged a pretty monstrance, three candles burning in cut-glass holders and a patch-box, or maybe a counter-box. Behind him swirls a detail from a large painting, a bare arm thrusting its way out of the surrounding chiaroscuro. The young man wears an open-necked shirt with the collar turned up. His arms rest on the board and his face, mask-like in the candlelight, is nervous and tense. It is the face of the perennial sick poet, and the candles with their short butts and tall flames tell one that his days are numbered. For those who felt his spell, there was no effeteness in the portrait, simply brilliance and doom. In fact, as a recent critic has pointed out, in the classic pathos of genius being allowed only a brief life to give of itself, 'we touch upon one of the most potent, and seductive factors in the whole Denton Welch case. His life as such forms an almost irresistible paradigm of what Mario Praz labelled the Romantic Agony – a desperate creative race against time.' Cyril Connolly placed him with Katherine Mansfield and Barbellion. Pain excused this category of writers their preoccupation with either the minutiae of their introspection or their possessions. When Denton Welch wrote preciously about his bric-à-brac he was given a mandate for doing so which was outside that given to other writers of the period. His obsessive descriptions of healthy soldiers and farm workers, usually stripping to wash or swim, appeared neither wholly self-indulgent nor silly, but oddly elegiac. Both they and the toys with which Welch surrounded himself, the class-consciousness and the banishment of all politics and wider social issues, were all part of a 'civilised structure' whose standards were well known and admired during the Forties.

Welch wrote and drew (and still rode his bicycle) through the decade and through increasing pain. At one time he considered suicide and went so far as destroying some of his diaries. Those that remain begin with a bounce:

10 July, Friday
And then we all met at Penshurst; I and Maurice and Filthy Freddie, RAF. And

first we had tea (I found them waiting for me with scones and butter on the table, when I came in from the rain) . . .

One of the things which had brought him in from the rain, as it were, had been an enthusiastic acceptance by Connolly of Welch's article on Sickert. '. . . Being ill made me think of being great and famous. They are always linked together in my mind. I must not be so ill that I cannot be famous.' Now that he had begun to be published all the things which had wrecked his boyhood, his loathing of Repton, from which he had run away at sixteen, his chilly family life, and even the accident itself, retreated. 'Now that is all gone. Broken away, lost and forgotten.' Curiously enough, the war atmosphere actually helped Welch, who was the kind of man, as Jocelyn Brooke said, who would hardly have found life easy in any circumstances. It left him isolated. Besides, others were soon to die as well as he.

Airmen flashed by on bicycles. They all wore that intent look of people who are grimly determined to enjoy themselves for their few free hours from slavery. It's an almost fanatical look. The anxious eyes seem to say, I *must* drink, copulate or what you will. I must, I must, I must, or I am nothing and my leave is wasted. O tomorrow and tomorrow and tomorrow; they'll all pile up until I die.

Unexpectedly, since it is preoccupied with the restoration of dolls' houses, kissing brass crusaders, picnics with ducks' eggs and cherry jam, and elaborate little treats and outings of all kinds, his *Journal* contains the very flavour of the war and its aftermath. Victory Day actually presented problems. Welch captures its peculiar ennui:

11 June, Tuesday. 10.15 pm
On Saturday, the Victory Celebration night, Eric suddenly suggested that we should go out to see the beacons and bonfires.

We had just heard that Evie had lost her job in Cornwall and might be coming back to us, and the upset had made us restless.

We drove in the car through the dark up the hill to Plaxtol, and there was a fire in the grounds of Fairlawne, huge, sullen, flat to the ground, with great boughs crumbling. A few people were gathered round it, staring into the flames, and some boys on a bench were singing sadly 'Oh my darling Clementine'. They were nervous of their voices, joking about them. The people stared, there was a great weight of emptiness. I felt that everybody was shamefaced and deadened – dumb, watching, waiting-for-death people.

We went on to Shipbourne Common and there was another larger bonfire with even fewer people about it. From the 'New Inn', several hundred yards away, the most extraordinary jig and blur of music was coming – demoniac in its clanging smashing smudge with the crooner's whisper frighteningly magnified.

Over the long bending grass it ran, through the blackness. It was sadder and more damned than a black monkey or a man in a stone cell clawing at the bars. The great voice was mourning and jigging and weeping all over the world. The blurs and atmospherics were like stabbing sparks. Eric and I watched the flames and the black shapes of the children running against them. There was a moping man too, who seemed to be searching in the grass, shoulders hunched, head sunk.

When rolls and plumes of sparks swept up out of the fire, then showered themselves down on the moping man and the dancing children, it was a medieval devil scene. The loud mechanical wailing, the sullen torpor, the life of the flames were all part of a hell picture.

When we drove on past the 'New Inn', we saw coloured umbrellas, drinkers and singers on the flood-lit grass. It was the only pub that had seemed gay. But its gaiety was like the deafening voice; merciless, made of tin, and mad.

I thought the whole night scene was a gaunt display of desperate failure. The people, for so short a time on the earth, watching their lives' hopelessness, as they stared into the flames . . .

During 1948, the year of his death, the snugness which the war had perversely allowed had quite gone and Welch no longer minded. Instead, the success of his books and the remarkable reputation he had made in such a short time caused him a great longing to be out in the world. It came over him suddenly 'that my life is really too limited to bear . . . Frustration like this has never come to me before. There is so much sensible, obvious reason for feeling it that I am made helpless . . . There should be many new words for what I mean, words that don't whine and pity.' On 10 August he wrote, 'Death seems so far away; it recedes and becomes more and more impossible as one grows iller.' Three weeks later he added his last entry, a very long one about a visit to Sissinghurst – 'Taste which is not one's own is a sort of holiday'. The last unfinished sentence reads, 'Even now, as I write, I . . .' He died on 30 December, all his energy during the final few weeks going into completing a novel called *A Voice Through a Cloud*.

Denton Welch wrote his diary in nineteen ordinary school exercise books, and in an old-fashioned schoolboyish script. He wrote quickly and did not correct. 'In Gide's Journal I have just read again how he does not wish to write his pages slowly as he would the pages of a novel . . . It is just what I have always felt about this journal of mine. Don't ponder, don't grope . . .'

No one can read Samuel Johnson's diary without pity, for here, most humbly set out, is the pathology of a virtuous and brilliant man. The famous definition in his *Dictionary* that a diary should be 'an account of the transactions, accidents, and observations of every day; a journal' implies something less profound than that which he made stabs at with his pen after his day's toil or sloth. But no one heeded the advice he gave to friends more when he urged them to keep diaries in which 'the great thing to be recorded is the state of your mind'. Pre-eminently and tragically, Johnson's diary is the troubled record of a troubled state of mind. 'A man loves to review his own mind', he would say. But did he? Could he? If so, it was a penitential love. He wrote his diary in order to learn from his own experiences, to become reconciled to the disparity between his discoveries and his hopes, as he told Boswell, and he also wrote it in what he believed was the full view of the eye of God. The result is awesome, and at the same time childishly intimate, like a Cowper hymn. He can never accept himself. He can never say, I am the kind of man who can't get up in the morning and who likes drink and women. These things weigh him down to such a degree that he can no longer see the eminence of his natural goodness and gifts. As the years pass and we find him still making New Year's resolutions, 'To rise early, to lose no time', etc, and we know by many confessions such as, 'I do not remember that since I left Oxford I ever rose early by mere choice, but . . . two or three times for the *Rambler*', we marvel at this inability to take himself as he is. And his guilt is terrible. 'I have now spent fifty years in resolving, having from the earliest time almost that I can remember been forming schemes of a better life. I have done nothing . . .'

It was not true, of course. Johnson's diary, though episodic and incomplete, reveals a great deal of activity. It is in one respect a stern and powerful meditation on the progress of the orthodox Anglican soul. In other ways it is a key to work in progress and a record of morbidity. Only now and then, as in the delightful account of his visit to France, does he actually spread himself in full and elaborate description. Eventually, with a horror unequalled by anything to be found in any other diary, Johnson moves from his habitual hypochondria into a monstrous medical account of his cumbersome journey to the grave, writing it chiefly in Latin and setting down all the pain and emotion of one who lies 'under dread of death'. Johnson's modern editors, in the Yale edition of his works, comment on the surprising fact that in August 1774 Johnson reveals that he had been reading Robert Southwell, the thirty-four-year-old poet-priest who was executed in 1595, and a writer practically unknown in the eighteenth century. Southwell had written,

> Before my face the picture hangs,
>   That daily should put me in mind,
> Of those cold names and bitter pangs,
>   That shortly I am like to find:
> But yet alas full little I
> Do thinke here on that I must die.

Like Southwell, like all men, Johnson finds it hard to contemplate his own death. His Christian faith seems to have simply intensified his terror of mortality. The diary shows a devout man with a graveyard view of the end which he longs to correct but cannot. Throughout his life he was depressed by his failure to achieve spiritual transcendence. On 21 April 1764, when he was sixty-eight, he wrote:

My indolence, since my last reception of the Sacrament, has sunk into gross sluggishness, and my dissipation spread into wilder negligence. My thoughts have been clouded with sensuality, and, except that from the beginning of this year I have in some measure forborn excess of Strong Drink my appetites have predominated over my reason. A kind of strange oblivion has overspread me, so that I know not what has become of the last year, and perceive incidents and intelligence pass over me without leaving any impression ... This is not the life to which Heaven is promised.

But whatever the depth of his melancholic despair, nothing finally unsettled the majestic balance of Johnson's mind and it is his sanity and honesty which causes the reader's heart to go out to him in his predicament.

The diary also contains a moving tribute to 'dear poor Tetty', the middle-aged widow whom Johnson had married when he was only twenty-seven and whom he loved most tenderly until her death in 1752 in spite of her addiction to drink and drugs, and much evidence of incompatibility in their two personalities. The entries concerning her memory are a study in remorse, but only thirteen months after her death, whilst on a pilgrimage to her grave at Bromley, he couples a wonderful commendation of her to God with the news that he is thinking of marrying again – a fact which Boswell suppressed in his *Life*.

Apr 23. Easter Monday. Yesterday as I purposed I went to Bromley where dear Tetty lies buried & received the sacrament, first praying before I went to the altar according to the prayer precomposed for Tetty and a prayer which I made against unchastity, idleness, & neglect of publick worship. I made it during a sermon which I could not perfectly hear. I repeated mentally the commendation of her with the utmost fervour *larme à l'oeil* before the reception of each element at the altar. I repeated it again in the pew, in the garden before dinner, in the garden before departure, at home at night. I hope I did not sin. *Fluunt lacrymae.* I likewise ardently applied to her the prayer for the Church militant where the dead are mentioned and commended her gain to Eternal Mercy, as in coming I approached her grave. During the whole service I was never once distracted by any thoughts of any other woman or with my design of a new wife which freedom of mind I remembered in the Garden. God guide me.

Eighteen years later he is still mourning her, wishing that when he saw the sea at Brighton she could have seen it with him and making his self-reforming resolutions over her name as others might do at a shrine. He constantly wonders what 'she would have said or done' and ten years later, while at the Palais Bourbon, he is once more regretting that Tetty was not with him to share its wonders. His love for her was frankly unbelievable to many of his acquaintances, and Garrick's cruel but probably truthful picture of her as 'very fat, with a bosom of more than ordinary protuberance, with swelled cheeks of a florid red, produced by thick painting, and increased by the liberal use of cordials; flaring and fantastic in her dress, and affected both in her speech and her general behaviour' made Johnson's lifelong sorrow at her death scarcely credible. Yet the diary exposes a real and poignant love, and a grief quite outside conventional mourning. The fact that she died about Easter became intertwined with his religious concept of renewal, and as time passed, Tetty, who had proved almost impossible to live with, became for Johnson an advocate in heaven. The older he got, the more he sensed their marriage to have had scandalous attributes for which they were equally to blame. Thirty years after he had buried her in the churchyard at Bromley he wrote, 'On what we did amiss, and our faults were great, I have thought of late with more regret than at any former time. She was I think very penitent. May God accept her repentance:

may he accept mine' and that night he suffered 'a night of great disturbance and solicitude, such as I do not remember.'

Johnson's diary is a dignified confessional in which the frailties of both body and soul are set down with great severity. The judgement of posterity is that the Doctor was too hard on himself. His practical kindness alone makes him a remarkable figure, for his philanthropy was not one of the adding his name to cheques and petitions sort, but belonged to that rarer category which puts up with lifelong difficulty and inconvenience because of its need to exercise love towards its fellow creatures. Boswell found it hard to stay in the same room whilst Mrs Williams fed. She was blind and ate with her fingers but, as Tetty's old friend, Johnson took her into his house and looked after her until the end. And he treated his black servant with the total affection and dignity which a good father would treat a son. He was profoundly religious, but Christianity appeared to afflict him more with fear than with joy, acerbating his highly-developed sense of guilt and enveloping him in worry. Also, throughout his days he was burdened with disease, badly disfigured even in the eyes of his contemporaries, accustomed as they were to physical ruin. It is little wonder that *The Anatomy of Melancholy* should be the only book that – according to Boswell – 'ever took him out of bed two hours sooner than he wished to rise'. So his diary is the account of the inner life of a great depressive and, as it unwinds in phrases of ponderous Augustan solemnity, the acute difference between the grand language and the privacy it describes is deeply affecting. It is little wonder that to those who knew him Johnson was like a modern Socrates in the Strand and the touchstone of all debate. That he himself frequently hated this role is revealed in those comic instances when he 'roared them off', as it were, Boswell often getting a goring for going too far, or coming too close. But if ever doubts about the essential humility and goodness of the Doctor should arise they are at once corrected by seeing his sad diary.

Some of Johnson's diaries were used by Boswell, two large quartos of them were burnt by the doctor just before his death, and others only came to light among the vast haul of papers discovered at Malahide Castle just before the last war. While staying with Johnson on 5 May 1776, Boswell managed to copy some of the large diary which Johnson was later to destroy. Two diaries, that describing Johnson's visit to

Wales in the summer of 1774 and his visit to France the following year, are filled out with descriptions, the Welsh diary so much so that the editors of the Yale edition of *Diaries, Prayers, Annals* believe that it might have been the intention to write a companion work to *Journey to the Western Islands*. Otherwise, in many respects, Dr Johnson's daily record is terse, full of gaps and fragmentary. In 1783 he had a stroke and began to send Mrs Thrale a day-to-day account begging her to 'forgive the gross images which disease must necessarily present. Dr Laurence said that medical treatises should always be in Latin.' And on 6 July Johnson began his 'Sick Man's Journal', the solemn description of his own dissolution, writing it in Latin and maintaining it to the last detail until within a month or so of his death on 13 December 1784. He prepared methodically for this, burning his papers, sending his works to Pembroke College, arranging to have all the prayers he had composed published by a clergyman friend, George Strahan, and making his will. The 'Sick Man's Journal' is a mixture of savage self-doctoring and heroism in the face of physical misery. It reminds one of how heartfelt were those prayers for an 'easy end' made by those who lived before the age of pain-killers and trustworthy sedatives.

A very different Johnson was William Johnson, an Eton master and author of the famous *Boating Song*, who maintained that he kept a diary during the school holidays for the benefit of 'about three readers'. He was correct when he called it 'a genuine, original book' but revealed more a lack of confidence than a pompous nineteenth-century morality when he described his activity as 'more wholesome than cooking novels'. That he should have, in the creative sense, cooked a great deal more than the faintly teasing fragments which have come down to us is all too plain. Friends must have said, 'You should write', immediately recognising Johnson's literary nature, and maybe its suppression, for every now and then, both in his journal and his letters, he gives defensive reasons for not doing so.

He began to write his holiday journal during the summer of 1863, beginning it with the strange statement, 'I am halfway through a long vacation, which may be my last'. He had taught at Eton for eighteen of his forty years and been a pupil at the school before this. It is true that at the start the barbarity of the school filled him with despair and that sometimes he would turn from trying to keep 'my mob in a state of quiet attentiveness when their blood is warm' to watch 'the plasterers and carpenters now working here, and envy them their weekly wages; for all my shoutings and questionings and mortifications, and all the ill-will I have to contract by punishing, I have not received a farthing.' The medieval chapel was being renovated in the midst of the uproar. Johnson battled with the disorder, noting with emotions which he himself called complex that the individual pupils who responded to his teaching were 'as virtuous as men, without men's pride and knowingness, as interesting as women, without women's timorousness and artifice'.

It had been saying goodbye to these favourites of the 1863 class which had temporarily decided him to give up teaching, not the earlier rowdyism. It was all too heart-breaking. One had no sooner acquired the perfect circle of friends and the most useful degree of discipleship than the whole thing was broken up by Oxford or the army. He felt that 'age has for youth a natural priesthood'. The creed he taught contained a nervous Hellenism and a kind of patrician freedom. Then, wherever they might happen to be in the future, in Anglican rectories or in politics, or worshipping 'the Union Jack in those famous but fetid towns of the gorgeous East', their duty was *Ephphatha* – 'utter thyself', 'cast thy bread upon the waters'. Johnson was reserved at first in showing that he intended to maintain a priestly role towards special pupils but later, convinced that his vocation was to transmit exciting and radical ideas to people who would one day form a new kind of aristocracy, he grew more reckless. 'I don't mind flooding you with this transcendental stuff about boys: you know it has been for a quarter of a century characteristic of me, and it is no use to *vieillize* . . .,' he wrote to a friend.

But in 1863, when the special friendships had become so important that Johnson could not bear to relinquish them even for the winter and summer hols, thus maintaining contact by his journal, he was less easy. Could it have been his activities as 'guerillero' within the education system were attracting crossfire, or was it simply that letters like the following told the full tale?

. . . he was always ready and glad to come to me, lunch, dine, breakfast, tea, sup, walk, drive with me: he was my comforter when I was ill (in Cambridge) nearly three years ago. When he left school I gave him all the volumes then published of the Cambridge Shakespeare, in perfect binding . . . His face in a dozen forms is with me; his innocent, rich, infantine voice, unchanged for fourteen happy years, is with me: I miss him still, though busy and not friendless.

It was to be a bereavement oft repeated, particularly during the summer.

I told M. to-night that tragic heartrending story of the two brothers who crossed and met and touched hands in the dark, going by train across Egypt, the one to India, the other from India, after years of separation. No Greek, no Arab could imagine the heroic flush and throb of such an exchange of Christian names in the midnight. Will they in ages to come say of us, 'Those poor Englishmen whom Newman stirred so deeply could not conceive our emotions? Love and part. Is it for this we are made? Strain tight then, whilst you may yet embrace, poor mortals . . .'

A few months before he started keeping his holiday diary, Johnson was in Torquay, his head full of ideas about his duty to help create a marvellous band of individuals worthy to serve imperial England, and about Eton. Reading Edwin Arnold's *Dalhousie's Administration*, a description of how one man had brought about speedy and excellent reforms in the Punjab, Johnson regretted that the growing practice of consultation held back natural leaders from getting things done. Lying in bed on the 9th of January, he was unable to get to sleep because of thoughts about the 4th of June. 'A half-humorous, half-sentimental boating song' was 'burning to be written out'. The tunes which ran through his brain as he composed his song were 'Waiting for the Waggon' and 'A Health to the Outward-Bound'. Years later he was still fiddling with it, saying that it lacked fusion and was a failure, and that he was too old for verse. 'The little slender vein is worked out. But I have my readers, like better men . . .' These readers, generations of them, would know William Johnson as William Cory, author of a much-anthologised poem entitled *Heraclitus*, eight unforgettable lines which summed up that mystical permanency which Johnson longed to discover in his close relationships. Like the Greek poet Mimnermus, he intended to fill his elegies with so much love that he would make them amorous instead of mournful. In *Mimnermus in Church* he challenges Christian transcendentalism.

> You say there is no substance here,
> One great reality above:

> Back from that void I shrink in fear,
>   And child-like hide myself in love:
> Show me what angels feel. Till then
> I cling, a mere weak man, to men.

He found the conventional worship in the school chapel increasingly odious and a major element in the destruction of the boys' spiritual nature:

Sunday, July 26. (1868) In desk at 3 p.m. Hateful service. A steaming crowd, a most lugubrious, wearisome anthem. When will this absurd sort of worship come to an end; this holocaust, this human incense, this Moloch-squeezing of innocents?

On 4 April 1872 Johnson left Eton suddenly, and in the October of that year he resigned his Fellowship at King's and changed his name to Cory. He had a little house in Halsdon, Devonshire and he retreated there. The reasons for the transformation are officially opaque. To one of his élite he wrote, 'Now the time is come for thinking where you will go, for I am gone – I have just resigned – "turned out to grass" – writing formal letters till I tire, and now getting a change by writing more at ease to you, whom I love and trust and long to see again . . . I am too sad and ill to write any more.' *Ephphatha*, he tells the master who succeeds him. Don't scold, don't grumble, never be sarcastic, don't be dry, never use a vituperative word like 'idle', tell boys outright what you like and what you hate, what you think about things and make yourself known to the shy and uncouth as well as to the engaging . . . To another of the élite he wrote, 'I have undergone a very strange wounding' . . . 'I go under a tunnel . . .' 'I break my heart every day.'

The tragedy is neither blacked-out nor floodlit. A luminous interest plays over it. Halsdon turns out to be a fine retreat and 'phots' are a rare comfort. They are all over the place, Lyttelton's (in cricket dress), Brett's, Wood's, Luxmoore's, Pollock's – all those beautiful, charming, assured, Victorian proconsular faces. And not only phots but, during the holidays, the still devoted originals, smiling and gay, and happy to accept inscribed copies of *Nuces* or *Iophon*. Johnson/Cory's intention was to direct all that was best in Eton youth to a highly personal form of Whiggery – 'If I were a Tory I should go to bed or to church, as it is I go to work . . .' He abhors what he calls 'kinks' in people. He is often desperate and ever in search of his beloved euphrasy – the mystic flower which clears the mind's eye.

William Cory's own phot shows a pale, rather formidable person. He has big thin ears like the emperor Augustus. Behind the marble brow one can almost hear the struggle between Plato and Christ. He might have made a good university representative, or a tortured don. His literary views were bizarre but somehow reminiscent of the *outré* opinions later to be held by characters in Wilde or Saki. 'Tea is mentioned too often in Turgenev.' 'Young Henry James goes a trifle far in Bret Hartery.' 'Ever since I found Ouida charming in French I fancy French would make me relish . . . Goethe's epigrams or his *Selective Affinities*.' 'As a poet Shakespeare moves me; as a dramatist less. I once saw *Hamlet* acted – I had rather not see it again.' 'I think *Othello* nearly as good as it was possible for anything to be before the human mind had by evolution become capable of *Kenilworth* . . .' Scott indeed is Johnson's hero and a yardstick for measuring everything. His novels are the direct descendant of the *Aeneid* and worth all the Lake poets put together.

On 26 March 1878 Johnson wrote from Madeira to his old friend Warre Cornish, '. . . I may as well now tell you . . . that I have a reasonable expectation of being married. It is a thing I cannot quite justify . . . "A new start" – possibly.' Earlier he had written, 'I am slowly exploring the headlands and bays of that *terra incognita*, girlhood . . .' The girl was the daughter of a Devonshire clergyman, the Reverend George de Carteret Guille. In August she became Mrs William Cory. The following July she gave birth to a son, Andrew. The family lived in Madeira until 1882 and the final decade was weathered at Hampstead. Johnson/ Cory died on 11 June 1892 in his seventieth year and shortly afterwards the group of Eton disciples, most of whom were now key figures in Victoria's establishment, published the holiday journals and letters he had devised for them.

There is a certain kind of diarist who writes with no thought of actual publication but who half hopes that his diary will be found. On 3 November 1874 Francis Kilvert wrote,

Why do I keep this voluminous journal? I can hardly tell. Partly because life appears to me such a curious and wonderful thing that it almost seems a pity that even such a humble and uneventful life as mine should pass altogether away without some such record as this, and partly too because I think the record may amuse and interest some who come after me.

He was thirty-three and the curious and wonderful thing, life, was already near its end. And although Kilvert was just under forty when he died, his marvellous diary is really that of an impassioned youth rather than that of a mature man. Its sensuous vision of nature, Anglicanism and society is not dissimilar to that of John Constable, and Kilvert's shimmering landscapes remind one of Constable's glittering statements of transient light and dewiness. His country is that of the Welsh border, Radnorshire and Herefordshire, and the artless account which Kilvert gives of its perfections and complexities is unequalled. He began his diary in 1870 and ended it abruptly in March 1879, the same month during which he had published an exquisite threnody on a little boy who had died and whom he had buried on the previous Christmas Day. Kilvert had gone to see the dead child, who was the shepherd's son, and had kissed him – 'I had not touched death for more than thirty years' – and in his poem he makes the boy request that the village stream, Clyro Water, should be his remembrancer. On 20 August, Kilvert married. A month later he died suddenly of peritonitis, and was buried within sound of the same stream. His diary was discovered just before the last war and selections from it, edited by William Plomer, were first published between 1938 and 1940. Since then it has become recognised as having a place among the few really great English diaries. Reading it casts an irresistible spell and the freshness of the writing permanently carries the freshness of girls, flowers, meals, games, prayers, creatures and sounds of a village of just a century ago.

Francis Kilvert was born at Hardenhuish, Wiltshire on 3 December 1840, the son of the rector. His father ran a prep school at the rectory and Kilvert was three when the nine-year-old Augustus Hare was admitted to it. Hare's horrific account of his experiences at the hands of Mr Kilvert and his pupils in *The Story of My Life*, his rape by the boys on his first night – 'At nine years old, I was compelled to eat Eve's apple quite up – indeed, the Tree of Knowledge of Good and Evil was stripped absolutely bare; there was no fruit left to gather,' – and the floggings he received from the rector, throws a disconcerting light on the exquisite Christian background to his life which is portrayed by the diarist. William Plomer believed that 'certain peculiarities' of Kilvert's character derived from what he had seen at his father's school. Yet, such is his art – and, indeed, his erotic heart – that even when he confesses those desires into his notebooks which should make the modern reader uncomfortable, if not outright condemning, he loses nothing in the process. His life remains that 'curious and wonderful thing'; it is all of a piece. It is, comparatively speaking, minutiae that fill it, the deepest, remotest, richest provincialism that speaks, yet the voice is neither quaint nor old-maidish but young, direct and vital. The only other writer who can equal him on the realities of country life is Hardy. Like Wessex, Clyro and Langley Burrell, Bredwardine and the Wye Valley are now the recognised landscape of genius. Although Francis Kilvert never flinched from mentioning the cruelties of existence and frequently demonstrates a Georgian – rather than a mid-Victorian – robustness towards the difficulties of his day, his diary generally is a convincing testimony to pleasure and happiness. Its tone is unselfconsciously anti-puritan, and Kilvert's treatment of his neighbours, whom he divides between 'gentle' and 'simple', provides an unparalleled account of the parish during the nineteenth century. Here is one of my favourite entries from a book which has always been for me a directly open door onto the still and heavy mid-Victorian afternoon.

Friday, 28 June 1872
I promised Mr. Venables in answer to his request that I would stay here through August till September 1st inclusive and go home for July if my father wants me. I hope this will be the last of the many changes and postponements that have been made in our plans. Going down the village I fell in with old James Jones the sawyer. 'I hear you are going away,' he said in a broken trembling voice. And he walked down the village with me weeping as he went.

Saturday, 29 June
Called at Hay Castle and went with the four pretty girl archers to shoot and pick up their arrows in the field opposite the Castle.
    This evening I went out visiting the village people. The sinking sun shone along the Churchyard and threw long shadows of the Church and the tombstones over the high waving grass. All round the lychgate and the churchyard wall the tall purple mallows are in flower and the banks and hedges about the village are full of them. Old Hannah Whitney was sitting in her cottage door at work as usual with her high cap and her little red shawl pinned over her breast, her thin grey-bearded nutcracker face bent earnestly upon her knitting till she glanced sharply up over her spectacles to see who it was that was passing.

Wednesday, 3 July

Tom Williams of Llowes and I had long been talking of going up to Llanbedr Hill to pay a visit to the eccentric solitary, the Vicar, and we arranged to go this morning. The day promised to be fine and after school at 10.30 I walked over to Llowes. When the postman, who followed me closely, had arrived we started up a steep stony narrow lane so overgrown and overarched with wild roses that it was difficult for a horseman to pass, but a lane most beautiful and picturesque with its wild luxuriant growth of fern and wild roses and foxgloves. The foxgloves were wonderful. They grew on both sides of the lane, multitudes, multitudes in long and deep array.

Tom Williams was on horseback, I on foot. As we mounted the hill, beautiful views of mountains and valley opened gleaming behind us, and Tom Williams pointed out to me some of the Llowes farmhouses scattered over the hills. The road seemed deserted as we went on our pilgrimage. All folk were busy in their hay fields. Here and there my fellow pilgrim from his point of vantage in the saddle spoke to a labourer or small farmer over the hedge.

As we went up the steep hill to Painscastle the huge green Castle mound towered above us. A carpenter came down the hill from the village. I asked him where the grave of Tom Tobacco lay on the moor, but he shook his head. He did not know.

In the village, a Post Office had been established since I was last here and the village well, the only one, which was formerly common and open to ducks and cattle had been neatly walled and railed round.

Society's need for villains being no less urgent than its demand for heroes, now and then one welcomes a monster-diarist. Villain—extraordinary for all of us in Suffolk is a seventeenth-century farmer from Laxfield named William Dowsing. In 1643 this strange man, then aged about fifty, accepted a commission from Lord Manchester to 'cleanse' the local churches. It was a task which turned out to be not only a duty but a pleasure, as they say, and its highly personalised completion has made Dowsing's name a byword for infamy ever since. So much so that any loss or dilapidation of the county's five hundred or more celebrated churches is now popularly attributed to him. The fact that his 'cleansing' was comparatively slight to what happened to these beautiful buildings under Thomas Cromwell, Elizabeth and Victoria is either unknown or ignored. Dowsing's mistake was to keep a diary. It is Suffolk's 'black book'. As one reads it, the de-mystification of Christianity which occurred under the Tudors and the architectural restoration which took place in the nineteenth century, both of which did untold damage to many an exquisite medieval structure, seem positively enlightened in comparison. Perhaps it is the sound of smashed glass which makes them so, and the crash of hundreds of 'mighty angels' from roofs and windows. Or did that careful and conscientious day-by-day account of wilful destruction reveal all too plainly the madness of zealots? Whatever it was, the diary which William Dowsing kept from 6 January 1643 to 1 October 1644 has been regarded since 1786 – when it was first published – as an appalling and shameful document. It was reprinted in 1818 and again in 1885, and few – not even those whose allegiance to East Anglia's inherent puritanism has been strict – have been able to read it without rage.

The order for removing scandalous 'pictures' – in other words, stained glass out of churches – was published in 1641. Soon afterwards regional committees were set up to implement the new law, and the Earl of Manchester put in charge of seven eastern counties. The Earl wrote to Dowsing and 'to such as hee shall appoint', that they were to put 'the said Ordinance in execution'. This was that 'all Crucifixes, Crosses, & all Images of any one or more persons of the Trinity, or of the Virgin Marye, & all other Images & pictures of Saints and superstitious inscriptions in or upon all and every ye said Churches or Cappeles . . . shall be taken away and defaced . . .' Dowsing employed the assistance of a man named Francis Jessop from Beccles and for the next year and a half the pair of them, with half a dozen or so ignorant assistants, set to with a will.

A book published in Oxford only three years after Dowsing's visit to Cambridge, *Querela Cantabrigiensis*, describes his arrival at the latter university.

And one who calls himself John (William) Dowsing, and by vertue of a pretended Commission goes about the Country like a Bedlam breaking glasse windowes, having battered and beaten downe all our painted glasse, not only in our Chapples but (contrary to order) in our publique Schooles, Colledge Halls, Libraryes, and Chambers, mistaking perhaps the liberall Arts for Saints (which they intend in time to pul down too) and having (against an Order) defaced and digged up the floors of our Chappels, many of which had lein so for tow or three hundred yeares together, not regarding the dust of our founders and predecessors, who likely were buried there; compelled us by armed Souldiers to pay forty shillings a colledge for not mending what he had spoyled and defaced, or forthwith to go to Prison . . .

But the indignation of those who witnessed Dowsing at work pales before the unease and disgust which can still overcome one as one turns the pages of his diary. It is devoid of spirituality. Here is simply the overthrow of one superstition by another. It is Dowsing's total lack of hesitancy which shocks. Also his henchmanship, his blind carrying out of orders. As the rich dark glass shivers and splinters, it never occurs to their destroyer to claim that he is letting in a better light. All he seems to understand is Lord Manchester's letter in his pocket. Generally speaking, the 1641 Order for further iconoclasm was not obeyed with any urgency or completeness by the country as a whole. The last – and most drastic – cleansing of the temples had taken place almost a century before, and ever since the death of Queen Elizabeth people had grown accustomed to a quiet and dignified repairing of their parish churches. So Dowsing's outrages on their fabric seemed ignorant and terrifying – incomprehensible to Christians for whom the stone and wood carvings and painted glass still remaining had largely ceased to be relics of the old religion and had become illustrations to the stories now being read to them from the new official Bible. No wonder the braver among them discovered that they had lost the Church key when Dowsing called.

His activity in other ways has puzzled historians. Why did he only tackle about a third of Suffolk's churches? Why did he miss out or pass over certain buildings? And why doesn't he mention the visit to Cambridge? Was the diary really an inventory written for Lord Manchester's benefit? Evelyn in his *Diary* describes the plundering of monumental brasses at Lincoln in 1654:

The souldiers had lately knocked off most of the brasses from the gravestones (in the Cathedral) so as few inscriptions were left; they told us that these men went in with axes and hammers, and shut themselves in, till they had rent and torn off some large loads of metal, not sparing even the monuments of the dead, so hellish an averice possessed them.

Dowsing lived to be eighty-five, a long time after those eighteen or so months when, at the head of a gang of villagers carrying staves, he wrecked some 150 churches. What did Suffolk say to him when the dust had settled? He was buried among his ancestors in the church at Laxfield on whose tomb the brasses remained intact. He had cleansed this church personally on 17 July 1644 and had taken up 'many superstitious Inscriptions in Brass . . .' He had also defaced the font in which he had been baptised.

His diary opens on Twelfth Night, 1643, at Haverhill, his first church.

We broke down about an hundred superstitious Pictures and seven Fryars hugging a Nun; and the Picture of God and Christ; and diverse others very superstitious; and 200 had been broke down before I came. We took away two popish Inscriptions with *ora pro nobis*; and we beat down a great stoneing Cross on the top of the Church.

At CLARE, Jan. the 6th. We brake down 1000 Pictures superstitious; I brake down 200; 3 of God the Father, and 3 of Christ, and the Holy Lamb, and 3 of the Holy Ghost like a Dove with Wings; and the 12 Apostles were carved in Wood, on the top of the Roof, which we gave orders to take down; and the Sun and the Moon in the East Window, by the King's Arms, to be taken down.

HUNDEN, Jan. the 6th. We brake down 30 superstitious Pictures; and we took up 3 popish Inscriptions in brass, *ora pro nobis*, on them; and we gave order for the levelling of the Steps.

WIXO, Jan. the 6th. We brake a Picture; and gave order for the levelling the Steps.

WHITHERSFIELD, Jan the 6th. We brake down a Crucifix, and 60 superstitious Pictures; and gave order for the levelling the Steps in the Chancel.

SUDBURY, Suffolk. *Peter's* Parish. Jan. the 9th 1643. We brake down a Picture of God the Father, 2 Crucifix's, and Pictures of Christ, about an hundred in all; and gave orders to take down a Cross off the Steeple; and diverse Angels, 20 at least, on the Roof of the Church.

SUDBURY, *Gregory* Parish. Jan. the 9th. We brake down 10 mighty great Angels in Glass, in all 80.

BARHAM, Jan the 22nd. We brake down the Twelve Apostles in the Chancel, and 6 superstitious more there; and 8 in the Church, one a Lamb with a Cross X on the back; and digged down the Steps; and took up 4 superstitious Inscriptions in Brass, one of them *Jesu, Fili Dei, miserere mei*, and *O mater Dei, memento mei – O mother of God have mercy on me!*

ALDBOROUGH, Jan the 24th. We gave order for taking down 20 Cherubims, and 38 Pictures; which their Lecturer Mr *Swayne* (a godly man) undertook, and their Captain Mr *Johnson*.

IPSWICH. At *Peter's*, was on the Porch, the Crown of Thorns, the Spunge and Nails, and the Trinity in Stone; and the Rails were there, which I gave order to brake in pieces.

IPSWICH *Margarett's*, Jan the 30th. There was 12 Apostles in Stone taken down; and between 20 and 30 superstitious Pictures to be taken down, which a (godly man) a Churchwarden promised to do.

Feb. the 3d. WENHAM *Magna*. There was Nothing to reform.

Feb. the 3d. We were at the Lady *Bruce's* House, and in Chapell, there was a Picture of God the Father, of the Trinity, of Christ, and the Holy Ghost, the Cloven Tongues; which we gave order to take down, and the Lady promised to do it.

COMEARTH *Magna* (Great Cornard) Feb. the 20th. I took up 2 Inscriptions, *pray for our souls*; and gave orders to take down a Cross on the Steeple; and to level the Steps. *John Pain*, Churchwarden, for not paying, and doing his duty injoyned by the Ordinance, I charged *Henry Turner*, the Constable, to carry before the Earl of *Manchester*.

Feb. the 23rd. At Mr Capt. Waldegrave's Chappel, in BUERS, there was a Picture of God the Father, and divers other superstitious Pictures, 20 at least, which they promised to break, his Daughter and Servants; he himself was not at home, neither could they find the key of the Chappel. I had not the 6s. 8d. yet promised it. And gave order to take down a Cross.

HELMINGHAM, Feb. the 29th. Adam and Eve to be beaten down.

FROSTENDEN, April the 8th . . . And Mr *Ellis*, an High Constable, of the Town, told me 'he saw an *Irish* man, within 2 months, bow to the Cross on the Steeple, and put off his hat to it.'

BLYBOROUGH, April the 9th. There was 20 superstitious Pictures; one on the Outside of the Church; 2 Crosses, one on the Porch; and another on the Steeple; and 20 Cherubims to be taken down in the Church, and Chancel; and I brake down 3 *orate pro animabus*; and gave order to take down 200 more Pictures, within 8 days. [The Blythburgh angels defeated Dowsing, being unreachable. He tried to shoot them down with musket balls and some of these can still be seen lodged in the ceiling.]

UFFORD, Aug. 31st. See No 26 Where it set down what we did, Jan. the 27th. [Dowsing had destroyed about half of the glass and had given orders for the rest to be broken. But apparently this was not done, and so, eight months later, 'some of them we brake down now'] . . . And we brake down the Organ Cases, and gave them to the Poor. – In the Church, there was on the Roof, above a 100 JESUS and MARY, in great Capital Letters; and a Crosier Staff to be broken down, in Glass; and above 20 Stars on the Roof. There is a glorious (Vain-glorious) Cover over the Font, like a Pope's Tripple Crown, with a Pelican on the Top, picking its Breast, all gilt over with Gold. And we were kept out of the Church above 2 hours, and neither Churchwardens, *William Brown*, nor *Roger*

Small, that were enjoined these things above three months afore, had not done them in May, and I sent one of them to see it done, and they would not let him have the key. And now, neither the Churchwardens, nor *William Brown*, nor the Constable *James Tokelove*, and *William Gardener*, the Sexton, would not let us have the key in 2 hours time. New Churchwardens, *Thomas Stanard*, *Thomas Stroud*. And *Samuel Canham*, of the same Town, said 'I sent men to rifle the Church' – and *Will. Brown*, old Churchwarden, said 'I went about to pull down the Church, and carried away part of the Church.'

ELMSETT, Aug. the 22d. *Crow*, a Deputy, had done before we came. We rent apieces there the Hood and Surplice.

The chilling thing about William Dowsing is not his radical approach to what remained of the symbolism of the old religion but his lack of love, feeling and understanding of the faith which was supplanting it. His orders were to deface and this he did with mindless obedience. He shows indifference to the sheer mess and expense left in his wake, and no consideration at all towards his neighbours. He lacks reverence for anything or anybody. How amazed he would be to know that he now occupies the place of devilishness in the imagination of his home county once occupied by those carved or painted demonic warnings which he obliterated.

Our other Suffolk diarist, George Crabbe, might be said to also have somewhat lacerated his native haunts, though in a very different manner. His sudden flight as a young man from the Suffolk coast to London, and what happened when, at the end of his tether, he begged Edmund Burke to help him, is one of literature's classic examples of fortuitousness. But the incident could not have its unique fascination among the annals of patronage had it not been supported by the brief but detailed diary which the poet kept at this period. Crabbe was not what one might call a natural diarist, and his later journalisings, as his son said, were often little more than lists of names. But his account of the few months covering his arrival in the capital, a near-destitute countryman of twenty-six, and the swift recognition of his genius makes this three-months' diary peculiarly exciting. It shows a young man taking the most important step in his life, the rejection of his background for a place where his intelligence and his personality both told him he naturally belonged. In Crabbe's case it was a step entirely without conceit, and it was taken as much with an East Anglian practicality as with visionary daring. As the odd-man-out son of the little, rough-speaking Aldeburgh saltmaster and as a self-educated, semi-qualified rural physician, Crabbe knew, long before he made his famous journey to Westminster, that he had been born into a kind of damnation and that he had a duty to somehow put the whole tragic inheritance behind him. He did so with such thoroughness that his son said that

no one so humbly born and bred, ever retained so few traces of his origin. His person and countenance peculiarly led the mind from the suspicion of any, but a highly cultivated and polished education; venerable, clerical, intellectual – it seemed a strange inconsistency to imagine him, even in early youth, occupied as a warehouseman . . .

Not that Crabbe repudiated either his parentage or his birthplace. What he burst free from was the limitation which his 'condition' imposed. Before he did so, as an apprentice physician and an expert psychologist, he had already taken a deeper look into the real nature of English rural society than any writer had done before. Its myths, strengths, multifarious sexual drives and circumstantial influences were an open book to him, and his knowledge of the heart of things made the conventional social patterns of little account. He never set out to destroy them and, as a Church of England parson, he correctly observed many of them, yet, as Edmund Blunden says, 'the poet prevailed over the professional man', and to the end of his life the man and his work 'remain majestically themselves'. Not only did Crabbe remain the acute spectator of things which happen to other people, adds Blunden, 'he was very willing to have them happen to himself. Literary success and fame did not affect him as genuine experience.'

At the beginning of the winter of 1799, clearly aware that he was a poet and must make up his mind either to fully live and work as one or to abandon such an overwhelming plan and force himself to practice medicine – something he was beginning to dislike – Crabbe walked to a dreary sheet of water known as the Leech-pond, stared into it, and 'determined to go to London and venture all'. The pond was on a cliff and 'venal' Aldeburgh lay below him, half-ruined by floods and inhabited by violence and ignorance. Calling God 'the Fountain of Happiness', the young poet begged that the new year should not hold for him the torment of the one which was ending. Part of the torment derived from the borough and part from his not having enough money to marry a girl named Sarah Elmy. Soon afterwards, with a box of clothes, his surgical instruments and three pounds, he sailed from Slaughden, the Aldeburgh quay where he had often been forced to work as a labourer.

In London Crabbe lodged with a Suffolk acquaintance and her draper husband, and concealed from them as best he could his dilemma. But for Sarah Elmy he kept a factual account of all that happened to him until that amazing day when Burke suddenly removed every obstacle from his path. Crabbe had attached a number of verses to his letter; Burke read both, immediately summoned the poet to his house and transformed the situation. Crabbe's son wrote, 'He went into Mr Burke's room, a poor young adventurer, spurned by the opulent, and rejected by the publishers, his last shilling gone, and all but his last hope with it; he came out virtually secure of almost all the good fortune that, by successive steps, afterwards fell to his lot . . .'

Crabbe's diary has always drawn a special response from me because he never managed to sustain it beyond the three most worried months of his lifetime, when starvation and even prison threatened to destroy him. He addressed it to 'Mira', his sweetheart Sarah, back home in Suffolk, hoping that it would afford her 'some amusement'. It is a lugubrious letter-journal to a girl, devised to elicit sympathy for a penniless and bewildered countryman at the mercy of a violent city. It is not surprising that his family were to know nothing about it until after his death in the light of what was so soon to occur, his rescue by Burke, the patronage of a duke, the justified fame, the return home of a celebrity. The diary is, in fact, a fearful little overture to the full recognition of early genius – not that it was the kind of genius which was to endear him to Aldeburgh. But there Crabbe is, most desperately, if temporarily, knocking on doors for work in a London made quite terrifying by anti-Catholic riots and a total indifference to what happened to any poor creature trapped in its streets, and his note of semi-controlled panic is one which I and probably most would-be writers and artists have felt when young. Diaries, often more so than novels, present an unadorned statement of their readers' as well as their creators' feelings.

May 12th, 1780 . . . I'm dull and heavy, nor can go on with my work. The head and heart are like children, who being praised for their good behaviour, will overact themselves; and so is the case with me. Oh, Sally, how I want you! . . . It is the vilest thing in the world to have but one coat. My only one has happened with a mischance, and how to manage it is some difficulty. A confounded stove's modish ornament caught its elbow, and rent it halfway. Pinioned to the side, it came home, and I ran deploring to my loft. In the dilemma, it occurred to me to turn tailor myself; but how to get materials to work with puzzled me. At last I went running down in a hurry, with three or four sheets of paper in my hand, and begged for a needle, &c., to sew them together. This finished my job, but that it is somewhat thicker, the elbow is a good one yet. These are foolish things, Mira, to write or speak, and we may laugh at them; but I'll be bound to say that they are much more likely to make a man cry . . .

Crabbe may have been a chilly provincial realist but he was never a cold fish. John Evelyn has always struck me as being near-Arctic, yet I read him avidly. No one knows why he felt a compunction to record what was going on all around him when he was only eleven years old and continued to do so, with various degrees of irregularity, until within three weeks of his death at the age of eighty-six. Like his near-contemporary and frequent companion Samuel Pepys, he wrote out of some deep inner need to put things down and yet with no intention of publishing. There is no sign that either man knew that the other was keeping a diary. Nor could there have been two more contrasting natures exposed in what they secretly stowed away at their desks. The two diaries remained hidden until the early nineteenth century and were then published within only seven years of each other, Pepys's – severely censored – in 1825, and Evelyn's in 1818. The light which they threw on the revolutionary seventeenth century continues to fascinate every kind of reader from the historian to anyone intrigued by the quirks and satisfactions of human nature.

John Evelyn was born on 31 October 1620 at Wotton, Surrey, the son of a country gentleman of whom we learn on page one that he was a stocky, prematurely white-haired, taciturn person with the tastes and outlook of a typical English squire. His mother was 'of a proper personage, well timber'd, of a browne complexion; her eyes and haire of a lovely black . . . for Oeconomiq prudence esteem'd one of the most conspicuous in her Country'. These opening pages, formal and yet capable of revealing intimacy through a kind of stylistic splendour, contain the essence of Evelyn's fascination. He keeps the reader at arm's length and yet, at the same time, he is courteously conducting him towards the heart of his existence insofar as he, a strictly orthodox and stiffly repressed individual, can approach it.

After three years at Balliol, and arriving at youthful independence by the death of his father, Evelyn set out on what was an early version of the Grand Tour of Europe. For seven years, until his marriage to a baronet's daughter in a chapel in Paris in the summer of 1647, he wandered leisurely through Holland, Belgium, France and Italy, describing what he saw in splendidly ornate language. He had a passion for spectacle, for gorgeous processions, architecture, gardens, paintings, delicious fruit, jewels, sculpture and customs, though the rich cataloguing of such things already contrasts with a primly observing, but not indulging, personality. And although scandalised by the unrestrained Mediterranean myth and fantasy encrusting the unreformed Church, his sedate Anglican temperament was frequently awed and overwhelmed by the sheer pomp of the Papacy. Nevertheless, it was at this time that Evelyn began to write 'perverted' for converted when he heard of English Protestants returning to Rome, a description which was to become very popular during the late nineteenth century when many High Churchmen followed Newman's example and became, in the eyes of their contemporaries, 'perverts'. During his travels, Evelyn's attitude towards Roman Catholicism is a mixture of bemused contempt and gentlemanly tolerance; it would be a different matter when, late in life, he was to catch James II and his Court hearing Mass in Whitehall 'with the doors wide open'. Similarly, while being inquisitively drawn to hospitals, torture chambers, operating theatres, executions and cruel sensations of all kinds, including watching the circumcision of a Jewish boy which he describes with exquisite indecency, Evelyn remains icy where sexual love is concerned and, so far as his *Diary* is concerned, we have to accept that he was chaste until his marriage to Mary Browne – whose Christian name he never even mentions – and faithful ever after.

The young couple walked from the altar into a Paris gaudy with banners and strewn with flowers. It was Corpus Christi. Unlike Elizabeth Pepys, that delightful, lazy girl who was to enchant and exasperate her husband in a fashion which makes his portrait of her one of the best accounts which we have of a true marriage, Mary Evelyn makes no real entrance into her spouse's diary. Although they were to be together for nearly sixty years and although there are countless references to 'my wife', Mary stays in the shadows. So do all their many sons and daughters. Even the daughter who, incomprehensibly, according to her father, eloped. In fact, the only occasions when the reader comes into close touch with Evelyn's family is around the deathbed and the grave. The funerals of his children are devastatingly numerous, and the *Diary* is dreadfully eloquent on the subject of family bereavement. As we follow these almost annual coffins to the armigerous vault at Wotton, we recognise that we are present at a terrible commonplace of the period. Evelyn himself tries to rationalise this horror in stoic Christian language but the grief and shock show through. This capricious giving and then taking away by the Lord, his scientific mind tells him, has more to do with human ignorance than divine wisdom.

He was twenty-seven when he and Mary returned from abroad to make their home in Surrey. During the few years of his absence everything had changed. Oliver Cromwell was virtually in power and the 'rebells', as he continued to call them right up till the Restoration, were everywhere. One day Evelyn slipped into the 'Painted Chamber' (the Banqueting Hall) in Whitehall and listened unbelievingly as Bradshaw and Peters discussed the killing of the king. When the time came, Evelyn found that it was one great event which he could not witness:

The Villanie of the Rebells proceeding now so far as to Trie, Condemne, and *Murder* our excellent King, the 30 of this Moneth, struck me with such horror that I kept the day of his *Martyrdom* a fast, & would not be present, at that execrable wickednesse; receiving that sad (account) of it from my Bro: Geo: & also by Mr Owen, who came to Visite this afternoon, recounting to me all Circumstances.

A few days after the execution, Evelyn walked to London, 'it being a hard frost', and saw Charles's possessions being sold and scattered. Not many weeks later, having been obliged to have Holy Communion celebrated in his parlour because 'it was now wholy out of use in the Parish Churches in which the Presbyterians and Fanatics had usurped', the Evelyns prepared to return to France. An inventory was made of their treasures, 'that had been dispers'd for fear of Plundering', leases on property settled in a businesslike fashion, farewell visits paid to old friends and some keepsake drawings made of familiar Thameside scenery, 'to carry into France, where I thought to have them Engrav'd'. It was while he was winding up his affairs in the City that Evelyn saw 'his

Majesties Statues throwne downe at St Paules Portico, & Exchange'. What could be more final? He swiftly obtained a 'Passe from the Rebell Bradshaw' and posted to Dover. On 1 August 1649, along with many other Royalists, he was in Paris. But a little less than a year later, back he was in London, his curiosity about the revolutionary English scene being too much for him and very much 'having a mind to see what doings was among the Rebells now in full possession at White-hall'. In February 1652 he saw Ireton's funeral and began his mordant commentary on the way saints and levellers, though swift to repress the old vanities in others, firmly retained such pomps for themselves. While reading Evelyn, it is always necessary to remember that in most matters his was a scrupulously biassed vision and that he was incapable of fairness towards any views which he does not share, be they religious, political or social. So the jaundiced but fascinating description of Henry Ireton's burial at Westminster and, a few years later, the grisly glee when the body is exhumed, along with that of Cromwell, and publicly hanged at Tyburn. 'Fear God, & honor the King, but meddle not with them who are given to change,' he wrote on that occasion; this text being the central pillar of his faith. John Evelyn is the conservative mystic whose Anglican faith and English nationality are inextricably intertwined in a single rigid spiritual knot.

In 1654 he was in Oxford and visited 'that miracle of a Youth, Mr Christopher Wren'. The diary from now on reveals Evelyn's fascination with science and we get his important accounts of the first meetings of the Royal Society, of which he was a founder-member, and many entries showing a fresh kind of intellectual awareness, in contrast with which his habit of sermon-tasting seems prim and reactionary. For the revolutionary nature of Christ's teachings are light years away from these severe pulpit conventions listened to and noted down with such approval by Evelyn, and recognised by him as divine instructions for the correct ordering of English life. During the Commonwealth he often had to search around in order to find a pulpit containing the authentic Anglican note – so often did they echo with the rantings of enthusiasts and the like. Its tedious quantity of sermons apart, the *Diary* does give a vivid picture of the Established Church emerging from political and social confusions to become a true spiritual expression of the English. During the 1650s Evelyn witnesses a great outbreak of iconoclasm to satisfy the 'scrupulosity of the times' and is horrified by the fervour with which the Puritans 'cleansed' Christianity of its art. What Thomas Cromwell's agents had allowed to remain was now destroyed under Oliver. Through Evelyn, we see the national church in a crude kind of vacuum. On 3 September 1658 he writes triumphantly, 'Died that archrebell *Oliver Cromwell*, cal'd Protector', and has no hesitation in seeing God reaping vengeance. The funeral did not take place until November.

To *Lond*, to visite my Bro: & the next day saw the superb Funerall of the *Protectors*: He was carried from *Somerset-house* in a velvet bed of state drawn by six horses houss'd with the same: the Pall held-up by his new Lords: *Oliver* lying in Effigie in royal robes, and Crown'd with a Crown, scepter, and *Mund*, like a King: the Pendants, and Guidons were carried by the Officers of the Army, The Imperial banners, Atchivements &c by the *Heraulds* in their *Coates*, a rich caparizon'd Horse all embroided over with gold: a Knight of honour arm'd *Cap a pé* & after all his Guards, Souldiers & innumerable Mourners: in this equipage they proceeded to *Westminster* . . . but it was the joyfullest funeral that ever I saw, for there was none that Cried, but dogs, which the souldiers hooted away with a barbarous noise: drinking, and taking *Tobacco* in the streetes as they went.

During the last months of the Commonwealth, Evelyn left his country house and went to live in an inn in Russell Street, Covent Garden, where he daringly published his *Apologie for the King* 'in this time of danger, when it was capital to speake or write in favour of him'. The next May, his ordeal was over, for there came 'the most happy tidings of his *Majesties* gracious *Declaration* . . . after a most bloudy & unreasonable Rebellion of neer 20 yeares. Praised be forever the Lord of Heaven, who only dost wondrous things. . . .'

Evelyn's account of the Restoration years is an enthralling document and made doubly interesting because of the conflict within the diarist himself. Everything he had hoped, prayed and longed for has happened. The God-ordered kingdom is established once more, a magnificent state-ordered Prayer Book is immediately published which will put paid to both innovation and the Papists once and for all, and England itself seems to be restored to its ancient vigorous health. The arts flourish and, except for such matters as the hanging, drawing and quartering of the regicides (whose 'smoking quarters' he was to observe, with satisfaction, being carted away from the gallows), the plague and the burning down of London, a new mildness seemed to prevail. And yet, and yet . . .

As the *Diary* plunges on and on, through the reigns of Charles II, his brother James, William and Mary, Anne and into an acceptance of, if not into the actual rule of the Hanoverians, the reader senses its growing disenchantment with kings. None of them makes the least effort to live up to his or her heaven-ordained role nor, so far as Evelyn can tell (and he is in constant personal contact with them in turn), do they make any serious attempt to achieve transcendence via the Sacraments, sermons, and prayer, over lust, greed & other temporal matters, as he does. He is stiffly honest but yet ungenerous, and where he is humorous, as in the incident about Charles and Nelly having a kind of slanging match over a garden wall, he doesn't mean to be. Never for one moment during all the long years which the *Diary* embraces is there a sign of personal let-up. Evelyn is the self-disciplined English gentleman from youth to dotage. He lives rigidly by Christian principles, yet never manages to convey the spirit of Christ, and the massive accounts of church services leave one intrigued only by what urged him to set them all down.

Parallel with Evelyn the lugubrious Anglican, there runs Evelyn the art-lover and Evelyn the scientist. Also Evelyn the guest whose frequent and various attendances at other people's tables belie the picture of a somewhat forbidding character. He is clearly welcome everywhere he goes, and intimacy has a habit of breaking into even the most formal occasions, as the following entry shows.

August 19th 1668
Standing by his Majestie at dinner in the Presence, There was of that rare fruite called the *King-Pine*, (growing in Barbados & W. Indies), the first of them I had ever seen; His Majestie having cut it up, was pleased to give me a piece off his own plate to tast of, but in my opinion it falls short of those ravishing varieties of deliciousnesse, describ'd in *Cap: Liggous* history & others; but possibly it might be, (& certainly was) much impaired in coming so far: It has yet a grateful accidity . . .

Evelyn's prose is a skilled mixture of the domestic, the learned and the sheer ornate, and contains periods which sometimes recall those of Sir Thomas Browne – whom he once made a special journey to Norwich to meet. Historic figures have a way of pushing through this handsome screen of words, to the constant astonishment of the reader. There is the account of Evelyn letting his house to Peter the Great, for example – who left it in such a mess that Evelyn had to send for Sir Christopher Wren to repair it. There are memorable glimpses of Lancelot Andrewes, Robert Boyle, Bishop Burnet, Marlborough, Dryden, Grinling Gibbons (whom Evelyn discovered), Sidney Godolphin, the mistresses and bastards of Charles II, Halley (whom Evelyn heard lecturing to the Royal Society), Hampden, William Harvey, Thomas Hobbes, Clarendon, Bishop Ken, Kneller, Lely, Louis XIV, Titus Oates, Pepys, Prince Rupert, Monmouth, Sheldon, Jeremy Taylor, Edmund Waller – and a vast range of public and private figures stretching from Shakespeare's to Pope's England.

But, except for such celebrated biographical essays as that written by Evelyn on Charles II, the pleasures of this great *Diary* lie in the many sentences which have a habit of bringing the reader up with an intrigued jolt by their strangeness and colour, and by its unique historical sweep as it records Britain struggling out of absolutism and many remaining medieval ideas, and into the modern age. When I read Evelyn I feel as though I have been shown to a front seat at the great parade of his time. Personally prim he may be, but what a commentator of the passing show!

There are early diaries which, with their easy jumble of pomp and homeliness, remind one of those florid seventeenth- and eighteenth-century tombs above which a fatherly peer, semi-nude, peruked and amiable, returns the adoring stares of marble cherubs with the same kind of sensible affection as at one time must have accompanied strict advice to his own little boys not to play too near the moat. The heroic paraphernalia of Greece and Rome on these monuments is supported on carved replicas of the hassock in the family pew, and their Latin inscriptions, oak-leaf mantling, stags heads, chained unicorns, pug-faced lions, swags of cannon, harness straps, rumpled drapery and extravagant gestures present a juxtaposition of formal myths too impersonal for the task they are asked to do, which is to commemorate an ordinary man.

The first Earl of Bristol's diary is a case in point. He kept it for fifty-four years, through two marriages, twenty births of sons and daughters, five reigns and countless vicissitudes on the racecourse. The entries are brief but they move so effortlessly from public to private experience, and are so ingenuously good-natured, that they leave one feeling that one has had complete access to the writer. His duties at Court never take precedence over the experiences at Ickworth, his beloved Suffolk home, and 'the sweet centre of my humble soul'. The deaths of his infant children and his dogs Fanny and Kickaninny are equally sensitively recorded. He rarely gossips but at the same time the news he has to give is always intimate and personal. Unlike Evelyn, Lord Bristol says a lot about his wife and family, and he also has an almost curiously balanced view of life in the country and life in town. In London he was the level-headed courtier, in Suffolk the ruler of local society. As his second wife wrote:

> When often urged, unwilling to be great,
> His country calls him from his lov'd retreat
> And then to Senates charg'd with common care,
> Which none less seeks and none can better bear,
> Where could they find another form'd so fit
> To pose with solid sense a sprightly wit?
> . . . Well-born and wealthy, wanting no support,
> He steers betwixt his country and the Court
> . . . He does with hands unbribed and heart sincere
> Twixt Prince and People in a medium steer.

The diary would seem to confirm the justice of this rhyme. John Hervey's good looks added to the general opinion that he was a model of leadership and attracted such epithets as 'the lovely Suffolk swain' and 'lovely Bristol'. His son Lord Hervey was to inherit this beauty to an ambivalent degree and it was, as he soon discovered when he dared to attack Pope, made the peg upon which to hang some scathing accusations. The diary contains many references to this brilliant courtier whose acidulous *Memoirs of the Reign of George II* are such a vivid exposure of the Hanoverians. He was the first of the sixteen children which John Hervey was to have by his second wife, Elizabeth Felton, and we hear of his father taking him to Cambridge and then, at twenty, setting him off on the Grand Tour 'to perfect him ye man I wish to see'. It was Lord Hervey's son Frederick, the Bishop of Derry, who began to build the present magnificent house at Ickworth. The Bishop, a magpie who had amassed a vast collection of furniture and *objets d'art*, needed somewhere to house it and conceived an immense oval drum flanked by single-storey quadrant wings. Scenes from Homer made a frieze round the drum, which is surrounded by a double ring of columns. The Bishop, who became the fourth Earl of Bristol in 1779, was a restless figure and appropriately gave his name to the Bristol Hotels which are now scattered all over the world. The modest country house which figures so frequently in his grandfather's diary as 'sweet Ikworth', and for which the diarist grew homesick the moment his carriages lurched Londonwards, is now no more than a stain on the summer grass.

John Hervey's diary displays good nature and a certain innocence. Also a personality which is in sharp contrast with those of his most famous son and grandson. He is like the principal figure in a splendid pastoral with his 'running horses' – My Hogg, Ball Manners, Grasshopper, Cobler, Mustard, Headpiece, Spider – his god-like descents on the assemblies at Bury St Edmunds, and in his unaffected magnanimity. Unlike many diarists, he kept the record of his expenses in a separate book, but this provides such an intimate inventory that it was an inspired decision by the clergyman who first edited both in 1894 to publish them together. Thus we have a truly remarkable list of the prices of eighteenth-century furs, lace, railings, silver, china, pictures, wages, tips, food, glass, rates, arms, upholstery, candles, books, etc.

Among John Hervey's accomplishments was music and he had an interest in the theatre. He played the flute and violin, and helped to rebuild the Haymarket Theatre. The diary ends on 13 April 1742 with the lonely old man – his wife had died in a sedan chair in St James's Park a few months earlier – back home in Suffolk, its final words being 'Ickworth', 'which I found not sweet in her absence'.

Its bland charm apart, Lord Bristol's reasons for writing his diary are hard to define. He is present at many historic events, but he tells us no more about them than could be discovered in the most straightforward history book. He meets a whole succession of monarchs and their families, their courts and the celebrities they attract yet, unlike his son, he does not think it either appropriate or worthwhile to describe what he hears and sees. He adores Suffolk and lives there surrounded by hordes of friendly neighbours, farming people, the citizens of Bury St Edmunds, clergy, artists and the Newmarket racing fraternity, yet here again he tells us little more of all these individuals than their names. On the other hand, he is never cold and the weight of the affection shown towards his huge family and to dogs and horses makes him appear the very essence of the good Englishman. So does his modesty, for though he rose from country squire's son to earl and although during his married life he spent nearly a third of a million pounds, an immense sum at that time, he has a way of conveying these things onto the page with a lack of pride and surprise which is faintly comic. More intimately, we hear of a cholic or two, but on the whole few physical discomforts, of endless bereavements and calm acceptance, of lots of dinners but no menus, of cellars and wine but no drunkenness; of his wife's near-continuous pregnancies, but no whoring. And what we never catch is Lord Bristol looking into himself as lover, Christian, politician, human being. Had he a biographer in mind when he took up his pen? How over fifty years did he manage to write so much that was personal and nothing that was really private?

Had Dorothy Wordsworth done no more than noted the day-by-day domestic routine against which her brother worked during the years of his highest creativity she would have remained a figure of rare interest. Yet, by setting out to do little more than this, she was to succeed in revealing a brother and sister relationship of such tenderness and intensity that it haunts the imagination of everyone who reads her quietly unflinching account of it. When, added to this, one knows that by her self-effacing genius the reader is admitted to the intimate presence of a young man who was changing the direction of English poetry even as she ironed his shirt or collected sticks with him in the wood, then the inestimable value of every small detail of Dorothy's *Journals* is easy to appreciate. Particularly when we know that William himself valued his sister not merely as his housekeeper-companion, but as his muse.

Dorothy Wordsworth's *Journals* differ from the main body of diary-keeping inasmuch as they were not written to satisfy a private need but 'to please William'. Her entire existence, as a matter of fact, was to please William. He in turn saw his sister as no ordinary recorder of weather, birds, flowers, trees and the natural history surrounding their homes in Somerset and Cumberland, of the talk of friends and neighbours, and of small rural events, but as his collaborator. 'She gave me eyes, she gave me ears', he wrote in *The Sparrow's Nest*, and in *The Prelude* he acknowledged her as 'the sister of my soul'.

There are two journals, the first written between January and May 1798 at Alfoxden, and the second between May 1800 and January 1803 at Grasmere. The first entry in the *Alfoxden Journal* declares Dorothy's quality as a writer.

Alfoxden, *January* 20th, 1798. The green paths down the hill-sides are channels for streams. The young wheat is streaked by silver lines of water running between the ridges, the sheep are gathered together on the slopes. After the wet dark days, the country seems more populous. It peoples itself in the sunbeams. The garden, mimic of spring, is gay with flowers. The purple-starred hepatica spreads itself in the sun, and the clustering snow-drops put forth their white heads, at first upright, ribbed with green, and like a rosebud when completely opened, hanging their heads downwards, but slowly lengthening their slender stems. The slanting woods of an unvarying brown, showing the light through the thin net-work of their upper boughs. Upon the highest ridge of that round hill covered with planted oaks, the shafts of the trees show in the light like the columns of a ruin.

The final entry in *The Grasmere Journal*, made almost exactly five years later on another January day, describes a visit made by Dorothy to a neighbour's cottage in the bitter cold. A man and his wife and his sister are sitting by the fire, formal in their Sunday best. The man is blind. A few weeks earlier Wordsworth had married his childhood friend Mary Hutchinson, and the evening scene in his house was of a man and his wife and his sister around the hearth. Dorothy loved Mary because William loved her. Harmony endured, but not the earlier joy.

Dorothy and her three brothers lost their parents as children, as did the Hutchinson girls. All of them were separated for years and all dreamt of the day when they could be reunited, Dorothy and William particularly. She was eighteen months his junior and was twenty-four before a legacy made it possible for William to keep his promise to live with her. This was in 1795, when he was extricating himself from his passionate involvement in the French Revolution and from guilt in another direction – his affair with Annette Vallon, which had produced a baby. In August 1802, some nine weeks before his marriage, William had taken his sister to Calais to see Annette and her child. Dorothy had walked with them on the sand while William bathed. They stayed together for a month and were happy. The journey home was portentous and leisurely, involving a stay with the Hutchinsons and William's marriage to Mary on 4 October, using the wedding ring which Dorothy had worn all the night before. Two days later they were back at Dove Cottage, William and Dorothy hurrying into the garden with candlesticks to see how their plants had grown. The purity and restraint with which these events are described is extraordinary.

But overshadowing even the interest of the delicately told personal story is the account of Wordsworth and Coleridge during the great years of their collaboration. *Lyrical Ballads* was published in 1798 and Dorothy witnessed another revolution at first hand, that philosophical interpretation of Nature which brought about the English romantic movement. It was during this time, when her every observation of the changing seasonal patterns of the countryside was of the utmost importance to him, that her brother began work on his masterpiece, *The Prelude*, although it was not to be published until after his death. So, in effect, we have in these *Journals* the day-by-day activity of a creative partnership of genius.

One other thing will strike the reader – Dorothy Wordsworth's humanity. Grasmere may have seemed like a rarefied retreat to those viewing it through hazes of cloud, peaks, streams and daffodils, but through it wandered the poor and sick and homeless. Her concern for them is total. The many sharp vignettes of beggars, lost children, wounded soldiers, stoical old men and victims of all kinds of a society in upheaval under industrial and military pressures offer a remarkable commentary on the times. Dorothy loved people, loved listening to them, and accepted each one of them as individual and unique. She approached every living soul with that special quality which her brother and his friends called 'imagination' – a kind of deep luminous truth. She could catch a particular voice so that its owner, who may have only rested an hour in Dove Cottage, stays in the memory like a character drawn by a great novelist.

Finally, I must confess an addiction to the tremendous diary kept by Virginia Woolf from January 1915 to her death in 1941. The selection her husband made from it in 1956 gave only the slightest indication of its range and power. It is the by-product of a solidly hard-working, professional life and what I most feel when I read it is the pressure of a freshly running stream which is not yet diverted by analysis or polluted by wash-back. Her policy when writing it, each evening after tea, with her favourite dip pen, was one of unpremeditation and immediacy. The pen had to fly fast and at a totally different pace and rhythm to when it was writing novels and essays. It had to outrun second thoughts and to surprise the diarist herself by where it often landed up. There was to be no re-phrasing, although she quite liked an occasional re-reading and she was frequently 'much struck by the haphazard gallop at which it swings along ... the advantage of the method is that it sweeps accidentally several stray matters which I should exclude if I hesitated, but which are the diamonds of the dustheap.' She thought it ought to be like

some deep old desk ... in which one flings a mass of odds & ends without looking them through. I should like to come back, after a year or two, & find that the collection had sorted itself & refined itself & coalesced, as such deposits so mysteriously do, into a mould, transparent enough to reflect the light of our life ...

When I read this sentence in her *Diary* covering the years 1915–19, I understood the fundamental attraction of all diaries. It was to watch particles of recorded experience catching fire and providing the final illumination I was likely to have of a past day.

The poet David Gascoyne kindly gave me a copy of his published 1936–7 *Journal* a few weeks ago, and on the first page his young self states, 'The whole question of journals is absurd . . . You are reading this? But I had to pretend that no one would ever read it!' So why is he writing it?

In order to find out who I am? Yes and no. To stretch the muscles of my ego, rather; to overcome a certain timidity where my own personality is concerned and in doing so, to resolve certain intimate problems which cannot be mine alone. All this embarrasses you? That was partly my intention. Where am I now? *For Future Reference*, then . . .

Six months later he admits to liking nothing better 'than notebooks or journals which give an exact, daily record of experience – feelings, self-analysis – the human being *chez lui*, naked. I think a journal should be a continual confession of an incurable passion for life.' So that could be it.